Understanding Jurisprudence

Jurisprudence considers general philosophical and theoretical questions about the nature, purpose and operation of law as a whole. This book introduces students to contemporary debates in jurisprudence and encourages them to think in a theoretical and critical way about the nature of law, legal reasoning and adjudication. Wider issues of morality, politics and society are discussed with reference to legal cases and examples to provide as broad a perspective on the law as possible.

Key features of this textbook include:

- introductions to each chapter
- analysis of how jurisprudential issues can arise in everyday life
- a wide range of cases to ground the theoretical discussion
- in-depth discussion of the relationship of law to force, morality and politics, as well as of rights, justice and feminist jurisprudence.

The text provides a concise treatment of all the major topics typically covered in an undergraduate course on jurisprudence, and succinctly explains the arguments for and against the different approaches to the issues raised.

Denise Meyerson is Professor of Law at Macquarie University, Sydney and Honorary Professor of Law at the University of Cape Town.

Understanding Jurisprudence

Denise Meyerson

Routledge·Cavendish
Taylor & Francis Group

First published 2007
by Routledge-Cavendish
2 Park Square, Milton Park, Abingdon, Oxon OX14 4RN

Simultaneously published in the USA and Canada
by Routledge-Cavendish
270 Madison Ave, New York, NY 10016

Transferred to Digital Printing 2008

*Routledge-Cavendish is an imprint of the Taylor & Francis Group,
an informa business*

© 2007 Denise Meyerson

Typeset in Times New Roman by
Newgen Imaging Systems (P) Ltd, Chennai, India

British Library Cataloguing in Publication Data
A catalogue record for this book is available from the British Library

Library of Congress Cataloging in Publication Data
A catalog record for this book has been requested

ISBN10: 1–85941–956–9 (pbk)
ISBN13: 978–1–85941–956–4 (pbk)

For Mike

Contents

Preface

This book draws on and elucidates the work of all the major contemporary jurisprudential scholars in the Anglo-American tradition as well as selected historical thinkers who have made important contributions to jurisprudential debates. I have tried to make theoretical and abstract views understandable while avoiding over-simplification. The reader should therefore not expect a 'Cook's Tour' or potted summary of various theories and thinkers. I try to do justice to the theories which are discussed, while also explaining them in ways that are, I hope, intuitive, accessible and stimulating.

The book carves up the subject matter of jurisprudence in a distinctive way. It is organised around issues rather than key figures or theories. So it does not contain chapters devoted to theorists like Kelsen or Dworkin, nor to theories like 'the natural law tradition' or 'realism'. I present the subject matter of jurisprudence via the arguments offered by different legal theorists in relation to the issues about which they disagree. As a result, most of the theorists discussed make several appearances in the book. The book also contains numerous cross-references designed to bring out the fact that the issues are not discrete but systematically related – that answers to one question invariably carry implications for the answers to other questions.

Though my own views will at times become apparent, the emphasis throughout is on an even-handed presentation of the reasons for and against the differing approaches to the various issues raised. I have not aimed to persuade readers to adopt a particular view but rather to give them the resources to arrive at their own assessments of the various theories and positions discussed, and to form views of their own.

I would like to thank a number of people for very helpful comments: Anton Fagan, Christina Murray, Peter Radan, Cameron Stewart, Max Taylor and Paul Taylor.

Table of cases

Introduction

0.1 What is jurisprudence?

Jurisprudence is a branch of philosophy – the branch which deals with philosophical questions about law. But what is philosophy, and why is the philosophy of law important?

A common answer is that philosophy deals with conceptual issues. In our everyday involvement with the law we take for granted a general conception of what law is – a grasp of what sets law and the practice of law apart from other institutions and activities. When someone appeals to the law to settle a dispute, for example, they know for all practical purposes what the implication of the situation is without having to reflect on what concepts like 'law' and 'legal' mean. Similarly, lawyers practise their areas of law for the most part without thinking about very general questions such as what sets *law* apart from other areas of life like *politics*, *religion*, *art* and *morality*. They manage by relying on an *intuitive* or *unreflective* grasp of what makes an issue a legal issue as opposed, say, to a moral, religious or political issue. The area of knowledge and expertise on which lawyers consciously draw in practising their profession does not normally include reflection on the very general concepts and principles that *define* their profession.

Studying jurisprudence means stepping back and reflecting on the ideas and assumptions that underlie and thereby define legal practices and institutions. Whereas in other law courses one studies areas of substantive law, jurisprudence studies law in a much more general way, and asks much more abstract and theoretical questions about law as such. It asks questions about where law fits into our lives and our society viewed as a whole. What is the function and value of law in society? Why is law important? What would a society be like without it? What contribution to the world is being made by those who have devoted a large part of their lives to legal practice? Why should we obey the law? A legal system provides norms by which we are supposed to live, but what is the difference between these norms and the norms prescribed by morality, or by a religion? Where does the authority of a legal system come from? Are laws necessarily good, in the sense of having a moral basis? What is the relation between law and morality? Is it possible for law and morality to be in conflict, so that we may sometimes be morally obliged to *disobey* the law?

Another way in which jurisprudence contributes to a deeper understanding of law is by providing the tools to engage in rational criticism of the law. Here we are interested in the shape the law *should* take – the standards, in other words, which *good* law should meet. Such standards can then be used to appraise existing laws. (Though these issues are clearly evaluative or normative, it would be too quick to assume that conceptual inquiries into the nature of law are *not* normative. As we will see, this is itself a disputed question in jurisprudence.)

Examples of questions which focus on the evaluation and criticism of existing law are the following. What role should the state play in our lives? What is the right balance between individual and collective interests? Are there, for instance, any moral limits on the authority of government over us – certain objectives which it is not legitimate for government to pursue and certain limits on the way it should pursue its legitimate objectives? And are there certain goods which government is under a duty to provide for us? The answers to questions like these are to be found in an understanding of rival moral and political theories. As we will see, familiarity with these theories generates powerful resources for criticism of actual legal rules and policies.

These are the kinds of issues that will be discussed in this book. Questions like this may seem bewildering, or so hard to deal with that you might think that no-one could come up with authoritative or rationally persuasive answers to them. But when approached systematically, and with the right philosophical tools, they can come to seem less daunting. There is also a long and luminous tradition of philosophical debate on the central issues of jurisprudence on which to draw – a tradition which has produced a rich and helpful literature. The purpose of this book is to enable readers to develop their own views about philosophical issues about the law, by becoming acquainted first-hand with basic methods of philosophical analysis and argumentation and with some of the most important contributions philosophers have made to the central questions of jurisprudence.

0.2   An overview of the topics to be covered in this book

Key conceptual questions about the practice of law relate to the similarities and differences between *law, force, morality* and *politics*. In Chapter 1 we tackle the question about the relation between law and force, asking whether law is essentially a coercive practice – a matter of *forcing* us to act in certain ways by threatening us with punishment – or whether it is rather an essentially normative practice which involves guiding our conduct by the use of standards of behaviour to which we *should* conform.

A related question is whether law can be understood from the outside as merely a matter of observable human behaviour – behaviour which can be studied in the way that we might study animal behaviour – or whether we have to take account of the beliefs and attitudes of those who participate in legal institutions in order to understand the nature of law. A theorist like John Austin, who believes that law is essentially a coercive practice, wishes to account for law purely in terms of observable regularities in human behaviour. Austin tells us to look for a person or body which is habitually obeyed by the bulk of the population and which does not habitually obey any other person or body. If we find such a person or body, then we have found the 'law-maker'. He also tells us to observe whether individuals are likely to suffer a punishment if they disobey the commands of that person. If we discover that this is indeed the case, then we have found individuals who are 'under a legal obligation'.

Austin's is not the only account of law which believes it unnecessary to attend to the perspective of those who participate in legal institutions. The realists, whom we study in Chapter 4, provide another such account. According to them, legal rules are merely predictions of what the courts will decide. Once again, a legal notion is analysed by reference to observable behaviour – in this case, the predictable ways in which courts decide legal cases.

By contrast, those who believe that law is a normative practice believe that it cannot be understood purely in terms of observable regularities of behaviour. They argue that laws function as standards of *correct* behaviour which are *accepted* by participants in legal institutions – accepted by virtue of an *internal* attitude which involves seeing legal rules as standards which *ought* to be followed. According to these theorists, failure to attend to this internal point of view amounts to a failure to understand the nature of law.

In Chapter 2, and also to some extent in Chapter 3, we turn to the relationship between law and morality. Law and morality are obviously *in practice* frequently connected, but we ask whether there is a *necessary* connection between law and morality – a necessary connection between what the law is and what it morally ought to be. Is there, for instance, anything about the nature of law which stands in the way of its being used for evil ends? Is law inherently something that serves justice? Are we, for example, willing to say that there was *law* in Nazi Germany? Clearly, Nazi statutes were enacted in a way which was recognised as valid by the Nazi legal system. But was there really law in the Third Reich?

Speaking broadly, *natural lawyers* believe that there is a necessary connection between law and morality, though they differ among themselves as to the precise nature of this connection. Some – who are often called 'classical natural lawyers' – argue that moral validity is necessarily a condition of legal validity: unjust rules cannot be legal rules or are not 'true' legal rules. The views of other natural law theorists are more complex. Lon Fuller argues that there are certain procedural 'virtues' or good qualities which a system of rules has to display in order to be regarded as a legal system. John Finnis argues that just law is the 'central case' of law. Ronald Dworkin believes that legal standards are whatever body of standards provides the best moral justification for a society's established legal rules. Since he sees legal argument as necessarily turning in part on moral argument, he can be counted among the natural lawyers.

Legal positivists, by contrast, believe that there are no *guaranteed* connections between law and morality. This is because they believe that what counts as law in a particular society is purely a matter of convention. In their view, legal standards are whatever standards conform to the criteria of legal validity which happen, *as a contingent matter of social fact*, to be accepted in a particular society. This view leads them to hold that legal standards are not necessarily morally defensible. Once again, though, there are differences in approach among those who can be broadly classified as positivists. Here the main distinction is between the inclusive positivists and the exclusive positivists.

Inclusive positivists, like HLA Hart and Jules Coleman, believe that it is *possible* (though not necessary) for moral principles to be part of a community's law, depending on the relevant conventions. By contrast, exclusive positivists, like Joseph Raz, believe that this is impossible. They identify the law with black-letter rules (the rules contained in the statute books and the law reports) and therefore believe that questions of law can always be answered by reference to 'hard facts' about statutes or decided cases. We examine these views in Chapter 2.

In Chapters 3 and 4 we explore the relationship between law and politics. We ask whether it is possible for the legal materials to determine the answer to legal questions. Is legal reasoning a distinctive kind of reasoning which is answerable to its own standards and which is able to supply objective answers to legal questions? Is it different from political reasoning in involving the application of the *existing* law rather than the creation of *new* legal rules in response to social needs? Is the ideal of impartiality and objectivity in judging – that judges should decide according to the law rather than according to their own personal values – a realisable ideal and not a myth?

In Chapter 3 we examine theories which answer 'yes' to these questions, though not all for the same reasons. Thus, as we will see, Hart believes there are objective answers to most legal questions because he believes that the meaning of legal rules is usually clear, and that when this is the case the law can be applied unproblematically or uncontroversially. By contrast, Dworkin's answer to this question is more complex. He believes that questions about what the law is are inevitably controversial, because the answers to them necessarily depend on wider views about which moral and political principles provide the best justification of the black-letter law. Yet this is not, Dworkin argues, an obstacle to the objectivity of law.

A connected issue explored in Chapters 3 and 4 is this: when the outcome to a particular legal dispute is not obvious, is this – as Hart thinks – because there is a gap in the law, a gap which gives judges the discretion to decide the case either way? Or is it rather the case – as Dworkin thinks – that there *is* law on the matter, though not of a kind which can be conclusively or uncontroversially demonstrated? Or is it perhaps the case that questions about what the law is are not so much controversial as *unanswerable*, because the legal materials can always be interpreted in conflicting and contradictory ways?

Those who take the last view are discussed in Chapter 4. Believing that the law is indeterminate and therefore not capable of generating uniquely correct outcomes to legal disputes, they reject the idea that legal reasoning is a distinctive kind of reasoning which is different in kind from political reasoning. They therefore believe that judges, like politicians, are necessarily in the business of making subjective, political choices, unconstrained by law. Once again, though, there is a wide diversity of views among those who think that the law does not have within it the resources to generate objective answers to legal questions. As we will see, the realists made this view popular in the United States in the first half of the twentieth century and it was subsequently radicalised by the Critical Legal Studies movement, under the influence of both postmodernism and Marxism. In Chapter 4 we also deal with the economic analysis of law which argues that the 'logic' of the law is really economics – that though judges rarely explicitly reason in economic terms, the true explanation of their decisions is usually economic in character.

After this, we turn to the second enterprise I described above, that of rational criticism of the law. When we engage in this enterprise we use philosophy to *evaluate* legal institutions, practices and the policies served by actual legal rules. Most of the questions falling under this enterprise are dealt with in Chapters 5, 6, 7 and 8. The views discussed in earlier chapters do, however, raise some normative questions of this kind. For instance, both realism and the economic analysis of law suggest that even if the law is on occasion capable of determining the answer to legal problems, judges should not regard the law as giving rise to rights which they are obliged to protect. Judges should, in other words, not try to do *justice* to individual litigants on the basis of the rights granted them by law, but should rather make decisions in *pragmatic* ways, based on their view about what decision would yield the best outcome for society. Thus judges should make decisions which will maximise wealth for society, for instance, or improve average welfare.

The resources to evaluate this pragmatic or instrumentalist approach to judging are contained in Chapter 5. This chapter asks whether there are certain interests of individuals which governments are *morally* obliged to respect and protect even if this is at some cost to society. As we will see, some philosophers argue that individuals have certain special interests which it is their *right* to have protected by government. They believe that there are interests which are so essential to the leading of a worthwhile life that they 'trump' or defeat the claims of the public interest. They point to such interests as freedom of speech and religion, the equal protection of the law and access to basic goods such as health care and housing.

In Chapter 5 we consider the pros and cons of this point of view. Is the demand for rights perhaps selfish, as the utilitarians argue, because it puts one's own interests ahead of the collective goals of society? Or are the communitarians right that, in prioritising the individual, rights undermine communal goods and values, such as solidarity and fraternity and a sense of belonging? Or is the idea of rights perhaps a merely Western value, as cultural relativists claim? Or is it rather the case, as the critical race theorists suggest, that it is only those who are socially and economically privileged who can afford the luxury of attacking rights?

In Chapters 6 and 7 we explore the arguments for and against certain specific rights. In Chapter 6 we ask: do we have a right to make our own choices free of state interference in certain areas of our lives, and, if so, how are these areas to be defined? We examine the views of liberals, like John Stuart Mill, who believe that there is a realm of private conduct which is not the law's legitimate concern. We also examine the views of their opponents – conservatives, like Lord Devlin, and perfectionists, like Aristotle and Aquinas. We then see how the philosophical debate about the right to make private choices can be used to illuminate the issues of pornography, abortion and euthanasia.

In Chapter 7 we consider whether we have a right to economic freedom, in which case any redistribution from rich to poor would be illegitimate. We examine the views of Robert Nozick, who thinks that there is such a right, as well as those of his critics, who argue against it. And, supposing that his critics are correct, we also ask by what principles, in that case, should government be guided when redistributing wealth? We consider both utilitarianism, which takes the view that wealth should be distributed so as to maximise total or average welfare, and John Rawls's theory of 'justice as fairness', which gives priority to the needs of the most disadvantaged members of society, on the basis that this is the arrangement that would be chosen if people were forced to choose principles of justice from a truly impartial perspective.

Finally, in Chapter 8 we explore feminist jurisprudence, which looks at law through the lens of women's experiences with the aim of demonstrating that law contributes to women's subordination. We ask about the ways in which it might be thought that the law is systematically biased towards the interests of men. And if gender-bias is a feature of the law, how should women's experiences and perspectives be brought into law? As we will see, feminist legal theorists answer this question in a variety of different ways. This chapter also uses feminist jurisprudence to revisit and reflect in more depth on issues dealt with earlier in the book. For instance, it returns to the topic of rights, this time from a feminist perspective, asking whether the concept of rights reflects a male perspective on the world. Theories about justice, the public–private divide and the adjudicative process are also reviewed and tested in Chapter 8 using feminist legal theory.

0.3   What is the point of studying jurisprudence?

There is a difference between education and vocational training. As John Bell explains:

> [t]raining is concerned with providing a person with the knowledge and skills to undertake a specific and immediate task. It is focused and utilitarian. Education is concerned with enabling an individual to understand and reflect upon knowledge and processes and to be able to act in a critical and responsible manner. It is concerned with critical self-awareness.
>
> (Bell, 2003, p 901)

It follows that legal education involves 'not just the study of law, but a study which also inculcates the ability to make use of law, to analyse it, and to criticise it as a member of the legal community' (Bell, 2003, p 905). Jurisprudence plays a key role in inculcating these and related abilities.

First, jurisprudence provides a broader perspective on the law. In asking questions about the nature of law and its point it gives us a general understanding of the relation of law to the other institutions making up our society, and its significance in relation to those institutions. For instance, jurisprudence alerts us to a variety of external perspectives on law, such as those offered by feminists, Marxists and critical race theorists. These critical perspectives aim to expose the biases of law, the interests it serves, the way in which it masks inequality and the injustices it does.

Another kind of external perspective to which jurisprudence alerts us is that offered by theorists in other disciplines such as economics and political science. These theorists claim that the law is best understood not according to its own self-image – as governed by internal standards of what counts as good legal reasoning. Rather, they claim, the law is best explained as a mechanism for allocating legal rights efficiently or as driven entirely by the ideological and political mindset of judges.

An understanding of critical and extra-disciplinary perspectives on the law like these promotes awareness of the social and economic context in which law operates and fosters the critical cast of mind which typifies the educated lawyer. In calling attention to the fact that law is an important social practice, and not just a set of rules, jurisprudence enables those who practise law, whether as solicitors, barristers, legal advisers or judges, to bring a broader perspective to their work. Decisions and actions previously guided by habit or rules of thumb will be guided instead by an awareness of the deeper issues, and by reasoning according to a broader vision of the law's purposes.

Second, jurisprudence requires us to think in a self-consciously reflective way about concepts which we normally use unthinkingly and take at face value, like the concept of law itself. For instance, everyone thinks they know what law is: it is the set of rules to be found in the law reports and the statute books (Simmonds, 1986, p 2). But is law really to be identified with these rules? If it is, what are we to say about cases in which the rules are unclear? Are we to say that in these cases there is no law on the matter and that judges are free to exercise a moral and political choice, unconstrained by legal standards? Does that make sense of how judges see their task? Does it show the law in a good light? If the answer to these last two questions is 'No', should we reconsider the way in which we think about law? This kind of critical questioning goes back to Socrates, who had a famous method of encouraging those who had gathered around to argue with him to spell out their own views in detail, until a point was invariably reached where it became obvious that their views were internally contradictory. In forcing us critically to examine our assumptions in this way, jurisprudence encourages us to take nothing for granted – to look deeper and to aim for a more fundamental understanding. This is, of course, another distinguishing characteristic of the educated lawyer.

Third, the aim of jurisprudence, as with all philosophical inquiry, is 'wisdom', not knowledge. Jurisprudence does not ask students to learn and reproduce different theories but shows students how to *use* these theories in critically and reflectively developing positions of their own. It is not interested in the history of legal philosophy for its own sake and it does not treat the great legal philosophers of the past as authorities. Instead it focuses on the reasons why these great figures held the views they did and it uses their work as a doorway into the subject so that students can begin engaging with the issues for themselves. Jurisprudence therefore empowers students to go on by themselves, independently of teachers and of other authority figures.

Fourth, lawyers have a responsibility to promote justice and fairness in the legal system, and jurisprudence gives lawyers the skills to detect the ways in which the law may fail to reflect the demands of justice and therefore to fulfil this responsibility. As we have seen, an essential aspect of jurisprudence is familiarity with moral and political theory. An understanding of moral and political theory in all its complexity alerts lawyers to the questions that need to be asked in evaluating proposed laws or undertaking law reform. It enables them to debate the issues in an informed, critical and analytical way, in full knowledge of the alternative views on offer.

Fifth, not only is an understanding of moral and political theory a prerequisite to evaluating the law and reforming it, moral and political reasoning is also frequently required in judging legal cases. This fact – acknowledged in one way or another by virtually all legal theorists – means that an understanding of moral and political theory is often indispensable to the resolution of legal cases. The most obvious examples (but not the only ones) come from jurisdictions in which moral rights are translated into law using the mechanism of a bill of rights. The protections granted by bills of rights are usually framed in a very abstract and general way which can be unpacked only by moral and political theorising. We will look, for instance, at the South African case of *President of the Republic of South Africa v Hugo* (1997). In this case, the court had to interpret a provision in the South African Bill of Rights which forbids *unfair discrimination* on the ground of sex or gender but gives no clue as to when such discrimination will be unfair. The court had to decide whether it was unfairly discriminatory for President Mandela to pardon mothers in prison who had children younger than 12 years old but not fathers of such children. A question like this can be resolved only by appeal to moral and political arguments of the kind discussed in this book.

The resolution of legal cases can also depend on an understanding of conceptual issues. For instance, in an Australian case we will discuss, *Milirrpum v Nabalco Pty Ltd* (1971), aboriginal claims to land were questioned on the basis that aboriginals do not have a legal system. The court was forced, as a result, to inquire into the *distinguishing characteristics of law*. And in another case we will discuss, the English case of *Oppenheimer v Cattermole* (1976), the court considered the question whether a Nazi law was so iniquitous that it should refuse to recognise it as a law, thus raising the *connection between the concepts of law and morality*. Thus jurisprudential issues are not tangential to the law. On the contrary, the perspective provided by jurisprudence is an indispensable prerequisite to an adequate understanding of the law.

Chapter 1

Law and force

Law is a way of regulating human conduct but it is not the only way. What is distinctive about law's way of regulating our conduct? How is law able to require certain conduct of us which was not required of us prior to its enactment? These questions are at the heart of many of the jurisprudential debates that will be discussed in this book. In this chapter we will look at the 'command theory' of law as articulated by the nineteenth-century British jurist, John Austin. This is the theory that law is distinguished from other social standards, like morality and religion, by the exercise of force. We will also look at the criticisms of the command theory put forward by HLA Hart, whose normative conception of law both transformed jurisprudence and laid the foundation for important later developments in the discipline. Finally, we will discuss the writings of Hans Kelsen, an Austrian legal theorist, whose 'pure theory of law' is another classic in the field of jurisprudence.

You should be familiar with the following areas:

- Austin's theory of law as commands laid down by the sovereign and backed up by sanctions
- Hart's theory of law in terms of rules and, in particular, of law as a combination of primary and secondary rules
- Kelsen's theory of law as an order of norms the validity of which rests on a presupposed 'grundnorm'

1.1 Austin's command theory of law

The aim of John Austin (1790–1859) was to show '*not what is law here or there, but what is law*' (Austin, 1863, p 32, Austin's emphasis), and he believed that he had found the key to answering this question in the command theory of law. Though he was not the first theorist to put forward the command theory – Jeremy Bentham and, before him, Thomas Hobbes and Jean Bodin had spoken of law in similar terms – Austin is generally acknowledged as having provided its fullest exposition. Austin also followed Bentham in aiming to extend the methods of science to the study of social phenomena. He was, in particular, a great admirer of James Mill's science of political economy and he expressly set out to put the study of law on the same scientific footing.

In his lectures entitled *The Province of Jurisprudence Determined*, published in 1832, Austin attempts to give an empirical account of law, that is, an account of law in terms of observable occurrences. Austin begins by distinguishing 'laws properly so called' from 'laws by analogy' (such as the laws of fashion or honour) and 'laws by metaphor' (these being the laws of science). He then turns in more detail to the category of laws properly so called and proceeds to make further distinctions within this category.

All laws properly so called are commands, says Austin, a command being an order backed up by a 'sanction' (a threat of harm) in the event of non-compliance with the command. Some commands are general – being directed to classes of persons and prescribing types of conduct – whereas some commands are directed to individual people. Furthermore, while all commands issue from a superior (a person or group of persons who has the power to inflict harm) – 'the term *superiority*', says Austin, 'signifies *might*' (Austin, 1832, p 30, Austin's emphasis) – some commands issue from God, while others issue from humans. And of those which issue from humans, some are laid down by the sovereign in a state, while others (like the commands of a father to his child) are not. Austin goes on to say that it is only those general commands which emanate from the sovereign which are laws 'strictly so called' or 'positive laws' and it is these laws which comprise the subject matter of jurisprudence.

Who or what is the sovereign in the state? The sovereign, Austin explains, is that person or body of persons which is habitually obeyed by the bulk of society and which does not habitually obey any other person or body. The sovereign may therefore be a specific person, such as an absolute monarch, or a body of persons, such as a democratically elected parliament. In either case, however, the sovereign can be identified as that person or body of persons which habitually receives obedience and does not itself display obedience.

This is therefore Austin's simple answer to the question posed at the beginning of this chapter: how do we distinguish legal standards from the many other kinds of standards which regulate and govern human conduct? Austin provides a straightforward factual test: laws are distinguished from other standards in being orders laid down by a supreme political superior or sovereign and backed up by sanctions. Here, Austin says, is 'the key to the science of jurisprudence' (Austin, 1832, p 21).

This answer is not of just abstract interest. Consider the Australian case of *Milirrpum v Nabalco Pty Ltd* (the *Gove Land Rights* case) (1971), in which Austin's account of law was directly relevant to the legal issues and the court had consequently to pronounce on its adequacy. The plaintiffs were certain aboriginal clans who claimed that a mining company had unlawfully interfered with rights they had under aboriginal customary law to occupy and enjoy certain areas of land in the Gove Peninsula in the Northern Territory. Blackburn J found that the clans in question had a religious basis and a connection with the land. They did not, however, have an internal organisation, were not ruled over by a chieftain, and were not in control of a definable territory. This raised the question whether in their world there was anything recognisable *as law*, because, if not, their relationship to their land could not amount to a proprietary right and their argument would have floundered at the first hurdle.

Clearly, on Austin's view, the answer would be 'No', since there was no identifiable sovereign authority giving the clans' customary rules about the use and enjoyment of the land a capacity to be enforced. Austin's view was, indeed, expressly relied on by the Australian Government in arguing that the clans' customs were of a religious not a legal nature, and that no invasion of legal rights had therefore taken place. But is Austin correct that force applied by the state is the defining characteristic of law? The court rejected his view and, as we will see, there are powerful arguments in favour of the position it took.

1.2   Hart's criticism of Austin's notion of obligation

On Austin's picture, as HLA Hart (1907–1992) points out, law is to be found in the 'gunman situation writ large' (Hart, 1994, p 7). A gunman who accosts you, saying 'your money or your life', achieves what he wants by threatening to kill you. We say that you have been coerced or forced into handing over your money. Law, for Austin, is coercive in the same way. The only points of difference are that the gunman's orders are directed temporarily at a particular individual and the gunman is not the supreme source of commands in the society, whereas, for Austin, laws are general, are obeyed over time and issue from the sovereign. The key notion of a command backed up by a threat of evil is nevertheless shared by both the gunman's orders and the law's dictates. For Austin, force or coercion is the essence of law: the state is a gunman on a large scale.

Hart objects to this picture on a number of grounds. For one thing, he argues that it cannot serve to elucidate the concept of *legal obligation*. Austin does not, it should be emphasised, offer his theory as a psychological explanation of why people obey the law, namely, that they obey out of fear of sanctions. He says, indeed, that even if the sanction is 'feeble or insufficient', we remain under a legal duty. We are, in other words, under a legal duty even in circumstances where the threat of punishment is insufficient to motivate us to obey the law. Nor is Austin making the factual observation that disregard of legal obligations usually leads to sanctions. He is making a *conceptual* claim about the *nature* of law. His view is that when we say that a person is under a legal obligation this is equivalent in *meaning* to saying that the person is likely to suffer a harm for disobeying an order issued by the person or body which the majority of people habitually obey. Sanction and legal obligation are, in other words, conceptually related. They are opposite sides of the same coin. Thus Austin writes: '[c]ommand and duty are . . . correlative terms: the meaning denoted by each being implied or supposed by the other' (Austin, 1832, p 22). Hart disagrees.

If the threat of being killed leads someone to hand over their money to a gunman, then we would describe them as *obliged* to hand over their money, in the sense that they have no real choice. But we would not, says Hart, say that they were under an *obligation* to do so or were *duty-bound* to do so (Hart, 1994, p 82). A gunman has the *power* to force me to act in a certain way but he has no *authority* to inflict harm on me and I am therefore under no obligation to obey him. If someone were to disarm him, I would have no further incentive to do what he orders. And if, for some reason, I were to resist the gunman, while this would no doubt lead to my suffering a harm, no-one would suggest that the harm was *justified* by my resistance. It makes no difference whether it is the state or a lone villain who plays the role of gunman. Threats backed up by sanctions do not translate into legal obligations. They may *explain* why I comply, but they do not imply that I *ought* to comply or that it is *justifiable* to punish me for failure to comply.

1.3   What Austin's account leaves out

Even if commands backed up by threats were capable of imposing obligations, Austin's account of law is too simple, according to Hart. It imposes on law a 'spurious uniformity' (Hart, 1994, p 49), for it is not the case that all laws order people to do or not to do certain things on pain of a sanction. Austin's picture comes closest to describing criminal laws which in some ways resemble commands backed up by a threat of punishment. But even criminal laws cannot be seen as analogous to a gunman's threats, because a gunman is above the law whereas criminal laws have to be obeyed by those who make them. Thus even criminal laws are not appropriately conceptualised in Austin's top-down way.

Furthermore, there are many laws which are even more difficult to force into Austin's model. Hart points in this connection to laws which confer powers, whether on private individuals or officials. Such laws do not impose duties or demands which require us to behave in certain ways whether we wish to do so or not. Rather, they provide the means to realise our wishes and they enable officials to act in certain ways.

There are, for instance, laws which empower us to make a will, or to enter into a contract or a marriage. And there are laws which confer power on courts to hear certain matters and on legislatures to make laws. Failure to observe the relevant requirements laid down by these laws leads to legal invalidity, not a threatened harm. If, for instance, someone fails to sign their will, they will not be punished. They will merely have failed to make a valid will. Likewise, if there is a law conferring power on a legislative body to pass laws which have the support of the majority, an attempt to pass a law which did not enjoy majority support would not be punished. It would merely be ineffective. Nor can it be said that legal invalidity is a kind of sanction, for the purpose of sanctions is to *discourage* certain conduct, whereas legal invalidity is not used for that purpose. Hart concludes that the command theory of law is incapable of adequately accounting for such power-conferring rules.

Hart argues next that there are certain typical features of legal systems that Austin's concept of sovereignty cannot explain. One such feature is that legal systems make provision for the uninterrupted continuity of law-making power when one law-giver succeeds another. When a new set of legislators take their seats in parliament, the first bills they pass are laws. When an absolute monarch's son succeeds him, the son's first orders are laws. But, for Austin, we can talk of law only when there is a habit of general obedience. It follows that when one law-maker succeeds another there is, for Austin, no law until the populace has acquired the habit of generally obeying the new law-maker: there will be an in-between period in which law cannot be made. Austin therefore cannot account for the fact that there is a seamless transfer of authority to the successor law-maker – that the first law made by the new law-maker is already law despite the fact that the new law-maker has not yet received habitual obedience.

A second familiar characteristic of legal systems for which Austin's concept of sovereignty cannot account, according to Hart, is the fact that laws made by an earlier legislator, now dead or now defunct, can still be valid law even though that legislator is no longer habitually obeyed. When one law-maker replaces another there is no reason to fear that all the old laws have disappeared. A law enacted 100 years ago can still be law today. Yet Austin's theory has obvious difficulty in explaining this phenomenon. How can the orders of previous law-makers still be law when they are no longer habitually obeyed? The only way in which Austin can attempt to account for this phenomenon is to say that if the new legislator has not expressly repealed the old statute then that amounts to 'tacitly' commanding it. In particular, by not interfering when the courts enforce the old statute the new legislator has given a tacit order that it should be obeyed. The trouble with this response, though, as Hart points out, is that it implies that the old law is not law until it is actually applied by the courts during the tenure of the new sovereign. But this is false. A statute does not become law only *after* it is applied by the courts. It is *already* law before any cases arise to which it may be applied (Hart, 1994, p 64).

Finally, a third feature of Austin's theory of law to which Hart objects is the sovereign's legally illimitable status: since, for Austin, the sovereign does not habitually obey any other person or body, there can be no legal limits on what the sovereign can command. This must, according to Austin, be the case in all societies in which there is law: where there is law there is a legally illimitable sovereign. Austin writes: '[s]upreme power limited by positive law, is a flat contradiction in terms... Every supreme government is legally despotic' (Austin, 1832, pp 212, 225). As Roger Cotterrell explains, this aspect of Austin's theory follows directly from his definition of law: '[e]very law is the direct or indirect command of the sovereign of an independent political society. But a sovereign cannot issue enforceable commands to itself... And no laws other than the sovereign's own commands can exist to bind it' (Cotterrell, 1989, p 69).

But, as Hart points out, there are many legal systems in which we do not find a sovereign which is legally illimitable. Austin's definition of sovereignty may seem to fit British constitutional arrangements, in which there is no written constitution limiting the legislative powers of the Westminster Parliament and – leaving aside certain complications arising from British membership of the European Union – the doctrine of unlimited parliamentary sovereignty has long been regarded as a fundamental rule. But there are many other countries in which the legal situation is different. In both the United States and Australia, for instance, there is a written constitution which divides power between the federal government and the States and which also prevents legislative interference with certain individual rights. To give just one example, s 116 of the Australian Constitution prohibits the federal Parliament from interfering with the free exercise of religion. This means that if the federal Parliament attempted to pass a law with such a purpose, the High Court would strike it down as invalid. The Parliament would, in such a case, have failed to make a valid law. But, though the power of the federal sovereign is subject to this and other legal limitations, it is obvious that Australia has a legal system.

At this point, someone sympathetic to Austin's view might point out that Austin does not, in fact, identify the sovereign with the legislature, but with the body of electors – a body which is perhaps more plausibly thought of as necessarily free of legal limitation. Thus, if we consider the Australian Constitution again, we will find that it contains a provision, s 128, which provides for alterations to the Constitution. Leaving aside certain special cases in which proposed amendments must pass an additional hurdle, the normal rule in terms of s 128 is that a proposed amendment has to be approved by a majority of voting electors in a majority of the States and by an overall majority of voting electors. This seems to suggest that the true sovereign in Australia is the people, not, as we first assumed, their elected representatives in parliament. And if it is the people who are sovereign – the people who issue the commands which provide for the legislative powers of the federal and State Parliaments – have we not found a body whose power is legally illimitable, in which case Austin would be vindicated, at least in this respect?

Hart's reply to this attempt to identify the sovereign body with the electorate is to point out that if it is the people who are sovereign, then it is impossible to understand their sovereignty on the original model of commands issued by a political superior and backed up by sanctions. After all, who is doing the commanding and who is doing the obeying? It seems that if the people are sovereign, and if sovereignty is defined in Austin's way, then the people must be issuing commands to themselves which they themselves obey. They must, in effect, be holding a gun to their own heads – an idea which is hard to comprehend.

In fact, as Hart points out, the only way to understand the concept of the people's sovereignty is not by reference to habits of obedience to the commands of a body *outside* the law but by reference to a legal rule – in this case, s 128 of the Australian Constitution – which tells us what *counts* as the sovereign body's will and therefore pre-exists and authorises any 'command' or 'sanction' that body may issue or impose. If it is the people who are sovereign, they are no more outside the law than the elected legislature: it is the law which gives both their law-making powers. Put simply: sovereignty cannot be the *basis* of law because it *derives* from law.

In sum, Austin's theory of law as the will of a sovereign ruler is crude. There are many features of legal systems which it lacks the resources to explain. It cannot, for instance, account for the fact that there are many legal obligations which do not have their source in a law-maker's will; that a law-maker's powers are conferred by law and can be limited by law; that legal powers may be used in ways which are not equivalent to prohibiting conduct; and that, when used in such ways, what has been done can be assessed for legal validity or invalidity. Hart does not deny that, in practice, some degree of coercion may be needed to *sustain* a legal system and that many people do, in fact, comply with legal demands out of fear of sanctions. His argument is the *conceptual* one that law cannot be *identified with* or *defined as* a set of coercive commands. As we will see in the next sections, this is because Hart thinks that the command theory cannot explain law's normative aspect – the fact that law guides our conduct by reference to *rules* or *normative standards* of behaviour.

1.4 A new start: law as a normative phenomenon

We have seen that Austin aspired to provide a scientific theory of law. He hoped to explain law from the outside, in terms of regularities in observable behaviour. All the elements of his theory refer to such external, observable patterns. Thus he cashes out the concept of legal authority not in terms of constitutional rules but in terms of habitual behaviour: the law-maker is that person or body of persons which most people are disposed to obey. As Cotterrell explains: '[t]he idea of a habit of obedience introduces a factual, indeed sociological, criterion of the existence of sovereignty' (Cotterrell, 1989, p 68). Likewise, what it means to be under a legal obligation or a legal duty is, for Austin, to be likely to suffer a punishment for failing to do what the law-maker has commanded. He understands statements about legal obligations, in other words, as assessments of the likelihood of being punished. In general, he makes no reference to individuals' attitudes and beliefs, nor to the way in which participants in legal institutions understand their own conduct. In short, he provides a behaviourist account of law which avoids all reference to mental states and attitudes.

And this, according to Hart, is the basis of all of Austin's mistakes. It is impossible to define concepts like legal obligation and legal authority in 'flatly descriptive' terms (Hart, 1982, p 253). For Hart, we cannot understand law unless we take into account the fact that those who participate in legal institutions take an *internal* view of the practice. In taking this view, Hart was influenced by an approach to social science which emphasises the differences between understanding human behaviour and understanding the physical world. On this approach we cannot explain and understand social phenomena such as law by using modes of explanation modelled on the natural sciences, which view human behaviour purely 'in terms of observable regularities of conduct, predictions, probabilities and signs' (Hart, 1994, p 89). We need instead to attend to the perspective of those who participate in the relevant institutions. This is not to say that we need to *adopt* or *share* their internal perspective. But we do need to understand the meaning and significance of their regular behaviour *to them*. Such an approach, which stresses the difference between the ways in which we understand natural and social phenomena, is often called 'hermeneutic' (MacCormick, 1981, pp 29–30).

Hart was also influenced by mid-twentieth-century developments in philosophy, and especially by the linguistic philosophy of Gilbert Ryle and JL Austin, which focuses on the way in which we talk about social phenomena as a means of enhancing our understanding of the realities our language describes. Hart draws attention to his use of this method in his Preface to the *Concept of Law*, in which he states: '[m]any important distinctions, which are not immediately obvious, between types of social situation or relationships may best be brought to light by an examination of the standard uses of the relevant expressions and of the way in which these depend on a social context, itself often left unstated' (Hart, 1994, p vi). Hart's application of the methods of analytical philosophy to the law revolutionised the way in which jurisprudence was understood in England, moving it, as William Twining observes, from an atheoretical study of legal principles and concepts to a new level of generality and abstraction (Twining, 1996, p 130). Neil MacCormick remarks similarly that in 1952 jurisprudence in England was 'moribund' and that Hart 'excited the legal imagination to reconsideration of the philosophical significance of legal problems' (MacCormick, 1981, p 19).

The hermeneutic and conceptual dimensions of Hart's approach converge in the crucial distinction he draws between a habit and a social rule, a distinction which in turn requires an understanding of the difference between 'is'-statements or factual statements and 'ought'-statements or normative statements. An 'is'-statement describes a feature of the world. An 'ought'- statement tells us how we should behave. Thus, 'some people steal' is an example of an 'is'-statement, whereas 'you ought not to steal' is an example of an 'ought'-statement. 'Ought'-statements or normative statements are 'practical' statements, where 'practical' means 'action-guiding'. They aim to guide our conduct and to provide a standard for its appraisal.

A habit, even one which is common to many people, is merely a matter of convergent behaviour. Suppose, for instance, that most people drive to work rather than take public transport as a matter of habit. This is a fact about their observable behaviour and the statement which describes their habit is an 'is'-statement. There is no *reason* for their habit. The habit may *explain* why they drive to work but it does not *justify* their behaviour, and if particular individuals start taking the bus to work they will not be criticised for their deviation from the habit.

By contrast, when it comes to social rules – such as the rule that everyone should drive on the left hand side of the road – the behaviour in question is not merely general. The regular mode of behaviour is in addition *perceived* in a certain way. It is treated by the members of a group 'as a general standard to be followed by the group as a whole' (Hart, 1994, p 56): they see the rule as *justifying* their driving on the left and serving as a basis for *criticising* those who disobey it. This perception is characteristically expressed in 'the normative terminology of "ought," "must," and "should," "right" and "wrong" ' (Hart, 1994, p 57): you *ought* to drive on the left; it is *wrong* to drive on the right. Social rules therefore involve not only external conformity or regular conduct. They combine regular conduct with a 'distinctive attitude' (Hart, 1994, p 85). Hart calls this distinctive attitude a 'critical reflective attitude' (Hart, 1994, p 57). It consists in taking up what he calls the 'internal point of view' – 'the view of those who do not merely record and predict behaviour conforming to rules, but *use* the rules as standards for the appraisal of their own and others' behaviour' (Hart, 1994, p 98, Hart's emphasis).

Hart describes those who take the internal point of view towards a rule as 'accepting' the rule, but he makes clear that people can accept rules without *morally* endorsing them. They might, for instance, adopt the internal attitude simply out of a wish to conform. Hart furthermore points out that to say that someone ought to do something is not necessarily to say that they are under a *moral* obligation to act in that way. Consider the statement, 'Burglars ought to wear gloves'. This implies merely that from the perspective of *self-interest* – if they do not wish to be caught – burglars should wear gloves. It is clearly not to say that burglars are *morally* obliged to wear gloves. These points are of great significance for Hart's legal philosophy and we will return to them in 2.7.

Thus, for Hart, the social rules of a group are constituted by a form of social practice which comprises the *regular following of a certain pattern of conduct* by most members of the group, as well as a *normative (though not necessarily moral) attitude* to the regular pattern of conduct. This normative attitude – 'acceptance', in Hart's terminology – consists in taking the regular pattern of conduct as a guide to behaviour and as a standard for its appraisal (Hart, 1994, p 255). In short: social rules exist when the members of a group behave in a certain way *as a rule*.

In his early work Hart seemed to think that all obligations, moral as well as legal, exist by virtue of social practices of this kind – practices which are supported by nothing more than the fact that all the members of the group regard certain regular forms of behaviour as appropriate. This supposition is, however, open to criticism. Perhaps the most obvious way in which it is flawed is that there can be moral obligations which are not acknowledged by the community in which one lives. Thus a vegetarian might say that we have no right to kill animals for food, regardless of whether this is or is not generally acknowledged (Dworkin, 1977a, p 52).

Furthermore, even obligations which *are* acknowledged by all the members of a community do not necessarily derive their normative force from the fact that they are generally practised. There are, as Ronald Dworkin points out, two kinds of consensus, a consensus of *convention* and a consensus of *conviction*. Dworkin explains the concept of a convention like this:

> [a] convention exists when people follow certain rules ... for reasons that essentially include their expectation that others will follow the same rules ..., and they will follow rules for that reason when they believe that ... having

some settled rule is more important than having any particular rule...Our reason for driving on the right in America and on the left in Britain is just our expectation that this is what others will do, coupled with our further belief that it is more important that there be a common rule than that it be one rather than the other.

(Dworkin, 1986, p 145)

A consensus of convention exists, in other words, when a standard is regarded as a reason for action *just because* it is accepted as a reason by everyone else. No rational support exists for the practice of driving on the left side of the road rather than the right, other than the fact that everyone does so. There is no need to provide a *substantive* argument in favour of accepting the standard. Rules of games are similar. All chess players accept that the king can move only one square at a time, not because there is any good *reason* to accept this rule but because *everyone else* accepts the rule (Dworkin, 1986, p 136).

By contrast, Dworkin points out, where there is agreement in *conviction*, though everyone follows the same rule they do so out of the *independent* conviction that the rule is right. They do not accept it *just because* it is the convention, or just because everyone else accepts the rule. An example of agreement in conviction is the fact that we all think it wrong to hurt other people gratuitously: our reason for obeying this principle is not that *others* obey it but that the principle is *right* (Dworkin, 1986, p 145). The shared morality of a group is therefore a consensus of conviction: the duties it imposes are not imposed by convention. Rather, they are imposed by virtue of the good reasons that are thought to support them. Thus even if moral rules are widely practised by one's community, they are not rules *because* they are practised.

Dworkin's distinction between consensus and conviction shows that Hart's account of social rules is not an adequate account of moral obligations. In the posthumously published Postscript to the *Concept of Law*, Hart concedes this. He says that he now realises that his account of social rules does not apply to morality, 'either individual or social' (Hart, 1994, p 256), but applies only to shared rules which are conventional. It applies, that is, only when the fact that certain behaviour is conventionally accepted is the *reason* why it is regarded as a standard to be followed. But his concession on this particular point leaves Hart's theory of *law* unscathed, because he believes, as we will see in the next section, that the foundation of all legal systems is a social practice supported by nothing but convention. In particular, Hart argues that the most important legal rule, which he calls the rule of recognition, exists by virtue of its acceptance. He therefore claims that as long as the social rule account is a faithful account of legal obligation, it does not much matter that it does not apply to *moral* obligation. As we will see in 2.10, Dworkin believes that the social rule account is as inapplicable to law as it is to morality, but that is a different point, resting on Dworkin's beliefs about the controversial nature of law. For the moment we need to concentrate on Hart's account of law.

1.5   Law as a union of primary and secondary rules

Hart offers his theory as a general theory about the institution of law – an institution, which has, he says, 'in spite of many variations in different cultures and in different times … taken the same general form and structure' (Hart, 1994, p 240). Hart's starting-point in the *Concept of Law* is 'the concepts that constitute the framework of legal thought' – such concepts as obligation, duty, authority, judge, court, jurisdiction, legislation, validity and power. Any adequate theory of law should be able to explain these concepts and Hart's aim is to provide such a theory.

Hart says that he is not concerned to *define* law, that is, to provide a rule for the correct use of the word. Rather, he wishes to 'advance legal theory by providing an improved analysis of the distinctive structure of a municipal legal system' (Hart, 1994, p 17). This is the 'central case' of law and Hart is more interested in analysing the central case – the legal system of a modern state – than in debating whether borderline cases such as international law and customary law should or should not be described as 'law'.

Let us begin with the phenomenon of obligation. As we know, Hart thinks that Austin's theory of law is incapable of elucidating the concept of obligation because threats of force may oblige us to act in certain ways but do not tell us why we *ought* to comply or why those who demand our obedience have a *right* to it. Habits of obedience are for the same reason incapable of conferring authority on anyone to impose obligations on us. The statement that someone is under an obligation is a *normative* statement which cannot be understood in terms of facts about externally observable physical behaviour, according to Hart, but only in terms of *rules*. For rules, as we saw in 1.4, have an internal aspect which consists in regarding a certain pattern of behaviour as a standard which ought to be followed. Rules furnish reasons to comply, and it is therefore rules to which we must refer if we are to explain the action-guiding role that notions like obligation play in our lives.

But this is only part of Hart's theory of law, for he believes, in addition, that the reasons for action which law provides are of a special kind. In order to understand Hart's views about law's distinctive kind of normativity we need to consider the role played in his theory by the concepts of primary rules and secondary rules. Primary rules impose obligations or duties. They directly govern our behaviour by telling us what we ought and ought not to do – refrain from violence, for instance, or keep our promises. Clearly, not all primary rules or obligation-imposing rules are legal rules. Primary rules may, for instance, be religious in nature, or moral. What, then, is the difference between a *moral* primary rule and a *legal* primary rule?

The authority of moral rules depends on their *content*. Their ability to give us reasons for action is a function of the *merit* of the arguments that can be provided on their behalf. By contrast, law's ability to give us reasons for action does not, according to Hart, depend on its rules having rational support. Though legal rules may and often do have rational support, and though their content frequently overlaps with moral rules, that is not the *basis* of their authority. We are under a legal obligation to do what the law tells us to do independent of the nature or character of the conduct that the law requires of us. The authority of legal rules is therefore 'content-independent': there is legal reason to do as they tell us independently of the merit of their content (Hart, 1982, p 254).

This is because primary legal rules bind us by virtue of being, as we say, '*valid*', and if we ask what their validity depends on, we see that it depends on their having been made in a way which conforms to certain criteria laid down in a *secondary* rule (or higher-order rule) which is used by legal officials to determine legal validity. Hart calls a higher-order rule of this kind the 'rule of recognition'. The rule of recognition identifies the sources of law in a particular society. A primary rule is legally valid if it accords with the criteria of validity prescribed by the rule of recognition.

The rule of recognition in a particular society might, for instance, test validity by reference to how a rule *originates*, stating that a primary rule is a valid law if it is an unrepealed enactment of parliament or if it is contained in a judicial precedent. In this hypothesised society, if a rule can be found in the statute books or the law reports, it is a *legal* standard. (Such a complex rule of recognition, which refers to more than one source of law, would also have to rank the sources, by, for instance, providing that precedent is subordinate to legislation in the sense that legislation can override common law rules.)

Notice, however, that Hart does not believe that in order to be a legal requirement a standard *must* have an *identifiable origin in an institutional or social source*, such as the decision of a court or legislature. As we will see in 2.9, Hart believes that the rule of recognition might authorise the use of standards in identifying law which are not tied to social sources. We will return to this important issue in some detail in the next chapter. For present purposes it is necessary only to note that in whatever way the rule of recognition tests validity, it enables us to speak of a legal rule as valid by providing us with authoritative criteria for determining whether a particular rule or norm is part of the society's law. It thereby enables us to distinguish valid legal rules from rules which are incorrectly argued to be rules of law and also to distinguish legal rules from other sorts of social rules, like moral and religious rules.

The key point to note about the rule of recognition is that it is a conventional rule of the kind explained in 1.4. As we saw there, the main feature of conventional rules is that there is no reason in favour of choosing one rather than another. They simply exist as a matter of fact or by virtue of being accepted as an appropriate standard of conduct. Likewise, Hart says that the rule of recognition is whatever rule is *in fact* or *contingently* used by judges in a particular legal system to decide legal disputes. It is not itself valid. It is simply a social practice that happens to exist and its binding force derives merely from the fact that legal officials accept it as a guide to their behaviour. It is entirely a matter of what they happen to accept – as contingent as driving on one side of the road rather than the other. It follows, as Hart says, that there is 'no logical restriction on the content of the rule of recognition' (Hart, 1983, p 361). And this means, in turn, that the primary legal rules valid under a rule of recognition are not guaranteed to enjoy rational support. But, however unmeritorious the subordinate legal rules may be, provided they conform to the criteria laid down in the rule of recognition, they remain *legally* valid and generate *legal* reasons to follow them. (This is not, however, to say that there are necessarily *moral* reasons to follow them, as we will see in 2.6.)

Hart goes on to argue that in order to account for the ability to make new legal rules and abolish old ones we once again have to invoke the concept of a secondary rule, in this case a 'rule of change'. Rules of change make it possible to change the primary rules.

Such rules specify who or what body has the power to create new legal rules and specify any procedures that must be followed by such a person or body. There is obviously a close connection between the rule of recognition and the rules of change. For instance, if society has a rule of change to the effect that parliament can amend or repeal laws, then the rule of recognition will state that what parliament enacts is the law. Rules of change also allow private persons to change their own legal position. For instance, by making a will, individuals can opt out of the law of intestacy. (It will be remembered that one of Hart's criticisms of Austin (see 1.3) was precisely that he did not recognise the different social functions that laws can have, including the fact that some laws do not impose duties on individuals but rather provide them with the means for realising their wishes.)

Finally, Hart argues that we need to invoke secondary rules to account for the fact that legal systems have mechanisms which enable disputes about whether a primary rule has been broken to be conclusively resolved. These are 'rules of adjudication'. In our society such disputes are resolved by courts which are constituted in certain ways and given jurisdiction to hear certain matters according to the rules of adjudication. Since the judge's authoritative finding on the matter will be a source of valid law, there will once again be a close connection between the rule of recognition and the rules of adjudication. Additional secondary rules give judges, at least in developed systems of law, the exclusive power to impose penalties for violation of the rules, thereby centralising the imposition of sanctions.

In general, then, secondary rules are rules which allow us to do such things as recognise, make, change and interpret primary rules. They are rules which refer to or are about primary rules. And Hart's claim is that if we want to understand the key features of the central case of law, such as obligation, validity, authority and jurisdiction, we need to invoke the concept of secondary rules: law is 'most illuminatingly... characterized as a union of primary rules of obligation with... secondary rules' (Hart, 1994, p 94). Since the rule of recognition is, for Hart, the most fundamental secondary rule – the 'master' rule or 'top' rule, giving unity to and systematising all the rules of the legal system – Hart sometimes explains his theory by referring to it alone. Thus he says: 'the... social situation where a secondary rule of recognition is accepted and used for the identification of primary rules of obligation...deserves...to be called the foundations of a legal system' (Hart, 1994, p 100).

Though the obligations which the law imposes must be *obeyed* by most individuals in society for a legal system to exist (by contrast, for instance, with one that has become defunct), Hart says that it is not necessary that such obedience be accompanied by *acceptance* of the criteria of legal validity *on the part of ordinary citizens*. They need not, in other words, think of their conforming behaviour in normative terms, as behaviour which is obligatory or right. Ordinary citizens may obey not because the rules give them a reason to obey but rather out of fear of sanctions, or unthinkingly.

Officials, by contrast, must accept the system's rule of recognition and its rules of change and adjudication. They must, in other words, regard the secondary rules from the internal point of view, as standards of correct official behaviour. Thus judges must, for instance, regard the fact that parliament enacted a provision as a *reason* for them to apply the provision. If this were not the case – if judges did not see the law as providing reasons and if deviations from the rules were not regarded with disapproval – 'the characteristic unity and continuity of a legal system would have disappeared' (Hart, 1994, p 116).

Thus a legal system is a combination of primary and secondary rules, in which the members of the population generally obey the rules that are valid according to the criteria of legal validity and legal officials accept the rules defining validity as common public standards. This situation is what, in Hart's view, fundamentally characterises law and distinguishes it from other social phenomena.

Hart also has another argument in favour of seeing law as a combination of primary and secondary rules. He argues that the function of law is to guide conduct and that a regime of primary rules is not capable of guiding conduct as efficiently as a regime of primary and secondary rules (Perry, 2001, pp 322–3). Hart asks us to imagine a society in which the only rules are primary rules. The people living in this society generally agree on the standards they use to guide their behaviour, in the sense that they share a disposition to praise certain kinds of behaviour and criticise other kinds. But now let us suppose that a difference of opinion has arisen as to whether a particular rule is or is not a rule of their society. If they had a rule which told them how to recognise valid rules of their society they would be able to settle this doubt. A rule specifying the ways in which valid primary rules can be identified is one kind of secondary rule. But we have hypothesised that the only rules they have are duty-imposing rules. They are therefore unable to ascertain if a putative rule is really one of their rules or has been falsely said to be one.

Let us now suppose that the people living in this society wish to abolish one of their primary rules or introduce a new one. If they had a rule which told them how to achieve such a change this would be easy. Once again such a rule would be a secondary rule. But, as we know, the only rules they have are rules for regulating their behaviour. They do not have rules for validly changing their rules.

Finally, let us suppose that a dispute has arisen in this society about whether one of their rules has been violated. They have, let us suppose, a rule against killing but it is not clear whether this rule also applies to acts of euthanasia. If they had a rule which gave power to a certain body authoritatively to determine how their rules should be interpreted, the dispute could be settled. Such a rule would be another kind of secondary rule. But they do not have rules for conferring such powers. The only rules they have are rules which impose duties. They are therefore unable to resolve the dispute.

A society of this sort – a society which has only primary rules of obligation and the rules of which are not systemically interconnected with other rules – will therefore suffer from certain 'defects' in so far as the ability to guide conduct is concerned. The defects are uncertainty, the static character of the rules and the inefficiency of the diffuse social pressure by which they are maintained (Hart, 1994, pp 92–3). The acceptance of secondary rules as binding by judges and other officials remedies these defects and, *in more efficiently guiding conduct*, marks the transition from a pre-legal to a legal system.

Hart's picture can be summed up in the following way. We cannot understand law other than as a normative practice, as a practice which uses the normative vocabulary of 'ought to', 'entitled to', 'authorised to'. Legal statements are practical. By contrast with descriptive statements, their function is to guide and appraise our conduct. But law's normativity is of a special kind. Moral standards, for instance, which are also practical, function as guides to conduct by virtue of the character or content of the actions they prescribe or prohibit. By contrast, according to Hart, the reasons for action which law provides are not a function of their content but depend instead on whatever conventions happen to be accepted by officials in a particular legal system.

The key difference between Austin and Hart is therefore this: Austin thought that what distinguishes law is its source in the will of a specific individual or body of individuals, whereas Hart argues that the key feature of law is the role it plays in human deliberation and, in particular, its ability to provide reasons for action which derive their normative force not from their content but from their relationship to rules for identifying, changing and enforcing standards which are accepted from the internal point of view. Law is essentially an institutional social practice. And it is the existence of a rule of recognition, accepted from the internal point of view by legal officials, which makes institutions possible. In a society in which there are no rules created by institutions, and no institution-creating rules accepted from the internal point of view, there is no law (Coleman, 2001a, p 109). Shared social practices therefore underpin the existence of legal systems.

In his later work, Hart also emphasises the fact that the reasons for action which law furnishes are 'peremptory'. By this Hart means that they are 'intended to preclude or cut off any independent deliberation... of the merits pro and con of doing the act' (Hart, 1982, p 253). Hart is here referring to the fact that the law claims to be the supreme authority in society, displacing our other reasons, whether these be reasons of self-interest, or morality, or religion. The law is therefore 'deliberation-excluding' (Hart, 1982, p 255).

1.6   Why Hart's account is superior to Austin's

We can now see how Hart's account of law, in terms of a system of rules – standards which are perceived as providing reasons for action – explains the features of law which Austin's austerely external account of law, in terms of statements which merely describe or predict regularities of behaviour, could not explain. Think of the gunman again. It is a fact, requiring explanation, that we see a distinction between a bank robber and a tax official. We regard the demands of the tax official as rightful in a way that the robber's are not. What does this difference consist in?

Austin cannot tell us, as we have seen, because he defines authority in terms of facts about habitual acquiescence to brute power, but Hart has a ready answer: the power of tax officials is conferred by higher-order standards in terms of which the officials are *authorised* to make the demands they do. Their demands therefore impose *obligations* on us – obligations which exist independently of whether we will in fact be punished, and which justify our punishment if we are in fact punished. Austinian predictions of punishment, by contrast, are not normative – they are made purely from the external point of view – and they therefore cannot explain why punishment is *appropriate* or *justified*. They fail to capture the distinctive way in which law purports to govern our conduct, namely, by imposing duties to comply, not by threatening us with harm. Austin thinks that rules are obligatory because sanctions are attached to their breach, but it is exactly the other way around: sanctions are used when rules are thought of as obligatory.

To avoid confusion, it is necessary again to emphasise that the obligations created by legal rules are not necessarily, according to Hart, *morally* defensible. It is tempting to think that the difference between the gunman and the tax official must be that the tax official's demands differ from the gunman's in being morally legitimate. But this is not Hart's view. Hart claims merely that the tax official's demands are *legally* justified, not morally justified, there being no guarantee that the law's demands will coincide with those of morality. Though law *should*, of course, be morally acceptable, Hart believes that it might not be.

Indeed, as Hart points out, a system of law may well be *more* unjust than a system of primary rules, in creating 'the risk that the centrally organised power may . . . be used for the oppression of numbers with whose support it can dispense, in a way that the simpler regime of primary rules could not' (Hart, 1994, p 202). An example might be a legal system which enforces slavery. Thus, for Hart, people can have legal rights and duties 'which have no moral justification or force whatever' (Hart, 1994, p 268). This point is of fundamental importance and we will return to it in 2.5. As we will see, it is the basis of Hart's attempt to carve out a position which is mid-way between the Austinian idea of law as founded on command and the natural law idea of law as founded on morality.

Hart's normative account of law is therefore superior to Austin's in being able to explain the difference between a bank robber and a tax official. Furthermore, Hart is also able to account for the other features of legal systems for which Austin cannot account: the continuity of the authority to make law, the persistence of law and the exercise of sovereign power by the electorate.

The reason why law-making power survives a change in individual law-makers is because the authority to make law is conferred on persons by virtue of their occupation of an 'office'. But how are we to understand the concept of 'office'? We cannot do so in terms of the sovereign's will, for the concept of office *defines* sovereignty, rather than the other way around. It is, in fact, a secondary rule which underpins the office of law-maker – a rule of constitutional law that names the new law-maker or specifies how the new law-maker shall be determined. It is therefore a secondary rule which explains the continuity of the authority to make law. In an absolute monarchy, for instance, there might be a rule specifying that the new ruler shall be the first-born son of the previous monarch. If so, the first-born son has the *right* to make law on his father's death and this explains why the laws he makes are already law before the bulk of the population has shown any disposition to obey him. Hart's account of law-making authority in terms of a legal right to make law therefore succeeds where Austin's factual account of sovereignty fails.

Again, it is a secondary rule which accounts for the fact that laws made by an earlier legislator, now dead or now defunct, can still be valid law. The reason why statutes passed by a previous law-maker and not repealed are still law is that they were enacted by a person or body of persons whose enactments are accepted as *authoritative* under our rules. We have a rule of what is to count as law which embraces, as Hart says, 'past as well as present legislative operations' (Hart, 1994, p 65).

And finally, if we wish to treat the electorate as the sovereign, then we will need to rely on secondary rules which define what the members of society must do in order to *function* as an electorate and therefore to speak as a sovereign body. For it is 'their qualifications under certain rules, and their compliance with other rules, which define what is to be done by them to make a valid election or a law' (Hart, 1994, p 76). Legal rules *create* sovereign status. It is not, as Austin mistakenly supposed, the other way around – that all rules emanate from the sovereign.

1.7   Norms and coercion in Kelsen's theory of law

Like Hart, Hans Kelsen (1881–1973) was interested in providing a general theory of law, that is, one not tied to any particular legal system. He aimed, he said, to 'discover the nature of law itself, to determine its structure and its typical forms, independent of the changing content which it exhibits at different times and among different peoples' (Kelsen, 1941, p 44).

This required, he thought, a 'pure' theory of law, because in order to discover the *essence* of law – what distinguishes law from other social phenomena – one would have to exclude all *extraneous* and *non-legal* elements, such as moral, sociological, psychological and political factors. 'The pure theory of law', Kelsen said:

> undertakes to delimit the cognition of law against these disciplines…because it wishes to avoid the uncritical mixture of methodologically different disciplines…which obscures the essence of the science of law and obliterates the limits imposed upon it by the nature of its subject matter.
>
> (Kelsen, 1967, p 1)

Kelsen believed that moral and political factors are extraneous to an account of law because he took the view that what is right and wrong is a subjective matter. He thought that value-judgments are based on 'emotional factors' and therefore cannot be verified by facts (Kelsen, 1945, p 6). Law, by contrast, he thought of as an *objective* matter and therefore susceptible to what he called 'scientific' study. He thought that it would contaminate the legal scientist's detached, objective descriptions of the subject matter if subjective moral tests were to be used in identifying law. Hence he concluded that moral considerations cannot contribute to determining what the law is (as opposed to determining what it ought to be).

Legal science is different from sociological and psychological accounts of law, in Kelsen's view, because the latter do not account for law's normativity. They describe the phenomena of law 'in propositions that tell how [men] *actually*…behave' whereas the science of law 'describes the phenomena of law…in propositions that state how men *should* behave' (Kelsen, 1941, p 52, my emphasis). Social scientific theories of law are therefore inadequate as a description of law because they fail to recognise that 'jurisprudence can describe its object' not 'in *is*-statements' but 'only in *ought*-statements' (Kelsen, 1959–1960, p 270, Kelsen's emphasis).

Notice, however, that Kelsen did not say that the law should not be studied in its moral, social and historical context. He claimed only that such study does not amount to *legal science*, which is the study of how people ought to behave according to positive law – according to the law as we find it, rather than the law as we would like it to be. As Joseph Raz explains, '[t]he picture of law dictated by the methodology of the Pure Theory is of law in the books, of an analysis of law using as the raw material only law reports and statute-books' (Raz, 1994, p 201).

Kelsen answered our question about the distinctive features of law in the following way. He said that law is not a fact, but a norm; that law, unlike morality, is a coercive order; that legal norms are created by acts of human beings; that such norms cannot be regarded as valid unless they are by and large effective; that the reason for their validity is a constitution which authorises their creation and that the reason for the validity of the constitution is a norm we presuppose; and hence that this presupposition is the condition under which every effective coercive order established by acts of human beings may be interpreted as a system of objectively valid norms.

This sounds very obscure but its meaning will become clearer if we pay attention to each of the building-blocks of the definition in turn: 'norms', 'coercion', 'validity', 'presupposition' and 'effectiveness'.

As we have seen, Kelsen insisted that law is a system of norms or 'ought'-statements, rejecting, like Hart, all reductionistic theories, such as Austin's, which aim to convert statements of law into descriptive statements. He thought that to say that a law is 'valid' is to say that an individual *ought* to behave in a way determined by the law. Kelsen further claimed that what distinguishes legal norms from other norms, like moral norms, is that legal norms are coercive in nature and that they are addressed to legal officials. Thus Kelsen thought that legal norms are authorisations to officials to impose sanctions, such as the deprivation of life, liberty, health or property. Thus a norm prohibiting murder can be translated, according to Kelsen, into the following instruction to a judge: 'if anyone commits murder, you (the judge) ought to impose a sanction on that person.' All legal norms can be formulated in statements of this kind, according to Kelsen.

Note, however, that when Kelsen talks about legal statements as 'ought'-statements it is legal 'oughts' he has in mind, not moral 'oughts'. In this respect his theory is similar to Hart's. Legal statements are, for Kelsen, statements which describe the circumstances under which law provides that sanctions ought to be applied. Whether such sanctions are *justly* applied is another matter entirely. The importance of this will be made plain in the next chapter.

Note also that we should not confuse Kelsen's theory about the role sanctions play in law with Austin's theory (McCoubrey and White, 1996, p 136). For Austin, legal obligations should be understood as predictions of the likelihood of being punished: law is what *is* enforced by coercion. For Kelsen, by contrast, legal statements convey information about the sanctions which officials (legally) *ought* to apply. For instance, the statement 'X is under a legal obligation to do Y' means 'if X fails to do Y, the law stipulates that coercion ought to be applied to X.' The statement does not *predict* the application of a sanction and remains true regardless of whether the sanction is or is not applied.

At the same time, Kelsen's and Austin's views are similar in one respect, namely, that both think that coercion is law's distinctive function, and Kelsen's views consequently suffer from the same defect that Hart identified in Austin's – the dogmatic attempt to reduce the complex phenomenon of law to just one element. The price of such 'spurious uniformity' is, according to Hart, distortion of the subject matter (Hart, 1994, p 49, 38). In particular, it conceals the fact that different kinds of laws serve different functions.

As we know from our discussion of Austin, Hart emphasises the fact that some laws play a facilitative role, not a coercive role. They provide us with options we would not otherwise have – the option, for instance, of disposing of our property on death (see 1.3). Hart concedes that, with sufficient ingenuity, legal rules which confer powers on us, such as rules which empower us to make a will, can be rewritten in Kelsen's format as conditional ought-statements. Thus the rule that states that two witnesses are required for the making of a valid will can be seen as a mere fragment of a more complete rule, stating: 'if there has been a will witnessed by two witnesses, and signed by the testator, and if the executor has not given effect to the provisions of the will, then the court ought to apply sanctions to the executor.'

But the trouble with this, as Hart points out, is that we do not really understand the nature of rules which confer powers on individuals, such as the power to make a will, if we leave out the perspective of those whom they empower. Such power-conferring rules are extremely valuable to us, and they therefore appear to us as 'an *additional* element introduced by the law into social life over and above that of coercive control' (Hart, 1994, p 41, my emphasis). Kelsen's analysis of legal norms as authorisations to officials to impose sanctions therefore conceals the distinctive nature and function of the different kinds of rules which go to make up a legal system.

1.8   Kelsen's hierarchy of norms

In order to explain the source of the validity of positive legal norms – legal norms laid down by human beings – and to explain what confers unity on a legal system, Kelsen, like Hart, took the view that the validity of any legal norm depends on its membership in a system of norms. In particular, Kelsen postulated a hierarchy of norms, each norm deriving its validity from a higher norm in the hierarchy. This hierarchy culminates in an ultimate source of validity which Kelsen called the 'grundnorm' or basic norm – a point at which the chain of validation can go no further. Kelsen writes: '[a]ll norms whose validity can be traced back to one and the same basic norm constitute a system of norms, a normative order. The basic norm is the common source for the validity of all norms that belong to the same order – it is their common reason of validity' (Kelsen, 1967, p 195).

In order to understand this, consider the following situation. Suppose you find a parking ticket on your car and you want to know if you are obliged to pay the fine. Does the law objectively require you to pay the fine? The answer to this question depends on whether you parked unlawfully. That will depend in the first instance on whether the local authority has made relevant regulations. But that is just the beginning of the inquiry. The validity of the regulations in turn depends on their conformity with another norm, namely an act of parliament authorising the authority to make regulations with respect to parking. The validity of parliament's statute likewise depends on another norm, namely, that in terms of constitutional law parliament has the legislative power to pass the statute, either because the statute is not in breach of any limits on its legislative power or because its legislative power is unlimited. The validity of the constitution may in turn be a function of the fact that it has evolved from an older constitution or was created in terms of the rules of an older constitution by way of constitutional amendment. At a certain point in this chain or hierarchy of norms we arrive at the starting-point of the current constitutional order. Kelsen calls this the 'historically first' constitution. It is a constitution that cannot be traced to an older constitution but arose either as a result of a revolution (that is, in a manner not consistent with the constitution valid until that point) or as a result of a grant of independence to a former colony. The historically first constitution in the case of England would be the settlement which followed the Glorious Revolution of 1688.

If we now ask why this 'historically first constitution' is valid we cannot trace its validity to a positive or created legal norm. Instead, according to Kelsen, we have to postulate a basic norm or 'grundnorm' – a *non-positive* norm which authorises the creation of all legal norms, including that of the historically first constitution, and which provides that '[c]oercive acts ought to be performed under the conditions and in the manner which the historically first constitution, and the norms created according to it, prescribe' (Kelsen, 1967, p 201). In short, the grundnorm provides that one ought to behave as the historically first constitution prescribes. When we reach the grundnorm we have, according to Kelsen, reached a point at which the enterprise of justifying legal statements must stop.

It is the existence of the grundnorm which, for Kelsen, makes the difference between a gangster's demands and a tax official's demands. Both demands express an individual's *subjective* wish that another person should pay over a certain amount of money, but the official's demands are authorised by a tax law, and ultimately by the grundnorm, and this confers *objective* validity on them. It is by virtue of the grundnorm that we can say that the official's demands objectively *ought* to be obeyed. By contrast, 'no basic norm is presupposed according to which one ought to behave in conformity with [the gangster's] order' (Kelsen, 1967, p 47). Once again, however, Kelsen does not identify legal validity with moral validity: it is not the *justifiability* of the official's demands which distinguishes them from the gangster's but the fact that they have been created in a way which is authorised by the grundnorm. To say that a legal norm is valid is merely to say that it exists within the legal system.

The chain of authorisation can also, of course, be followed in the other direction: from the abstraction of the grundnorm down to an actual decision or legal action. Kelsen calls this a process of 'concretisation', because at each point down the chain the norms become more specific and concrete. At the end-point we reach a norm authorising force in the particular set of circumstances which define the case at hand – for instance, a judge's order that a particular defendant should pay damages of a certain amount to a particular plaintiff, an order which will be backed up by the threat of seizure of the defendant's property should the defendant not pay what he or she owes.

Although both Hart's rule of recognition and Kelsen's grundnorm are ultimate norms, in the sense that there is no more fundamental norm from which they derive their legal authority and therefore no *legal* justification for them (Hart, 1994, pp 107–10; Raz, 1979, pp 68–9), there is also an important difference between their views. In particular, whereas Hart insists that the rule of recognition is identifiable empirically by reference to social facts – namely, the practice of the courts in identifying what counts as law – Kelsen conceptualised the grundnorm as a theoretical idea or hypothesis we have to make if 'we want to interpret the acts performed according to [the historically first constitution] as the creation or application of valid general legal norms' (Kelsen, 1967, p 200). This difference can be accounted for in part by the different influences on their thought. Where Hart was influenced by Bentham and Austin's social realism, and especially by their emphasis on law as a social construct, Kelsen was under the influence of Kantian philosophy.

Immanuel Kant (1724–1804) thought that knowledge is not independent of the human mind, but is partly constructed by it. In particular, categories like time, space and causality do not inhere in reality but are imposed by us on the world as a means of understanding it. Kelsen applied this analysis to the phenomenon of law, saying that the 'science' of law is a way of making sense of legal reality. 'Science', here, does not mean 'natural science'. It does not, in other words, mean the science which is concerned with evidence and causality. For Kelsen, the science of law aims to expose the *logical* structure of legal systems or the categories which must be imposed on the phenomenon of law in order to understand it.

According to Kelsen, the science of law has to hypothesise the concept of the grundnorm in order to make sense of the fact that we describe conduct as legal or illegal, that is, as conduct which objectively ought or ought not, according to law, to be done. This hypothesis or presupposition provides the logical basis, he says, for understanding how a subjective act of will (a demand that other people act in a certain way) can assume the form of an objectively valid legal norm. It is therefore a merely theoretical construction.

Kelsen explains: '[the basic norm] is presupposed to be valid because without this presupposition no human act could be interpreted as a legal, especially as a norm-creating act... The basic norm is the answer to the question: how ... are all these juristic statements concerning legal norms, legal duties, legal rights, and so on, possible?' (Kelsen, 1945, pp 116–17). It is, in other words, only by assuming that the grundnorm is valid – by assuming that all laws made in accordance with the historically first constitution ought to be obeyed – that we are able to make sense of the fact that we count certain standards as *legal* standards rather than as an 'aggregate of commands' (Kelsen, 1959–1960, p 276).

As JW Harris observes:

> [e]ffectively enforced acts of purported legislation come first and, indeed, could be recorded sociologically, without the help of any basic norm. But if we interpret them juristically, by speaking of their contents as 'legally binding', then we presuppose a basic norm. That presupposition adds a top-dressing of 'oughtness' to the power-facts on the ground.
>
> (Harris, 1997, p 77)

It should be obvious that Kelsen does not believe that legal norms manifest themselves or are explicitly formulated in the way he describes – that as we go about our daily business we are self-consciously invoking the grundnorm as the basis of the validity of our particular transactions.

1.9   Kelsen and revolutionary political changes

As we have seen, Kelsen believes that the grundnorm validates whatever constitutional order is currently in force. But how do we know what constitutional order is in force? Kelsen's answer to this is: whatever constitution is 'effective', a constitution being effective when the norms whose creation it licenses are on the whole applied and obeyed. This implies that if there is a revolution in a particular country (i.e., an unlawful break with the past rather than a change by constitutional means), and if the revolutionary leaders are effectively in control and generally obeyed, we have to postulate a new grundnorm as the reason for the validity of the new constitutional order.

Kelsen explains that he does not regard validity and effectiveness as *identical*. Effectiveness is a *condition* of the validity of legal norms but the *reason* for their validity is the grundnorm. Thus legal norms are valid only *while* the political order to which they correspond is effective, but the *reason* that the norms are valid is the presupposed grundnorm.

Kelsen writes:

> [s]uppose that a group of individuals attempt to seize power by force...If they succeed, if the old order ceases, and the new order begins to be efficacious, because the individuals whose behaviour the new order regulates actually behave, by and large, in conformity with the new order, then this order is considered as a valid order. It is now according to this new order that the actual behavior of individuals is interpreted as legal or illegal. But this means that a new basic norm is presupposed. It is...a norm endowing the revolutionary government with legal authority.
>
> (Kelsen, 1945, p 118)

Kelsen's pragmatic line of reasoning is easy to understand: if political reality no longer corresponds to the old order, that order must have ceased to be legally valid, and the usurpers must be acknowledged as the lawful government against the background of a new grundnorm. The new order may not be *morally* legitimate but that is an entirely different issue, relying on moral and political considerations which, as we know, fall outside Kelsen's pure theory.

There are some interesting cases in which courts asked to pronounce on the legality of a coup d'etat have validated the coup by reference to Kelsen's doctrine of effectiveness. Finding that the coup has been effective, they pronounce the new order lawful. Some scholars criticise this approach on the ground that it rewards and even encourages treason, though it is not, in fact, clear that Kelsen would have endorsed this particular use of his theory. For Kelsen, the grundnorm is a presupposition made by *jurists* – that is, people who are not officials – *after* an effective seizure of power has taken place. By contrast, judges who are asked to pronounce a coup valid are usually in the midst of events and are being asked to put their weight behind the seizure of power. This was exactly the situation in the recent case of *Republic of Fiji v Prasad* (2001).

In 2000, the military had overthrown Fiji's elected government and had issued a decree abrogating the 1997 Fijian Constitution. Prasad, a farmer who had been forced off his land during the upheaval, brought an action in the High Court of Fiji, seeking a declaration that the revocation of the 1997 Constitution was unconstitutional and that the elected government was still a legally constituted government. The High Court found for Prasad, at which point the Interim Civilian Government, established by the military, appealed to the Court of Appeal.

As George Williams explains:

> the High Court and Court of Appeal were not placed in the passive role of observers of an historical shift in the *Grundnorm* of Fiji. They were cast in the centre of an unfolding drama as important actors, and were asked by the coup leaders to recognise a new regime so as actually to lead to a shift in the basic norm of the nation.
>
> (Williams, 2001, pp 91–2)

Prasad is a very important case because the court refused to recognise the validity of the coup, saying that the overthrow of the 1997 Constitution was illegal. This makes it the only case in which a domestic court has pronounced a coup illegal (Williams, 2001, p 74). Though the court spoke the language of effectiveness, in fact it departed from Kelsen's understanding of effectiveness, saying that compliance with the new laws is not sufficient: obedience to the new regime must stem from popular acceptance and support, not from tacit submission to coercion or fear of force. It then went on to find that the Interim Civilian Government did not enjoy the required public support and that the revolution had therefore not been successful. Remarkably, the government agreed to implement the court's decision

Prasad was, it must be admitted, a very special case. The usurping government had been in existence for only seven months. The situation would obviously have been very different if many years had elapsed and the revolutionary government had decisively established itself in power. Furthermore, there had been no attempt to replace the court system of the old regime and it was the usurping government itself which made the legality of the new order the subject of a court case, promising to promote a return to constitutional legality if the court were to uphold the 1997 Constitution. *Prasad* nevertheless has something to teach us, namely, that while Kelsen is right that there may come a point at which the brute facts of political reality require legal acknowledgment, we should not be too quick to assume that this point has been reached.

Chapter 2

Law and morality

In the previous chapter we considered the relationship between law, force and norms. In this chapter we turn to the relationship between law and morality. Everyone agrees that morality can, and usually does, play a role in law. There is disagreement, however, as to whether there is any role it *must* play. In particular, while some theorists hold that any moral value or moral merit which law may have is merely contingent, others disagree, saying that there is a necessary connection between law and morality. They say it is *inherent* in the very *concept* of law that its content should conform to moral requirements. The former belong in the positivist camp and the latter in the natural law camp. This chapter will explore their rival views.

You should be familiar with the following areas:

- Classical natural law theory
- Finnis's restatement of natural law theory
- Fuller's 'procedural' version of natural law
- Legal positivism and the separability thesis
- The difference between inclusive and exclusive positivism
- Ethical positivism

2.1 Classical natural law theory

Natural law theory has been remarkably influential since it made its first appearance 2,500 years ago in ancient Greece. Its origins lie in the idea that there is a rational order which exists in nature and which is discoverable by human reason. This rational order is said to be the source of universal and objective moral standards, that is, standards of right and wrong in human conduct. Furthermore, these moral standards are thought to constitute a form of *law* – natural law (as opposed to 'man-made' law). Since this form of law owes its existence and authority to nature and not to human beings, it is irrelevant whether it is recognised by positive or human legal systems. Furthermore, it is a *higher* form of law and is therefore capable of invalidating human standards which are in conflict with it. At its most extreme, this view sees moral validity as necessarily a precondition for legal validity, holding that nothing can be law that is not moral. A less extreme version holds that it is only standards which *flagrantly* breach the standards of morality which cannot be regarded as laws or lose their character as laws.

We find these notions already in a rudimentary form in ancient Greece . For instance, in Sophocles' play, *Antigone*, Antigone has to decide whether to obey a command of the king, Creon, that her brother's body should not be buried but left to be devoured by the beasts. The Greeks thought that such a fate would lead to horrible suffering in the afterlife. Antigone scatters earth on her brother's body, and is arrested and brought to Creon. She defends herself by saying:

> These laws were not ordained of Zeus,
> And she who sits enthroned with gods below,
> Justice, enacted not these human laws.
> Nor did I deem that thou, a mortal man,
> Couldst by a breath annul and override
> The immutable unwritten laws of heaven.
> They were not born today nor yesterday;
> They die not; and none knoweth whence they sprang.
>
> (Kelly, 1992, p 20)

We find a more elaborate working-out of the idea of natural law in the Stoics, whose views in turn influenced Roman thought and were famously summarised by Cicero, a Roman writer of the first century BC, in his *De Republica*. Cicero wrote:

> [t]rue law is right reason in agreement with nature; it is of universal application, unchanging and everlasting...It is a sin to try to alter this law, nor is it allowable to attempt to repeal any part of it, and it is impossible to abolish it entirely. We cannot be freed from its obligations by senate or people...And there will not be different laws at Rome and at Athens, or different laws now and in the future, but one eternal and unchangeable law will be valid for all nations and for all times, and there will be one master and one ruler, that is, God, over us all, for he is the author of this law, its promulgator and its enforcing judge.
>
> (Cicero, 1928 edn, Book 3, 33)

Here we see all the essential elements of the idea of natural law: human beings are not the source of true law; the dictates of true law are universal, unchanging and discoverable by human reason; and human standards must conform with these higher moral standards in order to be legally valid.

These ideas passed subsequently into the teaching of the Christian Church, natural laws being understood as the commands of God. Thus the highest law for St Augustine (345–430) was the will of God. 'Lex iniusta non est lex', he wrote, which, translated literally, means: 'an unjust law is not a law'. But it is really mediaeval Christianity and especially the writings of Saint Thomas Aquinas (1225–1274) which are most strongly associated with the classical natural law tradition. In his *Summa Theologica*, Aquinas synthesised classical Graeco-Roman ideas of natural law as discoverable by human reason with the teachings of Christianity.

Aquinas was influenced by the Aristotelian doctrine that everything has its own nature or end which it is necessarily good to attain. To be an oak tree, for instance, is the optimum state of existence towards which an acorn tends. Aquinas fused these Aristotelian concepts with Christian thinking, saying that it is God who directs everything in nature towards its end. This divine plan he called 'eternal law'. Human beings, unlike other creatures, have the capacity for reason and Aquinas thought that reason allows us to discern what ends are natural for us and therefore the good we should pursue and the evil we should avoid, as directed by God. This part of the eternal law, which humans are capable of discerning with human reason, Aquinas called natural law: 'the natural law is nothing else than the rational creature's participation of the eternal law' (Aquinas, 1947 edn, 1a 2ae 91. 2).

Thus natural law for Aquinas consists in those rules for guiding our conduct which reason reveals are the route to human flourishing in the way intended by God. And the divinely ordained function of government, according to Aquinas, is to translate the dictates of the natural law into temporal or positive standards. Law, says Aquinas, is a rational ordinance made for the good of the community by those who have the powers of government. And human laws which deviate from this ideal standard are therefore a 'perversion' of law:

> [a]s Augustine says, 'that which is not just seems to be no law at all', wherefore the force of a law depends on the extent of its justice. Now in human affairs a thing is said to be just from being right according to the rule of reason. But the first rule of reason is the law of nature. Consequently, every human law has just so much of the nature of law as it is derived from the law of nature. But if in any point it deflects from the law of nature, it is no longer a law but a perversion of law.
>
> (Aquinas, 1947 edn, 1a 2ae 95.2)

Such laws are not binding in conscience, 'except perhaps in order to avoid scandal or disturbance' (Aquinas, 1947 edn, 1a 2ae 96.4).

Though human law must, for Aquinas, be compatible with natural law, it need not necessarily be derived from natural law in a deductive way. It may instead be derived by a process of 'determination of particulars'. Aquinas gives the example of a law providing for one type of punishment rather than another. It is a principle of natural law that an evil-doer should be punished, but when deciding 'that he be punished in this way or that way' (Aquinas, 1947 edn, 1a 2ae 95.2), there is a range of permissible punishments from which legislators may choose. In other words, they enjoy a degree of freedom. Aquinas therefore believes that there is a need for a system of human law, for human law is required to supplement or fill out the very general principles of natural law.

Classical natural law theory took a more secular and individualistic turn in the seventeenth and eighteenth centuries. Many trace these modern developments to Hugo Grotius (1583–1645), who announced that natural law would retain its validity even if God did not exist (Grotius, 1625, Prolegomena, para 11). Here we see the seeds of the idea that the law of nature can be elaborated without reference to theological presuppositions.

It was not long before the emphasis came to be placed not so much on natural *law* but on natural *rights* or rights enjoyed by all humans by virtue of their nature. (For a detailed discussion of such rights – now generally called 'human rights' – see Chapter 5.) Thus John Locke (1632–1704) saw the 'law of nature' as decreeing that 'no-one ought to harm another in his Life, Health, Liberty, or Possessions' (Locke, 1690, s 6), and he argued that it is the primary function of the state to respect the rights to life, liberty and property to which the law of nature gives rise.

The doctrine of natural rights would come to justify the American and French Revolutions, its iconic expression being the American Declaration of Independence of 1776:

> [w]e hold these truths to be self-evident, that all men are created equal, that they are endowed by their Creator with certain unalienable Rights, that among these are Life, Liberty and the pursuit of Happiness. That to secure these rights, Governments are instituted among Men, deriving their just powers from the consent of the governed. That whenever any form of Government becomes destructive of these ends, it is the Right of the People to alter or abolish it.

Finally, for a contemporary statement of classical natural law beliefs, consider the following statement made by Deryck Beyleveld and Roger Brownsword: '[i]n our view, iniquitous rules cannot be legally valid; and, for the record, we would not consciously speak of unjust *laws*' (Beyleveld and Brownsword, 1985, p 2 n 1, Beyleveld and Brownsword's emphasis).

2.2   Natural law in the courts

Courts have, on occasion, made use of classical natural law reasoning, especially when dealing with laws passed by murderous regimes. In unusual circumstances like these, they have sometimes been willing to invalidate formally valid rules of the previous regime. After the collapse of the Nazi regime, for instance, the German courts were faced with a series of cases called the 'grudge' cases. These involved the prosecution of people who had exploited the oppressive laws of the Nazis in order to settle a grudge or for some other malicious motive. One woman, for instance, who had tired of her husband, denounced him to the authorities, reporting that he had made critical comments about Hitler and the Nazi party.

The making of such comments was illegal in terms of Nazi law and the husband was sentenced to the death penalty. After the war ended, the wife was prosecuted for the offence of illegally depriving a person of his freedom. She, of course, defended herself by saying that since her husband's conduct was illegal in terms of Nazi law, she could not have been guilty of a crime. She had merely taken steps to ensure that the law was enforced. How, then, could she have committed an offence?

According to Hart, in his well-known discussion of this case, the German court took the view that the Nazi statute violated natural law. It held that although the Nazi statute in terms of which the husband was sentenced to death was valid in terms of all the standard criteria of validity for Nazi laws, it was so evil as not to be a law. The statute was so 'contrary to the sound conscience and sense of justice of all decent human beings' (Hart, 1958, p 619) that, in informing on her husband, the wife had acted not merely immorally but also, despite appearances, *illegally*. The court concluded that she was guilty of the offence with which she had been charged.

Though there is some debate about the accuracy of this interpretation of the case, it should be noted that it is not the only German case which appears to take the view that unjust laws may be invalid and can be ignored. After the collapse of the German Democratic Republic, for instance, a GDR law allowing East German border guards to shoot at people attempting to flee over the Berlin Wall was held to be invalid, and the guards were found guilty of manslaughter (Alexy, 1999, pp 20–2).

There are also some well-known seventeenth-century English cases in which judges invoked the *common* law as a proxy for natural law, appearing to suggest that there were certain moral principles, inherent in the common law, which could not be abrogated by acts of parliament or by the monarch. The most famous of these is *Dr Bonham's Case* of 1610 in which Chief Justice Coke said: 'when an Act of Parliament is against common right and reason, or repugnant, or impossible to be performed, the common law will controul it, and adjudge such Act to be void' (at 118a).

After the Glorious Revolution, it was assumed that the principle of the sovereignty of parliament had triumphed and that the courts could not invalidate acts of parliament. Yet the notion of fundamental moral principles higher than parliamentary sovereignty continued to make its presence felt. For one thing, the atrocities of Nazi Germany invited a resurgence of natural law thought not only in Germany but also in England. Thus in *Oppenheimer v Cattermole* (1976) a majority of the House of Lords indicated that it would refuse to recognise a Nazi law depriving Jewish citizens of German nationality (despite the fact that the law met all the standard criteria of legal validity in terms of English legal rules) because it was morally iniquitous. Lord Cross of Chelsea said:

> legislation which takes away without compensation from a section of the citizen body singled out on racial grounds all their property ... and ... deprives them of their citizenship ... constitutes so grave an infringement of human rights that the courts of this country ought to refuse to recognise it as a law at all.
>
> (at 278)

Second, it is worth mentioning recent developments in English public law and, in particular, the theory of 'common law constitutionalism'. This theory exemplifies an approach to the interpretation of statutes which, while formally acknowledging the unlimited sovereignty of the Westminster Parliament and therefore its ability to make morally repugnant legislation, in practice secures certain principles of justice very effectively. Those who adhere to this view hold that there are certain common law rights and principles of justice in the light of which all legislation must be interpreted and which are so fundamental that parliament can take them away only by legislating in the most unambiguous and unmistakable terms. The effect of this is to make it extremely difficult for parliament to repudiate fundamental human rights despite the absence of a written constitution expressly limiting its powers.

An example of this approach to interpretation can be seen in the recent case of *R (Anufrijeva) v Home Secretary* (2004). A regulation provided that an asylum seeker's income support benefit terminated on the date on which the Home Secretary's rejection of the claim to asylum was 'recorded'. In the context of the regulations as a whole, 'recorded' was not in the least ambiguous: it was quite clear that there was no need to notify the claimant of the decision. The majority of the House of Lords nevertheless found that the entitlement continued until notice of the rejection was sent some months later. Lord Steyn referred to the 'constitutional principle' that individuals have the right to know of a decision before their rights can be adversely affected, describing the proposition that uncommunicated administrative decisions can bind individuals as 'astonishingly unjust' (at 621 and 622). Since Parliament had not 'in specific and unmistakeable terms legislated to displace the applicable constitutional principles' (at 622), the decision could not have legal effect until the claimant had been notified. As Lord Cooke notes in his article, 'The Road Ahead for the Common Law', '[a] principle capable of transforming statutory regulations in this way seems so potent that the depth of common law constitutional rights is virtually measureless' (Cooke, 2004, p 278).

2.3   John Finnis's neo-Thomism

Classical natural law theory apparently asserts not simply that laws may fail to be *just*. Who, after all, would deny that? It seems to make the much stronger claim that rules which meet all the acknowledged criteria of legal validity in a legal system but are morally iniquitous might fail to be *laws*. Yet it seems obvious that there are morally reprehensible legal systems, such as that of apartheid South Africa, which are nevertheless truly describable as *legal* systems.

Some natural law theorists, responding to this difficulty, argue that natural law theory when properly understood does not make quite this claim. John Finnis, for instance, who is a contemporary natural law theorist writing in the classical tradition – he is heavily influenced by Aquinas in particular – argues that this claim is a caricature of classical natural law theory and he attempts to restate the theory in a way which avoids it.

In his important book, *Natural Law and Natural Rights*, Finnis distinguishes what he calls the 'focal' meaning of law from its 'secondary' meaning (Finnis, 1980, p 11). The focal conception of law is an ideal form of law, a form to which actual law is merely an approximation. The central case of law is the law of what Finnis calls 'a complete community', where a complete community is 'an all-round association' in which are co-ordinated 'the initiatives and activities of individuals, of families, and of the vast network of intermediate associations' (Finnis, 1980, p 147). Its 'point or common good' is to secure 'a whole ensemble of material and other conditions that tend to favour the realization, by each individual in the community, of his or her personal development' (Finnis, 1980, p 154).

Thus when 'law' is used in its focal or central meaning it describes rules which secure the common good by co-ordinating the different goods of individuals. This is the true purpose of law. It follows from this, says Finnis, that unjust laws are not laws in the *focal* sense of the term. They are not 'true' laws, or law 'in the fullest sense', in the same way that a neglectful parent may be described as 'no parent'. They are defective *as laws* and therefore, judged from the perspective of law's focal meaning, 'less' legal than laws that are just (Finnis, 1980, p 279).

But there are also, in Finnis's view, secondary meanings of the term 'law': here we are talking about instances of law which are 'undeveloped, primitive, corrupt, deviant or other "qualified sense" or "extended sense" instances of the subject-matter'(Finnis, 1980, p 11). When we are concerned with law in such a secondary sense – when we are concerned with what is merely 'in a *sense*' law – there is no point in saying that unjust laws lack legal validity. Rather, they are valid laws which fall short of the moral ideals which are contained in the concept of law in its fullest sense. The technical, lawyer's perspective, according to which any standard which meets the acknowledged criteria of validity in a particular legal system is valid, therefore sits alongside and can co-exist with the moralised account of law, on which 'true' law aims at the common good.

Natural law, for Finnis, provides the fundamental principles of any legal system that serves the true purpose of law. It does not function to invalidate human laws. Instead, it provides 'a rational basis for the activities of legislators, judges and citizens' (Finnis, 1980, p 290) and it furnishes a guide to deciding whether we have a moral obligation to obey the law in so far as positive law may diverge from the ideal standards of natural law.

In delineating the principles of natural law, Finnis's point of departure is, as it was with Aquinas, an analysis of human good. There are, according to Finnis, seven objective goods which, by virtue of our nature, make human life worthwhile. They are life, knowledge, play, aesthetic experience, sociability (especially friendship), practical reasonableness (bringing one's intelligence and judgment to bear in choosing how to live one's life) and religion (understood very broadly to encompass any interest in fundamental questions about the relationship between humanity and the cosmos).

All human societies, according to Finnis, show a concern for these values. Furthermore, these universal basic forms of good are equally fundamental or equally important: there is no objective hierarchy among them, though each of us can reasonably choose to treat one or some of them as of more significance in our lives. Finally, these goods are 'self-evidently' worth pursuing. By this Finnis means not that everyone will automatically recognise them, but that reasons cannot be offered for pursuing them: their status as goods is not inferable or derivable from more basic principles.

To think that these are objective values, Finnis explains, is not, as such, to think of them as moral values. Morality 'comes later' (Finnis, 1980, p 62). It enters by virtue of the fact that the basic goods can be pursued only in communal life. In particular, according to Finnis, we are guided in our choices among these goods in the context of communal life by certain universal requirements of practical reasonableness, each of which is 'a mode of moral obligation or responsibility' (Finnis, 1980, p 126). The requirements of practical reasonableness enable us to distinguish acts that are reasonable from acts that are unreasonable – acts that are morally right from acts that are morally wrong. They 'guide the transition from judgments about human goods to judgments about the right thing to do here and now' (Finnis, 1983, p 70).

One such requirement is the principle of impartiality or the principle that there should be no arbitrary preferences among persons: 'do to (or for) others what you would have them do to (or for) you' (Finnis, 1980, p 108). Another is the requirement of fostering the common good of one's community. A third – which is the basis of the notion of human rights, according to Finnis – is that one may never commit an act that of itself does nothing but damage a basic good, however beneficial the act's consequences. Thus I may not, for instance, sacrifice the life of one person (an act which of itself does nothing but damage the basic good of life) in order to save the lives of many others: the end does not justify the means. (For further discussion of rights as curbs on consequentialist reasoning, see 5.3.) There are also further requirements of practical reasonableness.

But the key point for our purposes is that the requirements of practical reasonableness provide the 'deep structure of moral thought' (Finnis, 1980, p 127) and that everything required by virtue of them 'is required by natural law' (Finnis, 1980, p 124). They therefore provide the fundamental principles of any legal system that meets the requirements of reason, and sound human laws will respect them and seek to implement them. It is, Finnis explains, one of the principal jurisprudential concerns of a theory of natural law to 'trace the ways in which sound laws ... are to be derived ... from unchanging principles – principles that have their force from their reasonableness' (Finnis, 1980, p 350).

Yet, as Lloyd Weinreb argues, it is difficult to see how the seven basic goods together with the principles of practical reasonableness can tell us with any degree of specificity or certainty what form sound law will take. As Weinreb says, '[t]he only principles that might plausibly be said to arise from reason ... are so general and abstract that they leave even the most basic legal obligations for further determination' (Weinreb, 1987, p 113).

What concrete legal obligations, for instance, can we deduce from the abstract requirement that we ought not deliberately to kill the innocent? Can such a principle tell us whether the law should allow you to kill, in self-defence, someone who is about to injure you seriously but not fatally? Or whether the law should allow killing to prevent theft of one's property? Or whether it should allow abortion or capital punishment and, if so, in what circumstances? It seems that it cannot. And, as Weinreb shows, the examples can be multiplied.

When we turn to the opponents of natural law we will see that there is much in Finnis's version of natural law with which they agree, raising the question as to how much of the natural law tradition Finnis has really retained. Hart agrees with Finnis, for instance, that sound moral principles should inform the law and that we may be obliged to disobey unjust positive laws (see 2.6). Where they are clearly at odds, though, is on the idea that just law is the *central* case of law. Hart writes:

> the identification of the central meaning of law with what is morally legitimate, because orientated towards the common good, seems to me in view of the hideous record of the evil use of law for oppression to be an unbalanced perspective, and as great a distortion as the opposite Marxist identification of the central case of law with the pursuit of the interests of a dominant economic class.
>
> (Hart, 1983, p 12)

2.4   Lon Fuller's internal morality of law

Lon Fuller (1902–1978) attempts to derive certain moral constraints on law from what he sees as law's essential characteristic. Like Hart, he takes issue with the view that the use of coercion or force serves to identify law. Though there is normally a mechanism ready to apply force in support of law, this does not mean, according to Fuller, that force is the identifying characteristic of law, any more than the fact that science depends on measuring instruments implies that the use of measuring instruments serves to identify science. In Fuller's view, the 'distinguishing mark' of law is that it is an activity with a certain *purpose*. In particular, law is 'the enterprise of subjecting human conduct to the governance of rules' (Fuller, 1969, p 106). And this enterprise, he goes on to say, contains a 'certain inner logic of its own' (Fuller, 1969, pp 150–1), imposing demands that must be met if it is to succeed in attaining its objectives.

Most obviously, if legislators were to attempt to decide every issue on an ad hoc basis, they would not be able to succeed in the enterprise of subjecting human conduct to the governance of *rules*. Likewise, if legislators did not promulgate their rules to those who are expected to observe them, the rules would not be capable of governing the latter's conduct. The same would be true if legislators were to make frequent use of retrospective rules; or use incomprehensible language in drafting the rules; or enact contradictory rules or rules with which it is impossible to comply; or change the rules so frequently that those subject to them would not have time to adjust to the changes; or if those who apply the rules were to depart from the law as enacted.

Because it is not possible for citizens to obey rules suffering from procedural defects like these, these defects would be 'routes to failure' in the enterprise of creating law (Fuller, 1969, p 41). And a total failure in all of these ways would result in something that is not simply bad law but not law at all. Just as we would not describe something that is totally incapable of cutting as a 'knife', so we would not describe a system of rules which is totally incapable of guiding conduct as a 'legal system'.

There are therefore certain procedural principles which make a legal system possible. Laws must be general, that is, refer to classes of people and circumstances, not individuals. Laws must be public. They must also be clear, non-contradictory, possible to obey, relatively constant and prospective. Finally, there must be congruence between official action and declared rule. Fuller calls these principles the 'principles of legality'. Though these principles do not need to be *perfectly* complied with, they must be *generally* complied with if a set of standards is to amount to a legal system. It is therefore a *necessary* truth, according to Fuller, that law consists of standards which by and large satisfy the principles of legality.

Fuller next goes on to argue that the principles of legality constitute a *moral* ideal. He points out, for instance, that retrospective laws, which punish us for conduct which was not unlawful at the time it was undertaken, are not merely incapable of changing our behaviour but are also widely perceived to be *unjust*. And rules which suffer from the other defects described above, like secret rules and incomprehensible rules, are similarly unjust.

Since for a system to be recognisable as law it must substantially conform with the principles of legality, and since, according to Fuller, these principles stand for certain moral values, it follows that we *cannot describe the nature of law without recourse to moral concepts*. The principles of legality are law's '*inner morality*' or 'the morality which makes law possible'. Law is therefore not an 'amoral datum' (Fuller, 1958, p 656) but an achievement worthy, at least to some extent, of respect.

Fuller thinks that Nazi Germany departed so far from the ideal of legal morality as to cease to be a legal system. He writes as follows about its procedural perversions:

> [w]hen a system calling itself law is predicated upon a general disregard by judges of the terms of the laws they purport to enforce, when the system habitually cures its legal irregularities, even the grossest, by retroactive statutes, when it has only to resort to forays of terror in the streets, which no one dares challenge, in order to escape even those scant restraints imposed by the pretence of legality – when all these things have become true of a dictatorship, it is not hard for me, at least, to deny to it the name of law.
>
> (Fuller, 1958, p 660)

Since Fuller believes that there is no law without substantial compliance with the principles of legal morality, his theory is a version of natural law theory. He describes it as a *procedural* version of natural law as opposed to the *substantive* version we find in classical natural law theory. Fuller explains that substantive natural law is concerned with the *content* of legal rules – with the substantive aims or ends that legal rules should seek to achieve. It holds that human laws whose aims are iniquitous are invalid by virtue of breach of a law that is *above* human law and that exists *independently* of human legal institutions. Fuller's natural law is not a *higher* law of this kind. Nor is Fuller concerned with the substance or content of legal rules. He focuses rather, as we have seen, on the procedural or, as he calls them, *inner* characteristics which must be displayed by a system of rules if it is to amount to a legal system – 'the ways in which a system of rules for governing human conduct must be constructed and administered' (Fuller, 1969, p 97) if it is to succeed in the enterprise of creating law – and, believing that there is a moral dimension to these procedural matters, he concludes that law and morality are necessarily connected.

For Fuller, therefore, the ideal of legality, which is a moral ideal, is built into the very *definition* of a legal system and the positivist attempt to draw a sharp distinction between legal obligations and moral obligations is misconceived: anything which is recognisable as law has an inbuilt claim on our moral allegiance. For Fuller this explains why we are thought to have a moral obligation of 'fidelity to law'.

Fuller's critics respond as follows. They agree with him that it is part of our concept of legal standards that they must be capable of being obeyed and therefore be generally framed, consistently applied, publicly announced, and so on. But – they say – this shows only that the principles of legality are essential to law's *effectiveness* or to effective law-making. It does not follow that the principles are principles of *morality* – any more than a recipe for successfully poisoning people yields a 'morality of poisoning' (Hart, 1983, pp 350–1). The principles of legality are ways of efficiently guiding conduct and legislators who depart wholesale from them will not succeed in influencing our behaviour. But though they are necessary for good laws, they are also compatible with bad laws. For instance, laws which discriminate on racial grounds can satisfy all the principles of legality. Indeed, if racist law-makers wish to succeed in their racist ends they would be well advised to enact laws which satisfy the principles of legality.

Fuller in turn replies that he believes that if law-makers respect the procedural ideals which are built into the concept of law they are more likely to pass good laws. He says that he will have to 'rest on the assertion of a belief that may seem naïve, namely that coherence and goodness have more affinity than coherence and evil' (Fuller, 1958, p 636). For 'when men are compelled to explain and justify their decisions, the effect will generally be to pull those decisions towards goodness' (Fuller, 1958, p 636). His critics remain unconvinced, regarding this as an article of faith, not an argument.

2.5   Legal positivism

So far we have discussed different versions of the natural law view that there is a necessary connection between the concepts of law and morality. They all have in common the idea that law is, as NE Simmonds puts it, the 'embodiment of a moral aspiration' (Simmonds, 2005, p 76): law is inherently something that serves justice and if it deviates too far from that path it is more accurate to describe it as terror than as law.

We turn now to the legal positivist view that there is no such necessary connection between the concepts of law and morality – that 'law is as serviceable for evil as for good' (Simmonds, 2005, p 61). This view is sometimes called the 'separability thesis'. It is a thesis to which Austin, Hart and Kelsen all adhere, despite their disagreements on other matters. Bentham (1748–1832) is also in their camp. Law, according to the separability thesis, is not necessarily just. The law as it *is* is not necessarily the law as it *ought* to be. 'A law which actually exists', said Austin, 'is a law, though we happen to dislike it' (Austin, 1832, p 157). '[T]he validity of positive legal norms', says Kelsen, 'does not depend on their conformity with the moral order' (Kelsen, 1967, p 68).

If we think back to the views of Austin, Hart and Kelsen about the identification of law, explained in the previous chapter, we will see why they think that law can assume any content, whether good or bad. For Austin, as we know, if a standard is to enjoy the status of law it must be traced to a command of the sovereign, and since the sovereign's commands may be evil, it follows that law and the standards of morality can come apart. For Hart, what makes a particular standard a legal standard is its conformity to conventionally accepted criteria of legal validity, and since there are no moral restrictions on what can come to be accepted as a matter of convention, law can be either good or bad. Finally, for Kelsen, the validity of any legal statement depends on the existence of an unbroken chain of norms which can be traced back to the historical starting-point of whatever legal order is currently in force, and ultimately to the grundnorm. Since the validity of legal statements depends solely on the fact that the norms have been created in a certain way – in a way authorised by the grundnorm – it follows, as Kelsen says, that '[l]egal norms may have any kind of content. There is no kind of human behaviour that, because of its nature, could not be made into a legal duty corresponding to a legal right' (Kelsen, 1945, p 113).

Thus our three thinkers all accept the separability thesis because for all of them the fact that a particular standard counts as law in a particular society is purely a matter of *chance events* or *contingent matters of social fact* – the fact that the sovereign happens to have commanded it, or that it satisfies criteria which happen to be accepted by legal officials, or that legal authorities have created it in a way which conforms to norms which happen to be contained in the constitution of an effective coercive order. From this 'social thesis' (Raz, 1979, p 38), or belief in the social foundation of the law, follows their distinctively positivist conclusion: 'nothing about the very existence of legal institutions, or about their lawness, tells us anything about their morality' (Schauer, 1998, p 70).

2.6   Some misconceptions about positivism

It is important to be quite clear on exactly what it is that legal positivists are claiming because their views tend to be caricatured in a number of ways.

First, they are not saying that there is no need for laws to be moral. They are not indifferent to the justice or injustice of law and they are therefore not 'amoralists'. On the contrary, they believe, of course, that laws *should* be just and that unjust laws should be exposed and criticised.

Second, legal positivism should not be confused with non-cognitivism or the theory that all moral judgments are subjective and that there are no right and wrong answers to moral questions. The philosopher David Hume (1711–1776) famously defended non-cognitivism. He argued that there is a fundamental difference between moral 'ought'-statements and factual 'is'-statements. Moral statements, he said, express our subjective attitudes of approval and disapproval, whereas factual statements describe the way the world objectively is. Thus a statement like, 'Many countries have the death penalty', is a factual statement, which tells us something objective about the world. It is, according to Hume, fundamentally different in kind from a statement like, 'The death penalty is wrong', which tells us something about the speaker's subjective attitude to the death penalty. Objective facts cannot dictate subjective attitudes. Moral statements therefore cannot be derived from factual statements and are incapable of rational defence. The so-called 'logical positivists' – who held that all knowledge derives from empirical experience – were led by their epistemological beliefs (beliefs about knowledge) to non-cognitivism in ethics. But we should not, tempting though it is, confuse *legal* positivism with *logical* positivism and its associated non-cognitivist ethics.

The temptation has two sources. First, there is the coincidence in terminology: the fact that both help themselves to the label 'positivism'. Second, legal positivism and non-cognitivism make apparently similar claims: legal positivism insists on the distinction between the law as it is and the law as it ought to be, while non-cognitivism asserts that what ought to be the case cannot be derived from what is the case. These sound like similar claims. But in fact they are very different.

Legal positivism is a theory about the nature of *law*, not about the nature of *moral judgments*. It is a 'positivistic' theory because it takes the view that all law is 'posited' – that contingent matters of social fact are what make a standard a legal standard. Holding that the foundations of law are social, it concludes that legal standards are not guaranteed to coincide with moral standards: however unjust a law may be, it is nevertheless a law. This is different from the non-cognitivist/ logical positivist view that moral standards do not have a rational basis. Legal positivists (from now on 'positivists' for short) *may* hold the latter view as well, but they are certainly not committed to it.

While Kelsen, for instance, distinguished law and morality on the basis that law is objective whereas standards of justice are relative and not rationally discoverable, Bentham and Austin believed that the standards of justice are no less universal and objective than legal standards. The particular moral theory which Bentham and Austin took to be objectively true was utilitarianism. We will discuss this theory in 5.3. It states that the standards of right conduct are to be found in the 'greatest happiness principle'. Laws which do not serve the end of maximum human happiness are therefore objectively unjust, according to Bentham and Austin, but – so they insist – their injustice is no barrier to their enjoying legal status. Their positivism is therefore not based on the belief that there is no objective basis on which to say what the law morally ought to be.

Third, positivism is not an *immoral* thesis which legitimates the laws of the state and encourages blind obedience to them, however tyrannical the laws may be. Though some legal theorists are guilty of this misunderstanding of positivism – Fuller is an example – many positivists argue that their theory has, in fact, the opposite effect. They say that there are *moral* as well as conceptual reasons for insisting on the separability of law and morality. They point out that their view highlights the potential for conflict between our legal obligations and moral obligations, noting that once citizens understand that ascription of legal status to a rule does not convey automatic moral approval of the rule, they will be *more* rather than less likely to resist tyrannical laws.

Certainly, one of the reasons why the early positivists like Bentham and Austin stressed the distinction between the law as it is and the law as it ought to be is because they thought the distinction facilitated a critical and reforming attitude to the law. And Hart finds positivism morally attractive for similar reasons. As Raz points out, Hart's attitude to the law is 'unromantic' (Raz, 1994, p 210). Instead of venerating the law, positivism encourages individuals to rely on their own conscience when confronting a powerful state. Hart tells us that the law does not automatically deserve our respect but must *earn* it:

> [w]hat surely is most needed in order to make men clear-sighted in confronting the official abuse of power, is that they should preserve the sense that the certification of something as legally valid is not conclusive of the question of obedience, and that, however great the aura of majesty or authority which the official system may have, its demands must in the end be submitted to a moral scrutiny.
>
> (Hart, 1994, p 210)

Fourth, positivists do not claim that law is 'neutral' in the sense of 'value-free', or that law and morality are always *separate* (Kramer, 1999, p 2). On the contrary, they believe that, in practice, law and morality usually overlap. This is not only because law is shaped by popular morality – the moral views endorsed by the population – but also because the law's demands are often objectively justifiable by reference to the standards of ideal or sound morality. Hart even thinks that because both morality and law are aimed at ensuring human survival, there is a certain minimum content which they *necessarily* share. Both morality and law must, for instance, include rules that restrict the use of violence. Every legal system *must* therefore contain some rules of moral value, according to Hart, though he also makes the point that such overlap is compatible with great iniquity and discrimination in the law. Thus slave-owning societies could meet this minimum standard (Hart, 1994, pp 193–200).

In fact, even if all the laws we happen to have come across were morally acceptable in terms of the standards of ideal morality, this would not disprove the positivist thesis because positivism does not say that law and morality *cannot* coincide. It says only that there is no *guarantee* of such a convergence. It says, in other words, that a legal system *could* exist in which law and morality do not coincide. Law and morality are, according to positivism, *separable*: though there are many important *contingent* connections between law and morality, and possibly even some necessary though limited overlap in content, laws are not *necessarily* just and unjust laws do not lose their character as laws by virtue of conflicting with moral standards.

Finally, positivists do not deny that judges sometimes decide cases on moral grounds. As we will see in 3.2, positivists believe that there are situations which are not covered by the existing law – that the legal rules, in other words, can run out. In order to resolve such cases, they say, judges have to exercise discretion. They have to choose what the law should become. And in so doing they are forced to rely on moral and policy considerations. Of course, the new legal rule created in the course of resolving such a dispute will now be part of the law which later judges in lower courts are bound by virtue of the doctrine of precedent to apply, but, consistent with the separability thesis, it is the fact that it can be found in a judicial decision, not its moral basis, which gives it its legal status.

Furthermore, some positivists – the so-called 'inclusive' positivists – believe that moral reasoning might even play a role in determining what the *existing* law requires. They believe that moral validity *can* be (though need not be) a condition for legal validity. It is therefore a mistake, though a common one, to associate positivism with the view that the law can always be ascertained in a morally neutral way and that it is the duty of judges to avoid moral judgments in *identifying* the law or saying what it *is*. We will return to this important issue in 2.9.

2.7   Is the normativity of law compatible with legal positivism?

Austin's theory of law and the view that law and morality are conceptually separate are obviously consistent. However, as we saw in 1.2 and 1.3, Austin's reduction of law to the brute exercise of power cannot explain the concept of legal authority or the fact that the law-maker has a right to our obedience. If commands based on sanctions could explain authority then a gunman would have authority – something that is evidently not the case, for we do not think that a gunman has the right to demand our money. We also saw that Hart's account of law (in terms of a conventional social rule accepted from the internal point of view by legal officials) is superior to Austin's precisely because it *can* explain law's *distinctive* way of making conduct non-optional by contrast with the use of force – the fact that law places us under obligations or tells us what we ought to do.

But does Hart's recognition that law is normative threaten his views about the conceptual separation of law and morality? Can an account of the normativity and therefore the authority of law really avoid any reference to morality? Beyleveld and Brownsword think it cannot. They think that there is no mid-way position such as Hart seeks to occupy between the command theory of law on the one hand and natural law theory on the other. They say that once it is recognised that legal phenomena have to be characterised from the internal point of view as *standards* of conduct, it follows that legal officials must regard legal demands as *morally* legitimate. Conversely, if legal officials who pronounce legal rules valid do not believe that it is morally legitimate to apply and enforce these rules, then it must be true of them that they do not regard the rules as *standards*, but merely as rules which constitute the 'practice of law' (Beyleveld and Brownsword, 1989, pp 505–6). Beyleveld and Brownsword conclude that if legal officials do not treat legal rules as imposing moral obligations, then 'law . . . is no more than a series of power-plays in which legal officials demand, "Obey or pay", with no more attempt at moral legitimacy than a highwayman' (Beyleveld and Brownsword, 1989, p 511).

Hart rejects this argument. He argues that 'the dichotomy of "law based merely on power" and "law which is accepted as morally binding" is not exhaustive' (Hart, 1994, p 203). He believes, as we know, that judges accept legislative provisions as authoritative legal reasons (see 1.5) and he also believes that there are no conceptual connections between law and morality. He therefore needs to show that judges can regard the fact that parliament enacted a provision as a *reason* to apply the provision without having to believe in the moral legitimacy of the legislature. His solution is to say that judges must have a '*comprehensible motive*' for accepting legislative enactments as determinants of the standards of correct judicial behaviour, but that these motives might have 'nothing to do with the belief in the moral legitimacy of the authority whose enactments they identify and apply as law' (Hart, 1982, p 265). 'Thus', Hart explains:

> individual judges may explain or justify their acceptance of the legislator's enactments by saying that they simply wish to continue in an established practice or that they had sworn on taking office to continue it or that they had tacitly agreed to do so by accepting the office of judge. All this would be compatible with judges either having no belief at all concerning the moral legitimacy of the legislature or even with their believing that it had none.
>
> (Hart, 1982, p 265)

Second, Hart argues that we should not read too much into the fact that both law and morality use the vocabulary of 'rights', 'duties' and 'obligations'. For Hart, these words do not have the same meaning in legal and moral contexts and judgments of legal obligation are not equivalent to judgments of moral obligation. Of course, judges may and usually do regard a person who is under a legal obligation as also being under a moral obligation, but it is not *necessary* that they should do so. 'Obligation' therefore means something different in law and morality: to say that I am under a legal obligation is to say merely that I am required to do something from the perspective of the law. Judges who speak of an individual's legal duty may therefore mean to speak in a 'technically confined way' – from within the specialised world of legal reasons – which does not carry the connotation that the obligation is morally justifiable: '[t]hey speak as judges, from within a legal institution which they are committed as judges to maintain, in order to draw attention to what by way of action is "owed" by the subject, that is, may legally be demanded or exacted from him' (Hart, 1982, p 266).

In support of Hart's argument that not all obligations make a claim to be moral obligations, consider the rules of a game. The rules of chess do not present themselves as morally legitimate but they are nevertheless authoritative, not coercive. As in the case of law, the rules of chess tell individuals what they should do and therefore provide a standard to which all chess players should conform and a basis for criticising those who depart from it. Legal rules may perhaps be analogously understood, though it is possible that this is *too* 'confined' a way in which to understand them and that any adequate form of positivism should explain how law can create rights and duties which, though not necessarily moral rights and duties, are nevertheless more 'real' than rights and duties arising within what is conceptualised as merely the 'game of law' (Coleman, 2001b, p 143).

2.8   Dworkin on positivism and plain facts

Ronald Dworkin is regarded by many as the most important contemporary legal theorist in the English-speaking world. His work contains a sustained challenge to positivism, to which it offers a highly sophisticated alternative. We will have occasion to return in Chapter 3 to Dworkin's positive contributions to legal theory, but for the moment we need to understand an important aspect of his attack on positivism, especially as found in his very influential early articles, 'The Model of Rules I' and 'The Model of Rules II'.

Dworkin attacks what he calls a 'plain-fact' view of the law. Dworkin explains the plain-fact view like this:

> [t]he law [on the plain-fact view] is only a matter of what legal institutions, like legislatures and city councils and courts, have decided in the past. If some body of that sort has decided that workmen can recover compensation for injuries by fellow workmen, then that is the law. If it has decided the other way, then that is the law. So questions of law can always be answered by looking in the books where the records of institutional decisions are kept.
>
> (Dworkin, 1986, p 7)

Thus, on the plain-fact view, what counts as law is always a matter of historical fact and never depends on morality (Dworkin, 1986, p 9). Or, as Dworkin also puts it, on the plain-fact view, the tests for identifying law 'have to do not with their content but with their pedigree or the manner in which they were adopted and developed' (Dworkin, 1977a, p 17). The criteria of legality are therefore exclusively social sources: what makes a standard a legal standard is the fact that it has, for instance, been authoritatively posited in legislation or a judicial decision and not the fact that it is just or fair. It is a matter of conforming to certain *formal* or *pedigree* or *non-moral* criteria.

Having described the plain-fact view, Dworkin sets out to argue that it is wrong. He points out in the 'Model of Rules I' that judges often resort to moral principles to resolve legal disputes, despite the fact that these principles are controversial and not to be found in explicit rules laid down by institutional office-holders. He then argues that such principles, though not part of the law by virtue of having been enacted in the right way by the relevant authorities, *are* part of the law by virtue of their *content* or their moral *merits*. Thus, even though the standards lack a pedigree in a social-fact source of law, judges are *legally obliged* to follow them when they apply (Dworkin, 1977a, p 40).

In order to demonstrate this point Dworkin makes reference to two US cases. In *Riggs v Palmer* (1889), the question was whether a grandson who had poisoned his grandfather so as to prevent him from changing his will could inherit under the will. The court noted that on a literal reading of the relevant statutes the grandson was entitled to take his inheritance. But it went on to say that 'all laws as well as all contracts may be controlled in their operation and effect by general, fundamental maxims of the common law. No-one shall be permitted to profit by his own fraud, or to take advantage of his own wrong, or to found any claim upon his own iniquity, or to acquire property by his own crime' (at 511). The grandson could therefore not inherit. Dworkin sees this as an example of a court declining to follow a clear rule, invoking a moral principle which stood in the way.

In *Henningsen v Bloomfield Motors, Inc* (1960), the question was whether a manufacturer of motor cars could escape liability for the expenses of persons injured in a crash due to defects in a car by invoking a clause in the contract which excluded such liability. There was no rule of law that prevented the manufacturer from relying on the clause. The court nevertheless held that the manufacturer could not rely on it, invoking several moral principles: car manufacturers are under special obligations by comparison with other manufacturers; courts will not allow themselves to be used as instruments of inequity and injustice; and courts will seek to protect those who are economically vulnerable.

In 'The Model of Rules I' Dworkin argues that the fact to which he calls attention – that judges in cases like *Riggs* and *Henningsen* do not rely on plain facts, but rather on value-judgments which are not to be found in the law reports or in statutes – presents an insuperable problem for legal positivism. This is because Dworkin assumes that positivism is committed to the plain-fact or pedigree view of law and therefore that it cannot explain why judges frequently draw on moral considerations in the process of determining what the law requires. But how accurate is Dworkin's conception of positivism as committed to a value-free model of law-identification? In order to answer this question we need to understand the important distinction between inclusive and exclusive positivism.

2.9   Inclusive positivism

Inclusive positivists accept Hart's picture of the conventional nature of law but reject the view that legal reasoning is necessarily factual – the view that what the law is necessarily depends only on empirically discoverable historical facts, such as legislation and judicial decisions, and that legal norms can therefore always be identified without recourse to moral argument. Since they are not committed to the view that law necessarily consists only of pedigreed or source-based standards, they are able to concede Dworkin's point that judges frequently regard moral considerations as part of the law by virtue of their moral merit or content, rather than their source.

Inclusive positivists, such as Hart (who refers to inclusive positivism as 'soft' positivism), Jules Coleman and WJ Waluchow, stress the fact that the rule of recognition is whatever rule happens to be accepted by judges in a particular society as setting out the criteria of legality. There is nothing in this picture, they say, which requires that the criteria provided by the rule of recognition be restricted to non-evaluative historical facts, such as acts of parliament and precedents. There is therefore nothing which stands in the way of a rule of recognition which specifies that laws must conform to certain moral criteria. As Hart says, '[t]here is, for me, no logical restriction on the content of the rule of recognition' (Hart, 1983, p 361). Which norms count as legal norms depends on social conventions and judges might be required by convention to use non-pedigree, moral tests in deciding questions of legal validity. If judges are under a duty to apply such tests, moral principles will be part of that community's law – as in the United States in which, as Hart says, 'the ultimate criteria of legal validity explicitly incorporate besides pedigree, principles of justice or substantive moral values' (Hart, 1994, p 247).

Hart is here referring to the fact that in the United States the validity of legislation is in part measured against very abstractly framed moral standards contained in the US Bill of Rights – such rights as rights to the 'equal protection' of the laws and to 'due process'. Laws which deny these protections will be struck down by the courts as invalid (see 5.9). This means that judges in the United States do not confine themselves to investigating whether a law has been duly enacted or adopted but are frequently engaged in political and moral theorising when they have to pronounce on the validity of laws. For instance, they have had to decide whether laws which allow for affirmative action violate the right to be treated equally. Or whether the procedures stipulated by a law are fair or unfair. Or whether the right not to be deprived of liberty without due process implies a right to abortion. These are questions of political morality, which means that in the United States sound morality is in certain circumstances a condition of legal validity.

In summary, positivists believe that which norms count as legal norms is just a matter of social convention. This implies on the one hand, as we saw in 2.5, that legal norms may be unjust. But by the same token, the inclusive positivists argue, it makes room for the possibility that judges might be required by convention to use moral tests in deciding questions of legal validity. Thus if, as is the case in the United Kingdom, judges accept the conventional rule that parliament is sovereign, they will not recognise moral constraints on parliament's law-making power and there will be no guarantee that the laws it passes will be just. By contrast, in a country like the United States, in which judges accept the conventional rule that laws must conform with the moral standards contained in the Bill of Rights, any attempt to pass laws in conflict with certain moral values will be invalidated by the courts.

Dworkin is therefore wrong that positivism is committed to the view that law is distinguishable from morality by virtue of being a matter of 'hard facts'. Inclusive positivists say that while it is an empirical or factual matter as to what *criteria of validity* the rule of recognition lays down – the empirical facts being facts about how legal officials decide disputes – this does not imply that the criteria must *themselves* be factual. And it therefore does not imply that *first-order* legal norms (norms valid under the higher-order rule of recognition) can be identified and their content determined by a purely empirical or factual or value-free inquiry. On the contrary, the rule of recognition might require putative legal norms to be tested by reference to their moral merits. If so, moral soundness (a standard lacking an *institutional* or *social* source) will be a source of law. And there will be *substantive* constraints on the *content* of first-order legal norms even though there are no substantive constraints on the content of the rule of recognition, which is merely whatever rule is *in fact* or *contingently* used by judges in a particular legal system to decide legal disputes. In short, for the inclusive positivists, though contingent social facts are the basis of any legal system, the identification of law need not depend only on social facts. Or, as Coleman puts it, the *existence conditions* of the criteria of legality are one matter, the *content* of the criteria another (Coleman, 2001b, p 172).

This is not a threat to the separability thesis, inclusive positivists say, because if this kind of connection between law and morality happens to exist, it is just another contingent connection of the kind that positivists do not deny. The separability thesis, they say, is about what *need not* be the case rather than about what *cannot be* the case. Thus the separability thesis states merely that morality is not *necessarily* a criterion of legal validity, not that it is *impossible* for morality to play a role in identifying valid law (Coleman, 1984, p 31). And since it is quite possible that the rule of recognition in a particular system might refer only to *non-moral* or social-fact criteria of legality, the separability thesis remains intact: morality as a condition of legal validity is not inherent in the very nature of law. Inclusive positivism is therefore able to account for the cases to which Dworkin calls attention, in which judges appear to regard moral principles as part of the law, while at the same time remaining a positivist thesis. It does this by combining, as Matthew Kramer notes, the following two theses: '(1) no legal system *has* to include moral principles among its criteria for ascertaining the law; and (2) any legal system *can* include moral principles among those criteria' (Kramer, 1999, p 152, Kramer's emphasis).

2.10   Dworkin's objections to inclusive positivism

Is inclusive positivism an acceptable theory of law? Dworkin thinks not, as do some positivists – positivists of the exclusive kind. Let us begin with Dworkin's objections to inclusive positivism. For one thing, he rejects the view that moral reasoning plays a role in legal argument as a contingent matter. As we will see in 3.8, though Dworkin does not accept the view of the classical natural lawyers that moral validity is necessarily a condition of legal validity, he does think that the identification of the law in every legal system is an interpretive enterprise which *necessarily* involves sound moral judgment. He is therefore a kind of natural lawyer, for he believes that questions of morality directly influence questions of law.

Second, faced with the inclusive positivist argument that positivism is not committed to the plain-fact view of law, Dworkin counter-argues that there are inconsistencies between inclusive positivism and other key positivist claims, and hence that inclusive positivism 'is not positivism at all' (Dworkin, 2002, p 1656). Dworkin argues for the incoherence of inclusive positivism in two ways.

Dworkin's first argument is that it is impossible to accept the inclusive positivist thesis that moral principles of the sort invoked in *Riggs* and in *Henningsen* can count as law while simultaneously holding to the view that in every legal system there is a conventional social rule supplying the standards of legal validity. This is because we speak of conventions only where there is *agreement* about how to behave. But morality is inherently *controversial* and judges will therefore inevitably disagree about what morality requires. Dworkin argues, in other words, that positivists cannot accept moral criteria of legal validity, which are in their nature controversial, while also conceptualising law as ultimately based on a conventional or agreed-upon test for determining which standards count as law and which do not. A rule of recognition which directs judges to have recourse to moral considerations therefore cannot be a conventional rule.

Inclusive positivists attempt to answer this challenge by distinguishing between controversy or disagreement about the *content* of a rule and disagreement about its *applicability*. They say that if there were widespread controversy about the content of the rule of recognition – if, for instance, judges were not agreed that moral validity is in certain circumstances a condition of legal validity under the rule – then it could not be a social rule. If judges were unsure as to what rule they were supposed to be following there could not be a social practice of following the rule. But disagreement about what the rule requires – disagreement about what the requirements of morality are in a particular case and therefore over which norms satisfy the conditions of legality set out in the rule of recognition – presupposes agreement about the content of the rule. Such disagreement merely involves disputes about the rule's correct application. And such disputes are not, inclusive positivists argue, incompatible with the rule's having conventional status (Coleman, 2001b, p 116).

But Dworkin also has another reason for thinking that inclusive positivism is incoherent. He argues that a rule of recognition which directs judges to have recourse to controversial moral considerations is incompatible with the positivist view of law's *function*, namely, that of providing reliable public standards of conduct (Dworkin, 1984, p 248). If moral argument were required to ascertain the validity or content of laws, the law would not be able to pick out in an uncontroversial way the patterns of behaviour which are required of us. Hence inclusive positivism is incompatible with the positivist view of law's function.

Inclusive positivists have two responses. One is to deny that law's primary or overriding function is to resolve social issues in ways that are certain and determinate. Thus Hart argues that values like certainty and determinacy compete with values like flexibility, and that there is no need to suppose that it is an essential feature of law that it should always choose to resolve disputes certainly rather than flexibly. Indeed, Hart takes the view that a margin of uncertainty is not only *inevitable* – he believes, as we will see in 3.2, that no rule, however precisely framed, can be *entirely* clear – but actually *desirable*. It is desirable because it leaves room for judges to make appropriate choices when unanticipated cases arise, instead of 'blindly prejudging what is to be done in a range of future cases, about whose composition we are ignorant' (Hart, 1994, p 130). Hart therefore thinks that law should deliberately be framed loosely, using terms such as 'reasonable' and 'fair', so as to allow judges the latitude to arrive at sensible results in unforeseen future cases.

A second response to Dworkin's argument against inclusive positivism is to question whether rules the validity of which depends in part on their meeting moral tests are necessarily incapable of providing reliable public standards of conduct. After all, some moral questions are uncontroversial and easily resolved. Thus Hart says we should not 'exaggerate...the uncertainty which will arise if the criteria of legal validity include conformity with specific moral principles or values' (Hart, 1994, p 251).

2.11   Exclusive positivism

It is time to turn to exclusive positivism. As we have seen, inclusive positivists say that there can be moral criteria of legal validity. They claim this is consistent with the separability thesis because – they say – the separability thesis asserts merely that morality is not necessarily a condition of legality. Exclusive positivists disagree. They say that, necessarily, morality is not a condition of legality (Coleman, 2001b, pp 151–2). They say, in other words, that the morality of a norm *cannot* be a condition of its legality, moral criteria of legal validity being conceptually impossible. They therefore take the plain-fact view of law: what the law is on any matter is determined solely by answering questions of fact about such matters as acts of parliament and judicial decisions. (This is not to say, however, that the relevant facts are necessarily easy to discover. They may depend on very complex reasoning.)

Kelsen can be regarded as an exclusive positivist for he insisted, as we have seen, that the identification of law must necessarily be value-free (see 1.7). I will focus, however, on the writings of Joseph Raz who is the most influential contemporary defender of this theory. Raz argues that *all criteria of legal validity must be source-based*. That is, the rule of recognition must stipulate conditions of validity that refer only to a norm's institutional or social source in, for instance, legislation or a judicial decision. Since, for Raz, the law necessarily consists only of source-based standards, the fact that a standard has moral value can never be a criterion of legal validity. Raz also argues that the content of legal rules can be established by facts about human beings – for instance, their intentions in enacting legislation – that once again can be described in value-free terms (Raz, 1979, pp 39–40, 47–8). Raz takes this view, which he calls the 'sources thesis', because he believes that moral tests for identifying the content of the law and determining its existence are *inconsistent with the nature of law*.

Raz's starting-point in arguing for this conclusion is the concept of an exclusionary or pre-emptive reason for action. When I am deciding whether to do something – go to the cinema, say – all sorts of reasons will be relevant to this matter, some of these for going to the cinema, some against. We can call these my first-order reasons. Suppose that if all the relevant considerations were taken into account, I ought, on the balance of all the applicable first-order reasons, to go to the cinema. Let us call this the conclusion of 'right reason'. Right reason is whatever I ought to do on the basis of all the reasons that apply to me. It might seem to follow that in deciding whether I ought to go to the cinema, I should rely directly on my own assessment as to what right reason requires. But Raz argues that this is not necessarily the case. For I might have a second-order reason for *not* acting on the balance of my first-order reasons as they appear to me. Such a second-order reason is an 'exclusionary' reason. It is a reason to disregard or *not* to act on my own assessment of what would be the best thing to do (Raz, 1979, p 17).

Submission to an authority involves acceptance of exclusionary reasons because when we accede to an authority's order we do what we have been told to do, regardless of our own view of the merits of the instruction. A private in the army, obeying the orders of an officer, submits to an authority in this sense. Authorities, in other words, give us reasons for acting which prevail over or *replace* the reasons we might otherwise have. They replace our 'dependent' reasons, these being our original reasons or the reasons we would otherwise take into account in deciding what to do. Thus Raz says: '[t]he fact that an authority requires performance of an action is a reason for its performance which is not to be added to all other relevant reasons when assessing what to do, but should replace some of them' (Raz, 1994, p 214).

When *should* a person be acknowledged to have authority over another person? Raz argues that authority is justified if we are more likely to comply with the dependent reasons that apply to us if we obey the authority than if we try *directly* to follow the reasons which apply to us. I might, for instance, be more likely to satisfy the demands of right reason if I rely on the opinion of an *expert* rather than my own opinion as to what the balance of reasons requires. Thus I am more likely to get well if I follow my doctor's instructions rather than my own idea of a cure.

Or, in cases where I am short of time or need to co-ordinate my actions with large numbers of other people, an authoritative directive may assist me to comply with the reasons that apply to me. Raz calls this a 'service conception' of authority because the authority performs a service for us. We hand over to the authority the task of weighing up the pros and cons of different courses of action and making a decision as to what we should do, the authority being better placed to do this than we are. The service conception therefore regards authorities as:

> *mediating* between people and the right reasons which apply to them, so that the authority judges and pronounces what they ought to do according to right reason. The people on their part take their cue from the authority whose pronouncements replace for them the force of the dependent reasons.
>
> (Raz, 1994, p 214, Raz's emphasis)

Raz goes on to argue that it is in the nature of law that it *claims* to possess legitimate authority (Raz, 1994, p 215). It is, in other words, a necessary feature of legal rules that they present themselves as exclusionary reasons. Law tells us that we must comply with *its* judgment as to the reasons which apply to us, even if we regard the law's judgment as wrong. This is not to say that the law necessarily *does* possess legitimate authority. Indeed, Raz is sceptical about the law's claims to legitimate authority. It is merely to say that standards which do not *purport* to affect our reasoning in this way cannot be legal standards.

Raz then goes on to argue that certain conceptual constraints on the criteria of legality follow from this fundamental truth about law. In particular, if law claims legitimate authority it must be *capable* of possessing legitimate authority – it must be capable of assisting us to act in accordance with right reason – and in order to be capable of possessing legitimate authority, rules must possess two features. First, they must be presented as the law-makers' view of how their subjects ought to behave. Second, the existence and content of the rules must be established by reference to their sources in empirically discoverable historical facts, such as legislation and judicial decisions, and therefore without reference to moral argument (Raz, 1994, p 218).

Why does Raz think that rules capable of possessing legitimate authority must have these features? His answer is as follows. First, the only plausible basis for thinking that individuals are more likely to conform to right reason by following the law rather than their own judgments is if the law can reflect *someone else's* superior judgment. Second, if it were necessary to investigate the moral merits or defensibility of a rule in order to ascertain whether it is law, or to determine its content, then the rule could not function *as an authority*. For one would then be obliged to revert to the dependent reasons the legal rule was meant to replace.

Let us examine the second point in more detail. Remember that, for Raz, authoritative directives *replace* our own judgments as to the reasons that apply to us, on the basis that we are *more likely* to satisfy the demands of right reason by following the directives than by following our own judgments. This, as we have seen, is the service authorities perform for us. It follows, says Raz, that if we could not identify a valid legal directive without first determining whether the directive *really* reflects the demands of right reason, law would not be able to perform this service. We would be inquiring into what the rule should be – evaluating its merits by reference to our dependent or background reasons – whereas the concept of an authority is of something that makes a *difference* to our deliberations, *replacing* the reasons on the basis of which we would otherwise decide, and therefore of something that *saves* us from having to engage in such an independent, open-ended evaluation. Think of the doctor example again. It would be of no use to you if the doctor instructed: 'do whatever will make you well.' If you knew what would make you well, you would not need a doctor. Similarly, if we were capable of complying with the requirements of right reason without help we would not need law.

Raz concludes that both Dworkin and the inclusive positivists are wrong in thinking that there can be moral criteria of legal validity, because their view erases the very point and purpose of law, namely, the service it claims to perform for us. Standards which do not have a social source cannot count as law because it is only sources of law like legislation and decisions that are able to replace our own judgments about what we should do in the way entailed by law's claim to authority. As Raz says:

> [s]ince it is of the very essence of the alleged authority that it issues rulings which are binding regardless of any other justification, it follows that it must be possible to identify those rulings without engaging in a justificatory argument, i.e. as issuing from certain activities and interpreted in the light of publicly ascertainable standards not involving moral argument.
>
> (Raz, 1979, pp 51–2)

Or, as Raz also puts it, we can benefit from law's decisions only if we 'can establish their existence and content in ways which do not depend on raising the very same issues which the authority is there to settle' (Raz, 1994, p 219). For instance, the identification of a tax law cannot depend on determining what a just tax law would be, because those are the very issues which the tax law was supposed to have authoritatively settled (Raz, 1994, p 225). Dworkin and the inclusive positivists therefore, according to Raz, include in law standards which are inconsistent with its mediating role.

But is it true that law would not be capable of possessing authority if it had to be identified via moral tests? Critics of Raz take issue with his assumption that if a rule is authoritative then it must *altogether* or *entirely* displace the individual's own assessments. Why, they say, should law's authority have to be understood in such an all-or-nothing way? Why should the existence of a legal rule imply that our own independent evaluations have *no* weight? Might it not rather be the case that law's claim to authority is merely a claim to give us reason for treating our own evaluations as having *less* weight? Thus Dworkin writes:

> [Raz] is right that any successful interpretation of our legal practice must recognize and justify the common assumption that law can compete with morality and wisdom and, for those who accept law's authority, override these other virtues in their final decision about what they should do.... [But] Raz thinks that law cannot be authoritative unless those who accept it never use their own convictions to decide what it requires, even in [a] partial way. But why must law be blind authority rather than authoritative in [a] more relaxed way?
>
> (Dworkin, 1986, p 429)

And in later work Dworkin adds:

> [w]e do not treat even those laws we regard as perfectly valid and legitimate as excluding and replacing the background reasons the framers of that law rightly considered in adopting it. We rather regard those laws as creating rights and duties that normally trump those other reasons. The reasons remain, and we sometimes need to consult them to decide whether, in particular circumstances, they are so extraordinarily powerful or important that the law's trump should not prevail.
>
> (Dworkin, 2002, p 1672)

If this argument is accepted, it leaves room for moral argument to play *some* role in determining the existence and content of law (Waluchow, 1994, pp 136–7).

We have seen that Raz thinks that standards which are not source–based cannot count as law. What, then, does he say about the fact to which Dworkin called attention in 'The Model of Rules I' – the fact that moral principles, such as the principle that people should not profit from their own wrongdoing, appear to be binding on courts by virtue of their merits, not their social source? Although Dworkin's observations are not fatal to the inclusive positivists, it may be wondered how a plain-fact positivist like Raz can deal with this apparent obstacle to his theory.

Raz has an ingenious way of accommodating Dworkin's observations without giving up his view that the criteria of legality must be social sources. Raz does not deny that judges often appeal to moral principles, *nor that they are binding*. Instead, he argues that where the law requires judges to apply moral considerations, the morality to which the law refers is not *incorporated* into the law. Rather, the legal duty which binds judges in such cases is to apply an *extra-legal* standard.

Suppose that a statute requires employers to pay a 'fair' wage. For a variety of reasons, legislatures may not wish to fix the details of what counts as 'fairness', preferring to leave the task to judges. In determining what is fair, the judge, says

Raz, is not answering a question to which the *law* provides the answer. Instead the statute places the judge under a *legal* obligation to go *beyond* the law – to seek guidance from *non-legal* norms, namely the norms of morality (Waluchow, 1994, p 83, 157). The statute therefore empowers judges not to determine what the *existing* law requires, but to *make* law on the matter of what constitutes a fair wage.

A somewhat similar situation arises in conflict of law situations when a municipal legal system requires judges to apply the rules of a foreign legal system. The rules of the foreign system are not thereby incorporated into the municipal system: they do not become the law of the municipal system (Raz, 1979, p 46). Moral standards are likewise foreign to the law, according to Raz: though judges may be obliged *by* the law to apply them, this does not imply that they are thereby converted into *legal* standards. Not all the standards which judges may have a legal obligation to apply are, in other words, necessarily legal standards. Or, put otherwise: reasoning *according* to law is not necessarily the same as reasoning *about* the law. The former may involve moral reasoning; the latter is always source-based (Raz, 1994, p 332). In this way, Raz is able to accommodate Dworkin's observations without giving up his plain-fact positivism.

2.12   Ethical positivism

There is one last version of positivism that needs attention. It goes under the name of 'ethical positivism' and its key thesis is that the separability of law and morality is morally desirable. Prominent ethical positivists are Thomas Campbell and Jeremy Waldron. Ethical positivists hold that moral criteria of legal validity are *conceptually possible* but not *morally desirable* and should be avoided in practice. Legal systems, they say, should not allow moral standards to play a role in determining the existence of law or its content.

Ethical positivism is therefore what Campbell calls a 'prescriptive separation thesis' (Campbell, 1996, p 71), by contrast with the conceptual versions of positivism we have been considering up until now. It is not a theory about the *nature* of law but a *recommendation* as to the form a legal system should take. The aim of ethical positivists is to prescribe what should be the case – in particular, that law and morals should be separate. They claim that 'the values associated with law, legality and the rule of law…can best be achieved if the ordinary operation of such a system does not require people to exercise moral judgment in order to find out what the law is' (Waldron, 2001, p 421). Ethical positivism is therefore a 'political theory of law' (Campbell, 1996, p 2). Instead of focusing on what law is, it focuses on what sort of law it is desirable to have.

Ethical positivism has its source in democratic values and is therefore also sometimes called 'democratic positivism'. It rests on the belief that, for democratic reasons, only the people's representatives in parliament should make law. For this reason, ethical positivists often attack the common law, as being too uncertain, leaving too much to the subjectivity of judges, and opening the door to judicial usurpation of the legislature.

Some of the inspiration behind ethical positivism goes back to Bentham, who thought that common law judges are in the business of making law with retrospective effect, thus treating us like dogs. 'Whenever your dog does anything you want to break him of', he wrote, 'you wait till he does it, and then beat him for it. This is the way you make laws for your dog: and this is the way the judges make law for you and me' (quoted in Postema, 1986, p 277). In place of the common law, Bentham wished to substitute a rational, codified legal system based on utilitarian principles of the general good (see 5.3).

Ethical positivists therefore believe that legislatures should assume full responsibility for the making of moral and policy choices, drafting legislation in precise and unambiguous language which reduces to the greatest possible extent the opportunities for judges to rely on their own disputed political and moral views in determining the existence and content of the law. Law *ought* therefore to be a system of rules drafted in such a way as to allow us to 'recognise without controversy whether actual conduct does or does not conform to the rule[s]' (Campbell, 1996, p 64). Those, like Hart, who, as we have seen, believe that law should be framed loosely will, of course, disagree. And those who think language is incapable of being clear and unambiguous, and therefore incapable of restricting the discretionary power of judges, will also disagree. We turn to the latter issue in the next chapter.

Chapter 3

Law and politics
Mainstream theories

So far we have canvassed the relationship between law and force as well as that between law and morality. In this chapter and the next we turn our attention to the issue of the difference, if any, between law and politics. We ask whether there is a distinctive form of reasoning – *'legal reasoning'* – which is different from 'political reasoning' or the reasoning of legislators. Is there an objective way of resolving legal questions on the basis of legal rules and whatever other resources may be contained within the law or is the idea that there are objective answers to legal questions a myth?

A connected set of questions relates to the nature of the *judicial task*. Obviously, if there is no objective way of answering legal questions, judges will necessarily be thrown back on their own subjective or personal moral and political views. The judicial task will be no different in kind from the legislative task. But if there is a difference between legal reasoning and political reasoning, a further question arises, namely, is it *always* possible for judges to reason legally? Or is it the case that only *some* legal questions can be given determinate answers, in which case judging will at least on some occasions require the exercise of a subjective choice? Finally, even if legal reasoning is *possible*, we can ask whether it is *desirable* for judges to reason legally rather than politically. We turn now to explore these issues.

> You should be familiar with the following areas:
>
> - Hart's views about the difference between clear cases and hard cases and the appropriate judicial response to them
> - Fuller's view of legal reasoning as purposive
> - Dworkin's interpretive approach and his theory of law as integrity

3.1 The mainstream view and its opponents

The classical common law theory of the sixteenth and seventeenth centuries made a distinction between natural reason, which every individual possesses, and the *artificial* or legal reason which underlies the common law and which requires, as Chief Justice Coke said in the famous case of *Prohibitions del Roy* (1607), 'long study and experience' (at 65).

In this distinction we see the beginnings of what can be described as the 'mainstream' view about legal reasoning. Mainstream theorists believe that there is a meaningful distinction between legal reasoning (reasoning about the law) and the reasoning of political decision-makers or legislators. They hold that legal reasoning is a *special* or *distinctive* mode of reasoning which is confined to a *limited* set of characteristic arguments and which involves the *rational* justification of legal outcomes. Legal reasoning is in important respects *constrained*, by comparison with ordinary moral or political reasoning which legitimately responds to the full range of moral and political considerations.

On the mainstream view, legal reasoning involves *applying* pre-existing law, not *creating* new law. It responds to reasons *within* the legal system, not reasons *outside* it. It is faithful to the *past* – to past decisions of legislatures and courts, in particular. Legal reasoning is therefore objective and impartial, not subjective and partial: when individuals reason in a legal way it is the *law* that determines the result, not their personal beliefs as to what would be a good outcome. Thus judges reason legally when, for instance, they apply the clear provisions of a statute or refuse to depart from a settled precedent, even though they think the precedent wrong or the statute misconceived. They decide *according to the law*, not according to political pressures or their own values. Politicians, by contrast, routinely make decisions with political goals in mind. They seek to shape society on the basis of their own beliefs about what is socially desirable. The politician's task is a *legislative, forward-looking* task, that of *creating* rules, not applying them.

Mainstream theorists do not necessarily believe that *all* the questions which judges are called upon to decide are resolvable by legal reasoning. Though Dworkin believes this, Hart and Raz do not. For Dworkin, as we will see, a theory of *adjudication* (a theory of the considerations judges may need to take into account in deciding cases) is also a theory of *law*: any consideration a judge may legitimately take into account is a legal reason. For Dworkin, 'legal reasoning' and 'adjudication' are therefore co-extensive. But Hart and Raz believe that what judges do is not necessarily to be identified with the law. This is because they believe that on certain issues there is no objective answer to what the law is and that where this is the case judges have no choice but to reason non-legally. Hence, on their view, adjudication does not always involve reasoning about the law.

Nor do mainstream theorists necessarily believe that the answers to legal questions are *obvious* or *logically deducible by formal reasoning* from the legal materials. Though this is a common caricature of the mainstream view, there are very few contemporary mainstream theorists who are 'formalists' – at least in the sense in which that word is used to refer to those who believe that the answers to all legal disputes can be logically or mechanically deduced from legal rules or concepts, and that judges are therefore mere 'mouthpieces' of the law. (For more about formalism in this sense, see the discussion of Christopher Langdell in 4.1.)

Dworkin, as we will see, discounts the role played by narrowly doctrinal rules of law in legal reasoning and believes that legal reasoning rests on controversial political and moral judgments which are not guaranteed to command universal assent. Dworkin is therefore not a formalist. Indeed, there are many respects in which Dworkin is influenced by the realists whom we will discuss in Chapter 4. But though Dworkin believes that resolving legal questions is creative and political in one sense of that word, he also believes that it *always* involves a specifically *legal* way of dealing with disputes and he does not think that judges should *ever* reason in the way that politicians do. He thinks that judges are under a duty to decide not on the basis of what decision would have the best *social* or political *consequences* but in a genuinely *principled* way, on the basis of the *pre-existing rights* of *individual* litigants, this being an objective matter about which judicial views can be right or wrong.

Dworkin does not, of course, deny that the application of pre-existing law *has* political consequences. Since judging is the exercise of power, judicial decisions invariably have political consequences. Dworkin and other mainstream theorists distinguish, however, between making decisions which *happen* to have political consequences and making decisions with their political consequences *in mind*. It is the latter which are incompatible, they say, with legal decision-making.

Radical critics attack this picture. They are much more sceptical about the determinacy of the law and its ability to justify legal outcomes, as well as about the associated distinctions between legal reasoning and the reasoning of political decision-makers, and between law-application and law-creation. The radical critics refuse to take the idea of 'legal reasoning' at face value. They believe it is a myth which is used to assert false claims to objectivity, deny judicial choices and camouflage the political realities of adjudication. They say that the aspiration to reason in a distinctively legal way – to seal off legal reasoning from the full range of moral and political considerations – is frequently if not always unrealisable. Judges are therefore really political actors in disguise – politicians with wigs on – deciding in a way which they personally think best in the circumstances.

We will discuss the sceptical position in the next chapter. In this chapter we consider the mainstream view. In particular, we discuss different ways of unpacking the idea that it is possible to reason in a legal way – a way which shows 'fidelity to law' or 'faithfulness to the past'.

3.2 Hart and the partial determinacy of the law

As we have seen, Hart thinks that the rule of recognition provides a clear, conventionally accepted test which tells us which of a society's standards count as law and which do not. It might seem that this would lead Hart directly to a view of the judicial task as involving nothing more than the straightforward application of the laws picked out by the rule of recognition to particular sets of facts, regardless of the judge's own personal beliefs as to what the law ought to be.

In fact, however, it is a mistake to associate positivism with the view that the legal system is a 'closed logical system' (Hart, 1983, p 168), and with the allied, formalistic belief that judges are mechanical decision-makers who simply apply the rules of law to the facts of legal cases, the answer to all legal cases being deductively dictated by rules the meaning of which is not in doubt. This is not Hart's view and, in fact, he regards it as one of two 'great exaggerations' (Hart, 1994, p 147). The second great exaggeration, according to him, is the sceptical view that the rules dictate the answer to no legal cases.

Hart occupies a position which is mid-way between the extremes of 'slot-machine' or 'mechanical' jurisprudence and what he calls the 'nightmare' that the rules of law do not constrain at all (Hart, 1983, p 126). In particular, he believes that legal standards are determinate in *most* cases but not all. In the *Concept of Law*, Hart makes a distinction between a core of clear meaning had by legal rules, whether these are to be found in judicial decisions or in statutory provisions, and what he calls their 'penumbra' of uncertainty.

Consider, Hart says, the rule 'No vehicles in the park'. There are obvious cases which the rule clearly covers. It is clear, for instance, that the general term 'vehicle' applies to motor cars and trucks. In the plain cases, the general terms 'seem to need no interpretation and . . . the recognition of instances seems unproblematic or "automatic"' (Hart, 1994, p 126). The reason why 'vehicle' clearly applies to motor cars or trucks is by virtue of agreement in the way we ordinarily use *language*, but Hart makes clear in later work that agreement that a case falls within the scope of a rule can also be based on other factors. For instance, the meaning of words can sometimes be 'clearly controlled' by the purpose of a statute as well as by special conventions relating to the legal use of words (Hart, 1983, p 106). Where there is *no doubt* that a case falls within the scope of a legal rule, the answer is uncontroversial and the law determines a uniquely correct outcome. The mainstream picture of legal reasoning as an objective form of reasoning is therefore vindicated.

But there are also cases, says Hart, in which it is *not* clear whether general terms apply. For instance, does the rule 'no vehicles in the park' apply to bicycles, roller skates and electrically propelled toy vehicles? There are reasons both for and against subsuming these under the general term 'vehicle', for they are like standard cases of vehicles in some ways but not in others. Such indeterminacy is a function, according to Hart, of the fact that language is necessarily 'open-textured': no rule, however precisely framed, can be entirely clear because unforeseen fact-situations will inevitably crop up which possess some of the features of the plain case but not all, and in which even reference to non-linguistic aids such as canons of statutory interpretation and the purpose of the rule will not be capable of settling the issue (Hart, 1983, p 103).

Since the rules which go to make up a legal system are 'open-textured', a legal system is, on Hart's view, not a closed logical system. There will inevitably be borderline or debatable cases in which there is no general agreement that the rule applies. In such cases, statutes or precedents are neither obviously applicable nor obviously not applicable: 'however smoothly [precedent and legislation] work over the great mass of ordinary cases, [they] will, at some point where their application is in question, prove indeterminate' (Hart, 1994, p 128). Another source of indeterminacy is the use of very general standards in legal rules – standards such as reasonableness and fairness. The application of such standards can likewise be uncertain. Since Hart identifies the law with plainly applicable legal rules or with what can be uncontroversially decided, it follows that where a rule does not plainly or unambiguously cover a particular situation, there is no law. The law has here run out or has 'gaps': there is no *legal* answer to the question which has cropped up.

Hart's theory of adjudication in the *Concept of Law* tracks the distinction between the core of determinate meaning and the penumbra of uncertain meaning. In the easy cases, where there is no doubt that a legal rule is applicable to a particular case, Hart believes that judges who wish to participate in the legal system ought to apply the rule as stated. They ought, in other words, to reason legally or apolitically, applying the pre-existing valid rule even if they believe the result to be undesirable. For Hart says that to think otherwise is to ignore the difference between the law as it is and the law as it ought to be: '[i]t is to assert that there is no central element of actual law to be seen in the core of central meaning which rules have' (Hart, 1958, p 615). The positivist distinction between the law as it is and the law as it ought to be therefore feeds into Hart's theory of adjudication, prescribing that when the law is clearly applicable judges should apply it as stated, without regard to their own personal views as to what it ought to be.

Notice that Hart's view about easy cases is not an empirical or descriptive claim. The claim is not that judges always do, *in fact*, apply clearly applicable rules. Such a descriptive claim is obviously false, as numerous judicial decisions biased by the race, class or gender of the judge attest. But to say that judges should apply clearly applicable rules is not an empirical claim. It is a normative claim which rests on a conceptual claim. The conceptual claim is that cases *can* be easy, in the sense that there are legal rules relevant to them which conclusively settle the dispute by virtue of various factors, including the language in which the rules are framed. The normative claim is that in such cases judges who refuse to apply the legal rules – because to do so would be unjust, perhaps, or would be inconsistent with the supposed reason why the rule was enacted – can be legitimately *criticised* for ignoring the law and taking into account considerations which are legally irrelevant. They can be criticised for not having done their job properly. As we will see in 3.3 and 3.4, Fuller disagrees with both of these claims.

What does Hart say about the cases 'at the fringe' – the hard cases which are at the edges of a rule's meaning – where the case is not clearly covered by the rule and the law is indeterminate? Here Hart says that judges are faced with a choice between alternative answers: they have discretion whether to subsume the case under the rule or not. And in exercising that discretion they have to rely on considerations which lie outside the currently existing law, such as moral considerations and policy considerations. In hard cases, it is therefore not possible for judges to reason in a legal way. In hard cases, courts have to perform a law-*making* rather than a law-*applying* function. They may not make arbitrary or haphazard choices, to be sure. And they make the law only in the 'interstices' created by the open texture of legal rules. Thus they are not able to undertake far-reaching law reform. But it remains true that, within these confines, they are *creating* new legal rights, not applying pre-existing legal standards. They are playing a role which is in all its essential features just like the role played by legislators when they enact legislation – making a decision which is, in their own personal opinion, the best decision in all the circumstances (Hart, 1994, p 273). Dworkin, as we will see in 3.6, disagrees with this claim.

The basis of Hart's picture is therefore a sharp distinction between clear cases and hard cases and a correspondingly sharp distinction between straightforward application of the law and the exercise of discretion unguided by the law. In clear cases the answer is uncontroversial and the law determines a uniquely correct outcome. Judges should in such cases apply the law. But it is only in the easy cases that the law provides answers, according to Hart, and the positivist ideal of judges neutrally or apolitically applying the rules of law therefore covers only one part of the judge's task. In hard cases, where there is no agreement that a rule applies, or on how it should be applied, there is no legal answer. The conventions and therefore the law have run out. In such cases judges have to reason like political decision-makers. They have no choice but to look outside the legal system and decide the case on the basis of their own subjective view as to what would be the best outcome in all the circumstances.

It follows that, for Hart, we cannot identify the *law* (the legal rules) with the *considerations which judges may legitimately take into account*. Though the task of adjudication is primarily a legal one, there are times, for Hart, when judges have no choice but to reason non-legally. At such times they are choosing what the law *should* be, in the process settling the issue for subsequent judges who may find themselves confronted by a case which is clearly covered by (i.e., within the core of) the newly made rule, and who will then be obliged, by the doctrine of precedent, to follow it.

We should not assume, however, that it is the reliance on moral and political arguments which is the source of judicial legislation in hard cases – that any recourse to moral and political reasons is, by definition, for Hart, an appeal to reasons which lie outside the legal system. This is Raz's view (see 2.11), but, though Hart does not make this explicit, he presumably does not believe that what defines clear cases is that in them the law is identifiable in a *morally* neutral way. He is, after all, an inclusive positivist who believes that judges might be required by the rule of recognition to use moral tests in deciding questions of legal validity (see 2.9). And since some moral questions have determinate or uncontroversial answers, it follows that a rule which contains moral terms can clearly cover a particular fact situation.

For instance, suppose a judge has to decide whether a constitutional provision outlawing cruel and unusual punishment applies to a case of punishment by stoning a person to death. Hart would presumably say that the provision straightforwardly outlaws such a punishment and that judges who find to this effect, though reasoning *morally*, would be *neutrally applying* rather than making the law. They would not be exercising discretion or injecting their own personal beliefs into the law. The dividing line between clear and hard cases is therefore the line between cases in which a rule uncontroversially applies and those in which it does not. It should not be understood as a line between cases in which judges consult 'hard facts' – legislation and judicial decisions – for the answers, and cases in which they reason morally.

3.3 Fuller's criticism of the idea that language can constrain

Fuller objects to Hart's picture on two grounds. Though he agrees with Hart that there are determinate answers to legal questions, Fuller rejects Hart's view that *language* can be a source of legal determinacy – that rules have a central core of plain meaning which can be read off from the language in which they are written. Fuller thinks that the idea of a rule having standard instances in isolation from the purpose of the rule is incoherent. 'If', he says, 'the rule excluding vehicles from parks seems easy to apply in some cases, I submit this is because we can see clearly enough what the rule "is aiming at in general" so that we know there is no need to worry about the difference between Fords and Cadillacs' (Fuller, 1958, p 663).

Fuller then considers Hart's example of the rule 'No vehicles in the park' and Hart's claim that, whatever else the term 'vehicle' refers to, it clearly refers to cars and trucks. Fuller asks what Hart would say if some local patriots wanted to construct a memorial by mounting a working truck used in the Second World War on a pedestal in the park. Though it is not clear why he does so, Fuller seems to assume that Hart would say that the word 'vehicle' clearly covers the truck on the pedestal. In fact, it seems more likely that Hart would say that this is an unforeseen situation which the language of the rule fails clearly to cover – that the rule clearly covers trucks which are being driven in the park but it is unclear whether it covers trucks on a pedestal.

But let us suppose, for the sake of argument, that Hart would agree that the word 'vehicle' clearly covers the truck on the pedestal. Fuller's opposing view is that in order to know whether 'vehicle' covers this situation we have to determine its meaning in the light of the purpose for which the rule was enacted. Since to prohibit the truck on the pedestal would be incompatible with any imaginable purpose behind the rule, 'vehicle' has, Fuller concludes, a different meaning in this context from the meaning it usually has: it does not cover trucks.

A second example Fuller uses is of a law which makes it an offence to sleep at railway stations. He asks what Hart would say about the following two cases. In the one case, an orderly businessman, waiting for a delayed train in the early hours of the morning, nods off while sitting upright. In the other case, a homeless person has settled down for the night on the platform with blankets and pillows but has not yet actually fallen asleep. Who is 'sleeping' in terms of the rule? Under the view that words have a clear core of plain meaning, the businessman would be asleep while the homeless person would not. But Fuller argues that we must have recourse to the likely purpose behind the law in order to interpret the word 'sleeping'. Having regard to this likely purpose, Fuller suggests that, in this context, the businessman is not 'sleeping' while the homeless person is (Fuller, 1958, p 664). Fuller thinks, in other words, that there is no such thing as context-independent literal meaning. The meaning of words in general, and therefore legal rules in particular, is entirely a function of the context in which they are used.

If Fuller is right, language does not constrain the interpretation of legal rules to any extent. The meaning of words is entirely a function of the specific context in which they have been used. How plausible is this as a theory of meaning? Frederick Schauer argues that it is implausible. He argues for the 'semantic autonomy' of language. By this he means that language can convey meaning independently of the communicative intentions of speakers.

Schauer points out that there is something shared by all speakers of a particular language which enables one speaker of that language to be understood by another even if the second knows nothing about the circumstances or context in which the first spoke. Schauer does not argue that language is entirely acontextual. He acknowledges that understanding the context is likely to *increase* our understanding of what has been said. But he maintains nevertheless that '*some* meaning exists that can be discerned through access only to those skills and understandings that are definitional of linguistic competence' (Schauer, 1991, p 58, Schauer's emphasis). Meaning can therefore be 'acontextual' in the sense that 'it draws on no other context besides those understandings shared among virtually all speakers of [a particular language]' (Schauer, 1988, p 528). 'That we might learn *more* from considering additional factors or from more fully understanding a speaker's intentions does not mean', Schauer says, 'that we learn *nothing* by consulting the language of the rules themselves' (Schauer, 1988, p 528, my emphasis).

Schauer asks us to imagine that someone who understands English but knows nothing of the history, politics, law or culture of the United States is given a copy of the US Constitution to read. Schauer points out that although 'their understanding would be primitive', and 'significant mistakes would be made', such a person would be able to glean just from the language of the Constitution some rudimentary idea of its content. They would know, for instance, the number of terms that may be served by the President (Schauer, 1985, pp 418–9).

Schauer also argues that the fact that language is not perfectly *precise* does not imply that it is therefore *worthless*. He agrees with Hart that language is open-textured and that every use of language is therefore potentially vague, in the sense that unforeseen situations may occur in which it is not clear whether a particular term is applicable or not. But this does not mean, he says, that there are no core cases. Think of a characteristic like baldness. We are sometimes not sure whether to describe someone as bald or not. But this does not mean that there are no indisputably bald people (Schauer, 1985, pp 421–3).There are likewise many cases which never leave the lawyer's office because litigation seems futile.

How can we explain this if the law does not speak at least some of the time with clarity (Schauer, 1985, p 412)?

Schauer therefore agrees with Hart: sometimes the rules are vague, in which case they produce hard cases, but some cases are easy and at least one source of their 'easiness' is that 'language can and frequently does speak with a sufficiently clear voice' (Schauer, 1985, p 416), the answer being dictated on such occasions by a straightforward reading of the rules. Schauer does not, of course, deny that judges sometimes ignore clear language. He claims merely that legal rules are frequently *capable* of generating determinate outcomes by virtue of the language in which they are written.

Some theorists attack the idea of clear, literal meaning on the basis that meaning is a human creation. Meaning, they point out, depends on arbitrary human arrangements and conventions: there is no magical relationship between words and the world which is a given. Hence, they conclude, there are no objective constraints on how words may be understood. But this is a *non sequitur*. It is, of course, true that it is completely arbitrary which words we apply to which objects. We might have called dogs 'cats' and cats 'dogs'. But it does not follow that words cannot have clear literal meanings. To say that 'dog' has a clear literal meaning is merely to say that any English-language speaker will agree on a certain range of ways of using the word.

3.4 Fuller's criticism of the idea of rigid adherence to rules

So far I have canvassed Hart and Fuller's disagreement about the ability of language to constrain interpretation. But Fuller also has a second objection to Hart's picture. Now seemingly agreeing with Hart that words *can* be understood acontextually, and that rules do have clear instances by virtue of the language in which they are couched, Fuller nevertheless disagrees with Hart that judges should always follow the rules in clear cases. Fuller says that judges should ignore the plain meaning of legal rules when the plain meaning dictates a result which defeats the rule's apparent purpose.

Hence Fuller advocates a 'purposive' approach to the interpretation of legal rules. When something falls within the letter of the law but not its spirit, the letter – its plain meaning – should give way to the spirit. Thus the businessman should not be found guilty of the offence of sleeping at the station and the truck on the pedestal should be allowed in the park. This is a *normative* argument about how judges should decide cases, rather than a *conceptual* argument about language. In fact, in saying that cases should not necessarily be decided according to their plain meaning, Fuller seems to concede that plain meaning exists.

Notice, however, that Fuller does not regard the purposive approach to interpretation as judicial activism or as a resort to non-legal or political reasons. When he tells us that the words in which the law is couched should not be regarded as decisive, this is not because he thinks judges are entitled to ignore the law in the service of *extra-legal* standards of morality or justice. Rather, he thinks that the *words* in which the law is couched should not be identified with the *'real'* law. It is, for Fuller, the *purpose* which is the source of the 'real' legal rule. Fuller claims, in other words, that when purposive judges ignore the letter of the law they are not *making* law, let alone *departing* from it. Rather, they are being *faithful* to the law – law which is latently *in* the statute, albeit not in its words as ordinarily understood. Purposive judges demonstrate intelligent obedience to the law, by contrast with the positivist's unintelligent obedience. In his well-known fictional case, 'The Case of the Speluncean Explorers', Fuller elaborates on this point, using Foster J, one of his fictional judges, as a mouthpiece. Foster J says:

> [n]o superior wants a servant who lacks the capacity to read between the lines. The stupidest housemaid knows that when she is told 'to peel the soup and skim the potatoes' her mistress does not mean what she says . . . Surely we have a right to expect the same modicum of intelligence from the judiciary. The correction of obvious legislative errors or oversights is not to supplant the legislative will, but to make that will effective.
>
> (Fuller, 1949, pp 625–6)

Fuller therefore agrees with Hart at least to this extent: he believes that there are distinctively legal reasons which generate the correct legal outcome. He accepts, in other words, the mainstream picture of legal reasoning. At the same time, he puts a natural law spin on the notion of legal reasons. For how does one determine the purpose of the law or what Fuller calls the 'legislative will'? It might be thought that one investigates the law-makers' intentions in enacting it – what they subjectively intended to say with the words they used, as opposed to what they actually said. This view, however, has well-known difficulties, among which is the fact that it is implausible to think that all those who vote for a particular piece of legislation will share the same mental states – that they will all have the same purpose for it in mind and exactly the same view about the range of factual situations which fall under the statutory words they have chosen. They may, in fact, have no clear view at all about these matters (Lyons, 1999, pp 17–22).

Fuller does not directly address this issue but he appears to downgrade the role of the law-makers' actual mental states in determining the purpose of the law, and to place more emphasis on the underlying policy goals of the legislation or the broad objectives it is intended to achieve, and even on the objectives that can be imputed to ideal or rational legislators of whom it can be presumed that their purposes are reasonable.

In his early book, entitled *The Law in Quest of Itself*, Fuller explains his views about legal interpretation. He compares interpreting a statute or decision to the retelling of a funny story. 'If I attempt to retell a funny story', he says:

> the story as I tell it will be the product of two forces: (1) the story as I heard it, the story *as it is* at the time of its first telling; (2) my conception of the point of the story, in other words, my notion of the story *as it ought to be* . . . If

the story as I heard it was, in my opinion, badly told, I am guided largely by my conception of the story as it ought to be ... On the other hand, if I had the story from a master raconteur, I may exert myself to reproduce his exact words ... These two forces, then, supplement one another in shaping the story as I tell it. It is a product of the *is* and the *ought* working together.

(Fuller, 1940, p 8, Fuller's emphasis)

A statute or decision likewise involves two things:

a set of words, and an objective sought. This objective may or may not have been happily expressed in the words chosen by the legislator or judge. This objective ... may be perceived dimly or clearly; it may be perceived more clearly by him who reads the statute than by him who drafted it. The statute or decision is not a segment of being, but ... a process of becoming ... By becoming more clearly what it is, the rule of the case becomes what it was previously only trying to be. In this situation to distinguish sharply between the rule as it is, and the rule as it ought to be, is to resort to an abstraction foreign to the raw data which experience offers us.

(Fuller, 1940, pp 8–9)

Thus, although Fuller claims that judges should be faithful to the law, he views fidelity to the law through a moralised or natural law lens. For he instructs judges to interpret the law so as to give effect to what the judge thinks it *should* be trying to achieve. For Fuller, legal reasons should not be identified with the reasons which appear on the face of the law – reasons which may, as we have seen, lead to an unjust outcome. They are rather the reasons which make the law a defensible or justifiable law, and which, when 'applied', lead to a reasonable result.

Schauer draws a useful distinction between 'formalistic' and 'particularistic' decision-making. Note that this is a different use of the word 'formalism' from that explained in 3.1. In 3.1 the word was used to refer to the theory that the answers to all legal questions can be mechanically derived by logical deduction from legal principles or concepts. By contrast, Schauer uses the word to refer to theories which tell judges rigidly to follow clearly applicable rules without regard to whether it is on-balance reasonable to do so (Schauer, 1988, p 521). In what follows we will be discussing formalism in Schauer's sense, namely, as a theory about *how rules should be applied*.

The key feature of a formalistic approach in this sense is that it treats rules as 'authorities' in the sense explained in 2.11; the rule is treated not as a mere 'rule of thumb' – as a provisional guide to decision-making which is usually useful but which should be ignored when the circumstances are unsuitable for its application. Rather, the rule is treated as a 'proper' rule – as precluding an independent evaluation of what should be done on the balance of reasons. Thus when judges regard themselves as bound by precedent they regard themselves as obliged to follow a previous decision even if they would have decided in a different way had there been no precedent. Formalistic decision-making is therefore 'acontextual': even in contexts when the rule is not apt to achieve its underlying purpose or leads to inequitable results, formalistic decision-makers will follow the rule (Schauer, 1991, p 135).

Fuller rejects the inflexibilities of formalism in favour of particularistic decision-making. Particularism 'focuses on the particular situation' (Schauer, 1991, p 77) and is sensitive to the 'needs of the instant' (Schauer, 1991, p 82). Particularistic decision-makers attend to all the moral and political considerations that are relevant to achieving the optimal result in each individual case. They are guided by their own assessment of what 'right reason' requires. (For the definition of 'right reason' see 2.11.) Rules are, as we have seen, a blunt instrument for achieving legislative purpose. They cannot cater for unimagined situations. They may also be badly drafted and not capable of being given sensible meaning even after attention has been paid to the statute in its entirety. A particularistic approach holds out the hope of a more fine-grained, individualised approach which avoids the errors attendant on the rigid following of rules.

Fuller's results-oriented argument against the inflexible application of rules is, on the face of it, more plausible than his claims about meaning. Instead of saying that rules do not always mean what they seem to mean – an argument which is dependent on controversial views about the nature of meaning – it seems more promising to argue that judges should not blindly apply rules according to their meaning. Why, after all, 'be enslaved by mere marks on a printed page' (Schauer, 1988, p 521)? Where following a rule would lead to inequitable results or results which do not seem to serve the rule's purpose, what possible reason can be given for rigidly sticking to the rule? Should judges rather not serve, as Lord Denning argued, the 'fundamental principles of truth and justice' (Denning, 1979, p 292)?

3.5   The formalist response

The appeal to justice has the look of a knockdown argument but formalists respond by pointing out the advantages of a formalistic approach. They concede that rigid rule-following is incompatible with the ideal of perfect justice. But they argue that it also has *benefits* – benefits which, they say, outweigh its costs. They say that there are values which compete with the ideal of perfect justice and which speak in favour of judicial deference to the plain meaning of rules. This view has become more popular in recent times.

First, formalists argue that adherence to the clear meaning of legal rules serves values we associate with the rule of law. For instance, it increases the likelihood that those who are subject to the law will know what conduct the law permits or prohibits. By contrast, if judges do not apply laws according to their publicly ascertainable meaning, but rather according to what the legislature must have had in mind but failed to communicate, citizens will be uncertain as to how the rules will be applied in practice. After all, the 'spirit of the law' is a much more controversial and unpredictable matter than its plain meaning. Where judges have recourse to the law's spirit, citizens will as a consequence be less able to plan their lives and to use the law to achieve their ends. Respect for clear rules therefore promotes predictability and certainty in the law, serving the ideal of government as 'a rule of laws, not men'.

The connection of formalism with the rule of law was spelt out by Deane J in the Australian case of *Federal Commissioner of Taxation v Westraders Pty Ltd* (1979) where, dealing with a taxation matter, he remarked:

> [f]or a court to arrogate to itself, without legislative warrant, the function of overriding the plain words of the Act in any case where it considers that overall considerations of fairness or some general policy of the Act would be best served by a decision against the taxpayer would be to substitute arbitrary taxation for taxation under the rule of law and, indeed, to subvert the rule of law itself.
>
> (at 319–20)

Second, formalists point out that judges may make mistakes in trying to do justice on a case-by-case basis. Schauer points out that there are two kinds of error. There are, as we have already noted, errors that result from the inflexible application of rules. But errors can also be made when decision-makers attempt to make the best decision, taking into account all relevant factors. Though their approach is *in theory* the optimal approach – whereas rules are necessarily sub-optimal – the truth is that, in the real world, particularistic decision-making may produce worse results on average than rule-guided decision-making. After all, real-world decision-makers are imperfectly rational and not usually in possession of all the relevant information. These human imperfections will inevitably lead them to make mistakes in trying to determine whether it is right to depart from the plain meaning of a rule. In fact, judges following the purposive approach may reach the wrong result *more* often than formalistic judges and therefore be *less* successful at achieving justice than judges who simply follow the rules (Schauer, 1991, pp 149–55).

Schauer's argument gains extra force when one takes into account the fact that judges tend to be drawn from a very narrow section of the community. Their class, race and gender are quite likely to contaminate their views about the underlying purpose of the law, or what justice requires in a particular case, and they may well subvert progressive legislative programmes if they are given *carte blanche* to depart from established or clear rules under the guise of doing justice or ensuring that the purpose of the law is realised. One person's sense of justice is not necessarily another's and there are many examples of judges exhibiting a bias against reform.

One interesting recent example of the use of a purposive approach to interpretation to inject conservative values into the law is the South African case of *S v Jordan* (2002). This case dealt with a bill of rights challenge to a law which subjected prostitutes (though not their customers) to criminal penalties. It was argued that the law was in breach of a section of the Bill of Rights contained in the interim South African Constitution which stated in unequivocal terms that '[e]very person shall have the right to his or her personal privacy'. The Constitutional Court of South Africa had previously found that prohibitions on homosexual sex breach the right to privacy because they intrude into the sphere of private intimacy. One would therefore have expected the Court to find that prohibitions on commercial sex suffer from the same flaw. But the majority of the Court found that the anti-prostitution provision was not analogous, relying on a purposive approach to the privacy clause. The majority reasoned that the purpose of the privacy clause must have been to allow people to establish meaningful and loving relationships. Prostitution, they said, is unlike homosexuality in having nothing to do with such relationships and prostitutes are therefore not entitled to the protection of the privacy guarantee.

Cases such as *Jordan* suggest that those who attack formalism may have a naïve faith in the judiciary to arrive at 'the spirit of the law'. The meaning of 'every person' in the privacy clause could not have been more plain. The interim Bill of Rights did not state that everyone except prostitutes has the right to privacy. It created a space of private intimacy for *everyone*, without exception. When the South African judges ignored the provision's plain meaning in order to give effect to the purpose of the guarantee, as they saw it, the effect was to deny the protection of the Bill of Rights to intimate relationships of which the judges happened to disapprove (Meyerson, 2004, p 152).

A third influence on formalism is democratic theory. Formalists argue that theirs is the correct interpretive method because formalism ensures that controversial moral and political choices are made by those 'with a superior democratic pedigree' (Sunstein, 1997, p 530), namely, elected and accountable representatives, not unelected and unaccountable judges. For this reason formalism is sometimes referred to as 'democratic formalism'. Though Fuller claims that his approach does not amount to an activist usurpation of the legislative role, formalists disagree. They say that Fuller's purposive judge is *not* reasoning legally: the notion of purpose is indeterminate and functions as a disguise for judicial law-making. They believe that formalism, by contrast, promotes democratic government by insisting that, as a matter of political legitimacy, judges should defer to clear rules of law, even when to do so will lead to evidently undesirable results. As Patrick Atiyah explains, 'formality is an important part of a system of distributing power in society.' In particular, it allocates law-making to parliament and law-application to the judiciary. If the law applied according to its clear meaning leads to injustice, then it is parliament's duty to reform it. It is not, Atiyah says, 'the job [of judges] to run everything ... [O]ther participants in the political process have an important role to play' (Atiyah, 1992, p 460).

The argument of the democratic formalists is therefore that even if a purposive approach *could* be relied on to achieve perfect justice, judges are not *entitled* to engage in the kind of reasoning which it requires. Lacking the political legitimacy which legislatures have, they are obliged to apply pre-existing legal principles according to their clear meaning. For the democratic formalists, the democratically elected legislature should occupy centre stage in legal theory. At the other extreme from this view is Dworkin's judge-centred approach. We turn to Dworkin now.

3.6   Dworkin's critique of Hart

Fuller's critique of Hart focuses on his claims about easy cases: that the language in which legal rules are cast settles most legal disputes and that the judge's responsibility in such cases is to apply the law according to its plain meaning. Dworkin's critique focuses, by contrast, on Hart's claim about *hard* cases. This is Hart's claim that, because the law is a system of accepted or social rules, in cases where there is no general agreement that a rule of law applies, the law has run out and judges are in such cases obliged to exercise 'strong' discretion – meaning that the judge has to make a choice unconstrained by legal standards, neither plaintiff nor defendant having a *right* to win. Dworkin agrees with Hart that in hard cases judges have to rely on controversial moral and political judgments. He disagrees, however, that the *law* is indeterminate in these cases and that judges have the discretion to decide them either way on the basis of what they think the law ought to be.

Dworkin opposes Hart's view about judicial discretion on two grounds, as a descriptive thesis and as a thesis which offers a normative justification for the structure of the institution of adjudication (Dworkin, 1977a, p 123). Thus Dworkin argues that judges do not see their task in hard cases as one of exercising strong discretion and he also argues that Hart's model is morally indefensible and fails to show law in its best light. (For more discussion on the need to show law in its best light, see 3.9.)

Dworkin claims, against Hart, that judges do not understand their task differently depending on whether the case is easy or hard. Even when it is controversial whether something is law, judges see themselves as obliged to make decisions according to their best understanding of what the law requires, rather than as making new law. They do not see themselves as casting aside their law books and they do not describe their task as that of creating new rights. On the contrary, it is clear from the way they speak and write that they are attempting to *find* the law – to discover which litigant has a *pre-existing* right to win. They may, of course, disagree on that matter. But if so, they disagree about who has the right. They do not take the view that neither party has the right.

Dworkin concedes that in a trivial sense judges do 'make new law' every time they decide an important case. They announce a principle that has never been officially announced before. But, he says, they see themselves as offering 'these "new" statements of law as improved reports of what the law, properly understood, already is. They claim, in other words, that the new statement is required by a correct perception of the true grounds of law even though this has not been recognized previously, or has even been denied' (Dworkin, 1986, p 6).

Dworkin also argues that Hart's views are inconsistent with fairness as well as with democratic values and the separation of powers. He points out that if judges did make new law in hard cases, the new law would be applied retroactively to the case before the judge. Losing parties would be held liable even though they had no duty at the time the events occurred not to act in that way. This would be, says Dworkin, grossly unfair. After all, laws are meant to guide our conduct, but retrospective law makes it impossible for us to plan our activities in the light of the law's demands. (We could also add, in the light of our earlier discussion about predictability, certainty and the rule of law in 3.5, that retrospective law is a breach of the rule of law.) Furthermore, because judges are not elected, and therefore not accountable to the electorate for their decisions, they do not, according to Dworkin, have the mandate to determine the political direction of society by making new law (Dworkin, 1977a, p 84). A related problem is that if judges make controversial policy choices, this may affect public confidence in their impartiality.

3.7   Dworkin's distinction between rules and principles

In explaining why judges do not make new law in hard cases, Dworkin's starting-point is the claim we encountered in 2.8, that there is more to the law than the explicit *rules* of law, as found in authoritative sources like constitutional provisions, statutes and precedents. In his early piece, 'The Model of Rules I', reprinted in *Taking Rights Seriously*, Dworkin seems to accept Hart's picture of hard cases – that these are cases in which the legal rules fail to provide clear guidance, either because they are silent or lack clear meaning. But Dworkin argues that there are also *moral principles* within the law. These are principles which the rules of law more or less perfectly express and which morally justify the explicit rules of law 'by identifying the political or moral concerns and traditions of the community which...do in fact support the rules' (Dworkin, 1977a, p 67).

Dworkin draws attention to a number of differences between rules and principles. He says that rules either apply or they do not: if it is clear that a situation falls under a valid rule, the legal consequences follow automatically. If, for instance, a rule of law provides that a will must be signed by two witnesses, then a will which has been signed by only one witness will not be valid. But principles do not work in this kind of way. A principle can be *relevant* to a situation but not necessarily *decisive* of the answer. Thus, though our law respects the principle that people should not profit from their own wrongdoing, there are cases in which the principle does not hold. This is because though relevant principles always have *some* weight, they do not always have *conclusive* weight. In order to decide whether a particular principle should apply or not, judges have to weigh up how strong it is in the circumstances of the particular case, which may include the presence of competing principles. But even if the principle does not ultimately prevail, it is not thereby invalidated. Rules, by contrast, cannot be assigned relative weight in this kind of way. If two rules conflict, one of them – Dworkin says – will have to be abandoned.

It is principles, according to Dworkin, which supply the answers when the settled rules of law have run out. Hence judges can go beyond established rules while still deciding *according to* law. In effect, judges decide hard cases by *theorising*: they invoke principles which in their view provide the best moral and political justification for the established legal rules. No doubt the application of principles will be controversial, involving, as it does, complex questions of moral and political theory. Judges who apply principles will therefore have to exercise discretion in one sense of that word – the *weak* sense in which we speak of discretion when the standards to be applied 'cannot be applied mechanically but demand the use of judgement' (Dworkin, 1977a, p 31). But judges are not required to exercise the kind of *strong* discretion postulated by Hart, because there is, in Dworkin's view, almost always a uniquely right solution even to such controversial matters. It will, in other words, very rarely be the case that the arguments on both sides are equally good, legally speaking.

As we saw in 2.8, Dworkin refers by way of example to the principle invoked in *Riggs v Palmer* (1889), that no-one be permitted to take advantage of their own wrongdoing. It is slightly confusing that *Riggs* was not a hard case in Hart's sense: the language of the rule was not, in fact, vague or ambiguous. The words of the statute were clear – the provision did not prevent the murderer grandson from inheriting under the will – and the principle was in fact used to evade the rule's clear meaning. The general point Dworkin wishes to make in 'The Model of Rules I' is nevertheless plain: he believes that when the rules of law are unclear, principles provide the answer.

As we saw in 2.9, Dworkin may have exaggerated the differences between himself and Hart. As we know, Hart accepts that moral principles can be part of a community's law. Hart also makes clear in his later work that he did not intend to imply by his use of the word 'rule' a standard which functions in an all-or-nothing way. He says in the Postscript to the *Concept of Law* that the difference between rules and principles is merely one of degree, rules being *more* conclusive than principles but potentially susceptible to being outweighed by more important rules. He also says that he agrees with Dworkin that arguments from less conclusive standards than rules (non-rule standards) are an important feature of adjudication and legal reasoning (Hart, 1994, pp 261–3).

An important point of difference between Hart and Dworkin nevertheless remains. Though Hart believes that moral principles may figure in a sound justification of the law, and therefore be part of a community's law, he also believes that such principles will at some point prove indeterminate, in the same way that authoritative explicitly formulated rules will prove indeterminate. He says that he finds it difficult to believe that, among the highly general and abstract principles which are part of the underlying justificatory theory of the existing law, 'just one principle or set of principles can be shown to fit the existing settled law better than any other' (Hart, 1983, p 157). Hence when judges reason on the basis of principles they will often be engaged in acts of judicial choice or law-making. For Dworkin, by contrast, there is never a need for the exercise of strong discretion.

In his later work, *Law's Empire*, Dworkin no longer relies on the difference between rules and principles. Furthermore, instead of focusing on disagreement resulting from the 'penumbra of uncertainty', or from borderline cases 'calling for some more or less arbitrary line to be drawn' (Dworkin, 1986, p 43), he now sees disagreement about the law as more fundamental – as involving theoretical disagreement as to what makes something the law. Hard cases are therefore 'pivotal', not marginal or 'penumbral'.

Riggs v Palmer, which, as we saw, is not really a good example of ambiguous or vague statutory language requiring recourse to a principle, now comes into its own as a good example of theoretical disagreement. The *words* in the statute considered in *Riggs* were clear, but – says Dworkin – the *law* was unclear. The judges disagreed about what the statute really meant. Did it mean what it *literally* said by virtue of the principle that democratically passed legislation should be applied according to its plain meaning (as formalists would argue)? Or was it necessary to read an exception for murderers into the clear language on the basis of moral considerations contained elsewhere within the law? This is a complex issue, the resolution of which involves, according to Dworkin, controversial and substantive moral argument directed at determining which of the competing principles provides the morally most acceptable justification of the law. Dworkin continues to insist, however, that such disagreements are not resolved by the exercise of strong discretion or judicial choice and that there are right answers to such disputes to be found within the law's resources.

How do we arrive at the right answer in hard cases when there appear to be alternative views as to what the law requires? To understand this we need to look closely at the arguments in *Law's Empire*, which, though supporting many of the same conclusions as *Taking Rights Seriously* – and especially the claim that the explicit law, as found in statutes and precedents, does not exhaust the law – adopts a different methodology. Instead of proceeding analytically, Dworkin's theory now takes an 'interpretive turn'. He argues for an interpretive approach to law, at the centre of which is a conception of legal argument as 'a characteristically and pervasively moral argument' (Dworkin, 2004, p 4).

3.8   Adjudication as an interpretive task

In *Law's Empire*, Dworkin analyses interpretation in general, before moving on to his interpretive approach to law. He explains that he does not mean by 'interpretation' the attempt to discover the *intention* of the author of a text. This is 'conversational interpretation' – interpreting what people say by focusing on what they mean to communicate. Though this is sometimes argued to be the correct approach to statutory interpretation – namely, that statutes should be understood in the light of what the legislators who enacted them had in mind – this is not what Dworkin means by an interpretive approach. He notes that we approach many social practices as well as works of art with the aim of 'imposing purpose on [the] object or practice in order to make of it the best possible example of the form or genre to which it is taken to belong' (Dworkin, 1986, p 52), and he explains that it is this kind of *argumentative* or *value-guided* interpretation that he has in mind and wishes to apply to law. He labels it 'constructive interpretation'.

Constructive interpretation begins by picking out the 'raw data' we wish to interpret. This is the 'preinterpretive' stage in which 'the rules and standards taken to provide the tentative content of the practice are identified' (Dworkin, 1986, pp 65–6). This is a primarily descriptive stage, though Dworkin does not deny that some interpretation is required even at this stage, as the scare quotes around 'preinterpretive' signal.

Then there is an interpretive stage, in which we focus on the point or value of the practice and attempt to provide a justification for the bulk of the practice which shows it in its best light: '[a] participant interpreting a social practice . . . proposes value for the practice by describing some scheme of interests or goals or principles the practice can be taken to serve or express or exemplify' (Dworkin, 1986, p 52). This is an enterprise which requires normative argument and different interpreters are likely to differ on which interpretation proposes the most value for the practice. However, if a justification does not fit enough of the practice it will not be an interpretation of it, but the invention of a new practice.

Finally, there is a postinterpretive stage in which we revisit and revise our views about the requirements of the practice in the light of its best justification. For instance, a previously accepted rule of the practice might now come to be seen as a mistake in the light of the justification that interprets the bulk of the practice in the best possible light (Dworkin, 1986, p 99).

Notice that there are therefore both formal or structural and substantive constraints on the process of interpretation. The formal or structural constraint is the requirement of 'fit' – the need for the interpretation to be consistent with the 'raw data' and not to be the invention of a new practice. The substantive constraint is the requirement of 'most value'.

In applying this account of interpretation to the judicial task, Dworkin compares adjudication with the writing of a 'chain novel'. Suppose a group of people decide to write a novel by each contributing a chapter. It must appear at the end as if a single author has written the whole work. Each novelist in the chain must continue the novel by building on what has gone before with the aim of making the novel the best it can be. In order to continue the novel, all the novelists, except the first, will have to interpret what has gone before. They will, for instance, have to decide what motivates the characters and what the point of the novel is. At the same time, their decisions must continue the novel in the best possible way.

There will therefore be two constraints on the creative activity of the novelists. First, they have to *continue* the novel, not start a new one. This means that their chapter will have to be consistent with or fit the material that has been constructed so far. This is not to say that the fit must be exact. It must, though, fit the bulk of the text. If a new chapter entirely disregards what has gone before, the interpretation will be disqualified. This is the constraint I previously called formal or structural. Second, in choosing between different interpretations which both fit the bulk of the text, the novelists should choose that interpretation which they believe makes the work in progress the *best* work it can be. What is 'best' is here judged from the standpoint of aesthetic value. This is the constraint I previously called substantive.

Stanley Fish argues that Dworkin assumes that there are 'hard facts' about texts which any interpretation must accommodate as a matter of brute, recalcitrant reality – an assumption which Fish argues is misplaced. He claims that 'information only comes in an interpreted form' (Fish, 1982, p 554) – that there is nothing 'obviously and unproblematically there' (Fish, 1982, p 562) to constrain interpretation – and that to the extent that it seems that there are hard facts about the text which present an obstacle to the interpreter's freedom, this is only because certain interpretations have become orthodox among the community of interpreters.

Dworkin's response to this is to concede that judgments about fit are to some extent a controversial, interpretive matter. He points out, nevertheless, that the chain novelist is in a different position from an ordinary novelist. It is obvious that the chain novelist has *less* freedom than someone engaged in what Dworkin calls 'more independent creative writing', and this can only be explained on the basis that the pre-existing material makes structural demands which can compete with the independent demands of aesthetic value (Dworkin, 1986, pp 231–2). If Fish were right, there would be no constraint of consistency, but – Dworkin responds – there clearly is.

Adjudication – interpreting a statute or a line of precedents – is similar in important ways to the writing of a chain novel, according to Dworkin. He says that judges should think of themselves as authors in the chain of common law. They should think of earlier cases on related matters as part of an ongoing story which requires interpretation and continuation. And when interpreting statutes, they should likewise think of the legislature as an author earlier than themselves in the chain of law, their responsibility being to continue to develop, in the best way, the statutory scheme the legislature began. In both cases, judges are not entitled to strike off in a new direction: their interpretation of the law must to a significant extent cohere with or fit the 'data', whether these be common-law precedents or the words of a statute. They must weave these into a story which is recognisably continuous with what went before. They must, in other words, be faithful to the past.

But their interpretation must also make the story (the legal record) the best story it can be. Judges should decide in a way which provides the *best justification* for the precedents or the legislation. What is 'best' in the case of law is judged from the standpoint of political morality – the moral standards which apply to the evaluation of social institutions. The idea is to 'achieve equilibrium between legal practice ... and the best justification of that practice' (Dworkin, 1986, p 90).

It is therefore impossible to draw a sharp distinction between the law as it is and the law as it ought to be – between legal standards on the one hand and moral standards on the other. Moral reasoning is required to identify the law and the judicial task, on Dworkin's account, is therefore an inescapably theoretical or philosophical one, carrying 'the lawyer very deep into political and moral theory' (Dworkin, 1977a, p 67).

In *Law's Empire*, the distinction between hard and easy cases recedes in importance. 'Hard' is just a label which is used when people disagree about which reading of the law shows the legal record as a whole in its best light, irrespective of how linguistically clear the words in which the law is couched may be. Conversely, even if the words of a statute are vague or ambiguous, the *law* may nevertheless be clear, because there may be no doubt that one reading of the statute would be 'a better performance of the legislative function' (Dworkin, 1986, p 353). The same interpretive method is used in both cases, hard and easy, but just because there is no disagreement about the correct interpretation in an easy case we may not be aware that the theory is at work (Dworkin, 1986, p 354). Thus, contrary to Hart, Dworkin believes that adjudication *always* involves moral and political reasoning, not only in hard cases.

3.9   Law as integrity

Why should we accept Dworkin's account of the nature of adjudication? In order to understand Dworkin's answer to this question we have to appreciate that he believes that theories about the nature of law are not morally neutral. He takes issue with an 'Archimedean' view of jurisprudence, meaning by this a view of jurisprudence as 'not participating' in law, but 'look[ing] down, from outside and above' on law (Dworkin, 2004, p 2).

According to Dworkin, law is that practice which constrains the exercise of state power by insisting that when the state coerces citizens (by punishing them, for instance, or forcing them to pay damages), it should do so only in ways which 'flow from' past political decisions of courts and legislatures (Dworkin, 1986, pp 93–4). Dworkin claims, furthermore, that all legal theorists are in the interpretive business of showing from the perspective of a participant in this practice – because one cannot, according to Dworkin, interpret a practice without joining it – how their particular theory or conception of law serves values that *justify* the practice of constraining governmental coercion by reference to past political decisions. 'A conception of law', says Dworkin, 'is a general, abstract interpretation of legal practice as a whole. It offers to show the practice in its best light, to deploy some argument why law on that conception provides an adequate justification for coercion' (Dworkin, 1986, p 139)

Or, as Dworkin puts it in more recent work, all legal theories are in the business of proposing a reading of the value of 'legality' – some putative point it serves or political end it promotes – legality being the value that insists that 'the coercive power of a political community should be deployed against its citizens only in accordance with standards established in advance of that deployment' (Dworkin, 2004, p 26). All legal theories, in other words, aim to demonstrate that their theory of law explains most satisfactorily why pre-established standards, as laid down in cases and statutes, provide appropriate grounds for governmental coercion.

Hence, for Dworkin, those who do jurisprudence or theorise about the nature of law are involved in the same kind of activity as judges and lawyers. Just as judges have to appeal to moral arguments when they determine what the law is on a particular matter, so legal theorists have to appeal to moral arguments when they theorise about the nature of law in general: 'no firm line divides jurisprudence from adjudication or any other aspect of legal practice' (Dworkin, 1986, p 90).

Thus Dworkin claims that Hart's positivism, for instance, is best understood as an interpretive theory which takes the view that the point of legality is to guide conduct *efficiently* as well as to give *fair warning* before coercion is used. It is for these *moral* reasons, according to Dworkin, that Hart conceives of law as a set of conventions which authorise the making of legal rules. Legal conventions are clear and therefore give 'crisp direction' to citizens as to when force will be used. They '[make] the occasions of coercion depend on plain facts available to all'. In this way they serve the values of efficiency and fair warning (Dworkin, 1986, p 117, 2004, p 28).

Dworkin believes, of course, that his account of law shows law in a better light than its rivals and that this is why we should accept it. But before turning to his arguments for this conclusion, it is necessary to point out that Dworkin's characterisation of legal theory is controversial: many legal theorists reject his claim that explaining the nature of law involves the interpretation of law in a way which shows why it morally justifies state coercion. Even theorists who accept Dworkin's argument that legal *practice* is interpretive do not necessarily agree that legal *theory* is interpretive (Moore, 1989, pp 947–8). Many positivists likewise argue that their aim is to provide a *morally neutral, descriptive* account of law. Stephen Perry calls this view 'methodological positivism' as opposed to the 'substantive' positivism we considered in the last chapter – substantive positivism being the view that there is no necessary connection between morality and law, and methodological positivism being the view that there is no necessary connection between morality and legal theory (Perry, 2001, p 311).

Substantive positivists are not necessarily committed to methodological positivism. For instance, the ethical positivists discussed in 2.12 are not methodological positivists. They defend positivism on *moral* and *political* grounds, namely, as a way of cutting back on the political power of judges. Hart, by contrast, is both a substantive and a methodological positivist. He describes his method as follows: it is '*descriptive* in that it is morally neutral and has no justificatory aims: it does not seek to justify or commend on moral or other grounds the forms and structures which appear in my general account of law' (Hart, 1994, p 240). Hart therefore takes issue with Dworkin's argument that positivism is best understood as an interpretive theory. He says that his account of law, in terms of criteria of validity conventionally accepted by officials, does not rely for support on the claim that it shows law in a good light, by making it clear and uncontroversial. Rather, Hart thinks his account should be accepted because it is *descriptively* true.

Hart says that he can see no reason why those who do legal theory should have to share the internal viewpoint of participants in the legal system like judges. Of course, as we know, Hart thinks that an adequate account of law must make *reference* to the internal point of view – the view of those who accept the law as a guide to conduct. But – he argues – this does not mean that the *theorist* must *share* or *endorse* the internal point of view, or 'in any other way...surrender his descriptive stance' (Hart, 1994, p 242). Even if those who accept the law as a guide to conduct also believe that there are moral reasons for conforming to the law's requirements and that the law's use of coercion is morally justified – something which Hart argues is not necessarily the case, as we know (see 2.7) – the theorist would merely *describe* or *record* these moral beliefs, not share them (Hart, 1994, p 243). In short, Hart argues that legal theory *describes* the normative stance of participants in legal institutions without *adopting* that normative stance.

Dworkin's view of legal theory as a value-laden, interpretive enterprise is therefore open to question. Let us assume, however, for the sake of argument that Dworkin is right that all theories of law aim to show law in its best light, and turn now to his reasons for thinking that his theory of the nature of law gives the best such account.

Dworkin explains that his theory makes the idea of *integrity* central to understanding the point of constraining the exercise of state power by reference to pre-established standards. He explains the idea of integrity first in individual terms and then in political terms. When we speak of *individuals* as having integrity we mean, Dworkin says, that they act 'according to convictions that inform and shape their lives as a whole, rather than capriciously or whimsically' (Dworkin, 1986, p 166). Integrity as a *political* ideal, says Dworkin, makes an analogous demand on the state. Law as integrity requires 'government to speak with one voice, to act in a principled and coherent manner toward all its citizens, to extend to everyone the substantive standards of justice or fairness it uses for some' (Dworkin, 1986, p 165). And integrity in adjudication is, in turn, one aspect of law as integrity: it requires judges to see and enforce the law as coherent in principle, as a body of law to be administered as a whole so that rules which violate the principle of integrity are not treated as part of the law.

It is easy to see why Dworkin's account of adjudication obeys the principle of integrity. It 'instructs judges to identify legal rights and duties...on the assumption that they were all created by a single author – the community personified – expressing a coherent conception of justice and fairness' (Dworkin, 1986, p 225). It requires a judge 'to test his interpretation of any part of the great network of political structures and decisions of his community by asking whether it could form part of a coherent theory justifying the network as a whole' (Dworkin, 1986, p 245). As JW Harris explains, the aspiration 'in arriving at propositions of law is...that of displaying the constitution, all unrepealed statutes and all non-repudiated precedents as a consistent and coherent scheme of just coercion' (Harris, 1997, p 192). (No wonder, then, that Dworkin calls his ideal judge 'Hercules', for this holistic approach to identifying the law is undoubtedly a Herculean task.)

Dworkin then argues that the single vision of justice presented by law as integrity does a better job of justifying the coercive authority of the state than its rivals and therefore shows the practice of law in its best light. Law as integrity obliges judges to decide new cases in a way which is consistent with the moral principles which best justify the previous cases, 'so that each person's situation is fair and just according to the same standards' (Dworkin, 1986, p 243). In thereby precluding coercion on the basis of arbitrary distinctions (see also 4.4), law as integrity *affirms the right of citizens to be treated as equals*. It insists that government must govern under a set of principles applicable to *everyone* and it is therefore the conception of law which best legitimises the coercive authority of the state.

3.10　Judging and legislating

Dworkin seems to have the best of all worlds. He accepts the mainstream picture of the law as providing right answers to legal disputes which judges are under an obligation to find. Indeed, he goes further than Hart, in claiming that there are no legal problems which fall outside the legal system. All legal problems can be solved in terms of the application of pre-existing law. Judges, according to Dworkin, do not have the freedom of legislators and never reach outside the law to make new law: they never create new duties and impose them retrospectively. Thus Hercules is never in the business of law-making, which would be an illegitimate exercise of judicial power in Dworkin's view.

Yet Dworkin is not guilty of mechanical jurisprudence – of the view that judges are 'computers in robes', to borrow a phrase from Martha Minow and Elizabeth Spelman (Minow and Spelman, 1988, p 53). He does not claim that judges are mechanically constrained by rules of law which inexorably dictate the answer to all legal cases. On the contrary, like the realists (to whom we turn in the next chapter), Dworkin discounts the role played by the formal rules of law in legal reasoning. He sees legal reasoning as involving complex and controversial moral and political judgments and he likens it to an act of creative interpretation. It may be wondered whether it is really possible to incorporate all of these 'desirables' in a single theory. Can law really be, as Dworkin claims, 'deeply and thoroughly political', yet not 'a matter of *personal* or *partisan* politics' (Dworkin, 1982, p 179, my emphasis)?

Dworkin offers a number of reasons in support of this claim. He argues, for one thing, that the moral and political reasoning in which judges are necessarily engaged is constrained to some extent by the fact that any satisfactory interpretation will have to fit the pre-interpretive legal materials, as contained in precedents or statutes. Thus, although judges' moral and political convictions will influence their views as to what rights individuals have under the law, judges may not justify their decisions by reference to their own *idiosyncratic*, personal convictions or political beliefs – the political morality they would like the law *ideally* to reflect. Instead, they are obliged to justify their decisions by reference to the best justification for the society's *actual* legal record (Dworkin, 1984, p 254). Hence their view of what the law is may diverge from their view as to what it ought to be.

Dworkin gives the example of a Marxist judge who thinks that the rich should share their wealth with the poor. Marxist judges will find that the need to decide cases in a way which fits the bulk of the prior legal record prevents them from interpreting the law in the way they would prefer. In this way, 'the brute facts of political history will... limit the role any judge's personal convictions of justice can play in his decisions' (Dworkin, 1986, p 255). Legislators, by contrast, are entitled to draw on their own moral and political beliefs in deciding what laws would be desirable.

Dworkin argues that judges are also in a different position from legislators in another way. He draws a distinction between two *kinds* of political argument – arguments of *principle* and arguments of *policy* – and he goes on to argue that legislators may rely on policy arguments but judges may decide cases only on the basis of principle. Arguments of policy justify a decision in terms which appeal to the *collective interest of the community as a whole* rather than in terms of pre-existing moral rights. Dworkin gives the example of an argument in favour of a subsidy for aircraft manufacturers on the ground that such a subsidy will serve the ends of national defence. Arguments of principle, by contrast, justify a decision by showing that the decision protects an individual's *rights*. They focus on what individuals are entitled to, *even if the majority would be better off if the relevant entitlements were denied* (Dworkin, 1977a, p 82). (For further discussion on how, in Dworkin's view, rights 'trump' collective goals, see 5.3.)

Dworkin argues that legislators may legitimately justify their decisions by using policy arguments but judges, in deciding to hold people liable in damages, may not appeal to community goals. Even in hard cases, when judges construct rules of liability not previously recognised, they do so on the *principled* basis that the parties actually had the relevant rights and duties at the time the events occurred. They are obliged to decide in a way which is consistent with the moral principles which best justify the previous cases, 'so that each person's situation is fair and just according to the same standards' (Dworkin, 1986, p 243). This may come at a cost to the community but that is not a consideration by which, in Dworkin's opinion, a judge should be swayed.

There is also another reason why Dworkin believes that it is possible to have the best of all worlds – that adjudication can be based on controversial moral and political judgments while still remaining an objective enterprise. He believes that there are right and wrong answers to moral questions and that there are therefore objective answers to the interpretive questions of political morality which judges are, in his view, required to consider. He disagrees, in other words, with the non-cognitivist views about morality discussed in 2.6.

Dworkin does not, of course, deny that judges will, in practice, quite commonly disagree about the answers to legal questions. This is virtually inevitable given the prominence he gives to the role of controversial and complex moral and political reasoning in resolving legal cases. Nor does Dworkin claim that it is possible mechanically to *demonstrate* that a particular answer is the right answer. But this does not, he says, prevent one answer from *being* the most reasonable answer. For – as he points out – a proposition can be true even if it is not *uncontroversially* true or cannot be *proved* to be true to everyone's satisfaction.

Once again, he gives a literary example. Suppose we are discussing the question whether David Copperfield had a sexual relationship with Steerforth. Dickens does not directly tell us about this aspect of David's life. There can, nevertheless, be said to be a right answer to this question in the sense that one hypothesis 'provides a more satisfactory explanation of what [David] subsequently did and thought than the [opposite hypothesis]' (Dworkin, 1977b, p 78). The same is true of the law. Propositions of law can be true even if they cannot be conclusively proved to be true. (Contrast Hart: the right answer is the 'clearly right' answer.)

Dworkin has, as a result, a much more expansive view of the law than Hart. For Hart, the law is what legal officials agree upon and legal standards are therefore standards about which we can give uncontroversial information. The result is that there is *less* law than we might assume there is. For Dworkin, by contrast, law is something 'pervasively contestable' (Dworkin, 1986, p 411). For Dworkin, our legal rights extend *beyond* those which judicial decisions and legislative enactments uncontroversially grant us. In his view, legal rights are identified, as we have seen, through the process of constructive interpretation. The principles revealed by this approach represent the real law behind the institutional or explicit law – the law which shows the explicit law in the best moral light.

In fact, what the legal materials uncontroversially grant us may be a pale reflection of our legal rights because they may contain mistakes – which is to say that they may be in conflict with principles which are more fundamental to justifying law as a whole, in which case they will need to be jettisoned when we revisit them at the postinterpretive stage. The cases and statutes are therefore merely 'raw material' (Coleman, 2001b, p 166), which judges fashion and modify in the service of presenting the law as a regime of justified coercion. In the postinterpretive stage, we adjust our sense of what the law 'really' requires in the light of the justification we see the legal record as serving and it is this idealised, if controversial, law which courts are obliged to enforce: what the law *is* therefore depends on *moral* judgments as to which principles best justify past political decisions, and legal standards are whatever body of standards provides the best moral justification for a society's established legal rules and institutions. (Contrast Hart: legal standards are whatever standards conform to the criteria of legal validity which happen, *as a contingent matter of social fact*, to be accepted in a particular society.)

Dworkin does not go so far as to postulate *universal* legal standards *unrelated* to human law which are capable of invalidating it. For Dworkin, it is the *actual* legal practice of a *particular* community which judges seek to show in the best light. Something might therefore be the law even if, according to 'some pure objective or natural law' (Dworkin, 1982, p 180), it ought not to be. Dworkin therefore insists that there is a distinction between interpreting the *existing* law and postulating an *ideal* law: judges are not entitled to invent a better legal record. He is therefore not a classical natural lawyer. It should, nevertheless, be clear that Dworkin's theory, in asserting that the identification of the law necessarily involves sound moral judgment – that judgments of morality are *part* of the grounds of law (part of what makes legal propositions true), even though they are not law's *only* grounds (Dworkin, 1986, p 429) – is on the natural law side of the positivism/natural law divide.

It should also be clear that once one has expanded the available pre-existing legal standards in this way, it becomes more plausible to say that all legal disputes can be decided *according to* the law. If the law should not be identified with what legal officials agree upon, but depends instead in part on moral argument, then, despite the existence of cases to which there are no obvious answers, there need be no gaps in the law which judges are obliged to fill by the exercise of discretion.

3.11   Some criticisms of Dworkin

As we have seen, Dworkin attempts to distinguish between the activities of judging and legislating, while simultaneously asserting that judges make controversial moral and political judgments. Many critics argue, however, that, in reality, Hercules is exercising exactly the same kind of law-making power which Dworkin finds so objectionable in Hart's model judge, Herbert. (It will be remembered that Hart's first name is 'Herbert'.) The only difference, according to these critics, is that Hercules *disguises* the fact that he is imposing his own personal views by claiming that they are contained in the law. His claim that the law provides answers for all disputes is therefore just 'rhetoric' or 'ritual language' (Hart, 1994, p 274). These critics point out that from the perspective of the litigants it really makes little difference whether they come before Hercules or whether they come before Herbert – a judge who sees his task as that of exercising discretion in a hard case. Since Hercules' arguments are not guaranteed to persuade, and since his decision could not have been predicted in advance, he is exercising power just as unpredictably as Herbert (Bell, 1983, pp 213, 222–3).

It does not change this picture – the critics say – to say that, objectively, there is a right answer to the issue in dispute. Even if there is a right answer, if two judges conscientiously applying their mind to the problem may disagree about the answer, it is hard to deny that they have the discretion to decide the case either way. Kent Greenawalt gives the example of standards of beauty. Suppose a group of judges is told to pick the most beautiful flower. Let us also suppose that there are objective standards of beauty in flowers but no way of telling what they are. 'Then everyone would believe that one choice was "right" but would be unable to ascertain which one. The judges themselves would be thrown back on their own judgments' (Greenawalt, 1975, p 369). If this is not the exercise of discretion, what is? How can judges be said to be under a duty to decide in one way rather than another if they cannot say with any confidence which is the correct decision? Greenawalt concludes:

> [w]hen authoritative standards yield no clear answers, when a judge must rely on debatable personal assessments to decide a case, and when more than one result will widely be regarded as a satisfactory fulfillment of his judicial responsibilities then it does not make good sense to say that a judge is under a duty to reach one result rather than another; as far as the law is concerned, he has discretion to decide between them.
>
> (Greenawalt, 1975, p 378)

Another criticism of Dworkin, made by Finnis, relates to the 'incommensurability' of the two dimensions – fit and moral value – in terms of which different interpretations must be assessed. When two things are incommensurable, it is impossible to compare them by saying that one is better than another. One cannot, for instance, normally say that spending the afternoon reading philosophy is better or worse than spending the afternoon going for a walk (Bix, 1993, p 99). Finnis says that judgments of fit and moral merits may be incommensurable in this kind of way. One solution to a legal problem may be slightly better on the dimension of fit, whereas the other may be slightly better on the dimension of value. In such circumstances, he says, there is an open choice between the two answers: there is no uniquely right way to resolve the dispute (Bix, 1993, pp 96–101; Finnis, 1987, pp 371–6).

Chapter 4

Law and politics

Challenging the mainstream

We turn now to a group of theories which reject the mainstream idea of the law as a distinctive realm of reasons which is capable of constraining or controlling decisions according to its own inner 'logic' or 'artificial reason'. These theories put the emphasis on *external* or *non-legal* factors as the explanation of judicial decision-making, and they are favourably disposed to the idea that judges should openly make decisions politically, that is, with an eye to their policy implications and future social consequences. While mainstream theorists stress the need for law to show fidelity to the past, their critics, in other words, wish to use law to improve the future.

The primary focus of this chapter is on American legal realism and Critical Legal Studies, with attention being paid to the influence of Marxism and postmodernism on the latter. We will extract some broad themes from these umbrella movements while also noting the differences of opinion and disagreements among the theorists who fall under them. The chapter will also explain the main claims of critical race theory. Finally, it will examine the economic analysis of law, especially as expounded by its most influential defender, Richard Posner.

You should be familiar with:

- Realism
- The economic analysis of law
- Postmodernism
- Marxism and law
- Critical Legal Studies
- Critical race theory

4.1 Legal indeterminacy

The American legal realists were a group of legal theorists and lawyers whose heyday was in the 1920s, 1930s and 1940s. Among them can be counted

Karl Llewellyn (1893–1962), Jerome Frank (1889–1957), Herman Oliphant (1844–1939) and John Chipman Gray (1839–1915). Oliver Wendell Holmes, Jr (1841–1935), who was a Justice of the Supreme Court of the United States, was a key influence on the realists. He talked of the need to 'wash…with cynical acid' (Holmes, 1897, p 462) the traditional view of law, on which existing legal doctrine supplies uniquely correct answers to legal problems. In place of this traditional view, the realists wished to substitute a 'realistic' theory, focusing on the 'real' determinants of judicial decisions – not on what judges *say* they do, but on 'what the courts…do in fact' (Holmes, 1897, p 461). They were therefore 'realists' in the sense that they aimed to bring legal theory down to earth, puncture the illusions in which it trades, and describe the practical realities of the legal system in its social context.

At the time the realists were writing, legal reasoning was widely seen as involving the deductive application of rules of law, as found in judicial decisions and statutes, to known facts. The judicial task therefore involved the mechanical, uncontroversial derivation of legal conclusions without regard to their practical consequences. The views of Christopher Columbus Langdell, who was Dean of the Harvard Law School at the end of the nineteenth century, were highly influential in the development of this orthodoxy. Langdell had seen law as a science, which involved identifying the principles on which a field of law is based and working out the subordinate principles logically entailed by them, the aim being to construct a logically connected system of rules. Law was thus like mathematics. In challenging this view, the realists went to the other extreme, arguing that in so far as judicial decision-making is concerned, legal rules are merely 'pretty playthings' (Llewellyn, 1930a, p 14) and that the notion of legal reasoning is a myth or sham.

It is important to understand the exact character of the realists' claim. Their claim is not that, as a matter of fact, judges ignore the rules of law in reaching their decisions. Rather, they take the view that legal rules are *in their nature* not capable of yielding uniquely correct answers in any of the cases that come before the courts. There is, in other words, no such thing as a legally correct decision in these cases. (Contrast Hart's less extreme view (see 3.2), that the rules of law do not *always* dictate the outcome.) Holmes expressed the realist view by saying: '[g]eneral propositions do not determine concrete cases.' He also said: 'I always say in conference…that I will admit any general proposition you like and decide the case either way' (quoted in Rumble, 1968, pp 39–40).

In support of this view, realists argue that there are so many different rules potentially relevant to any legal case that there is virtually always precedential support for both sides in a legal argument. There are also conflicting ways of interpreting precedents. A precedent can be read both narrowly and broadly. It can be confined to its facts or it can be read as standing for a wider proposition. This means that there are different possible readings of a precedent, of which one will support one side, one the other. The same precedent can, in other words, be used to justify opposing outcomes. And the same, according to the realists, is true of the interpretation of statutes. They too can be read in contradictory ways.

Jerome Frank, who was a 'fact-sceptic' as well as a 'rule-sceptic', went even further. He said that even in situations where the rules are clear, the factual findings of trial judges and juries can never be predicted: trial judges and juries can make any factual finding they please, so as to bring the facts under the rule which will generate the outcome they want to reach. In fact, Frank thought that the 'elusiveness of facts' generates even more unpredictability and uncertainty in the judicial process than the difficulties which attend the application of rules. But, whether by virtue of the indeterminacy of rules or the manipulability of facts, the 'law in the books' is – according to the realists – not capable of generating answers to the legal problems which come before the courts and is therefore not on its own a reliable basis for predicting judicial decisions.

How do mainstream theorists respond to these claims? Hart, for one, thinks that the realists are right about some legal cases, namely, hard cases. But he denies that 'all legal questions are fundamentally like those of the penumbra'. As we know, he thinks that rules have a core of agreed-upon meaning. Thus, while 'it is good to be occupied with the penumbra', the realists have, in his view, become 'preoccupied' with it (Hart, 1958, p 615).

Dworkin believes, as we have seen, that even in hard cases, where a statute is unclear or there is disagreement about whether a precedent is applicable, there are nevertheless right and wrong ways to read the statute and the precedent. One example he gives is of a precedent case which awarded compensation to someone who suffered emotional injury on witnessing serious injury to a close relative at the scene of the accident. Now a later court is presented with slightly different facts: the shock does not occur at the scene of the accident but some hours later and in a hospital when someone sees the serious condition of their relative. Is the precedent applicable?

The realists would say that there is no *legal* answer to this question because the precedent can be read both narrowly and broadly. Dworkin disagrees. He says that the answer depends on whether the *moral principles* which explain the earlier decision also apply in the later circumstances. Is there any difference of principle between the case of a mother who suffers emotional injury witnessing her child hit by a car and a mother who suffers identical injury seeing her injured child in hospital? Can the bare fact of suffering the injury later, away from the scene, be a *morally good* reason to deny compensation? If not, the mother deserves compensation in both cases and the precedent cannot be confined to its facts.

4.2   Paper rules and real rules

If law should not be identified with what Llewellyn called the 'paper' rules – or the law in the books – what is it, according to the realists? What are we talking about when we talk about legal rights and duties? The realist answer to this question – one which again goes back to Holmes – is that if you want to know what the law is, you must look at it not in terms of the *idealistic* abstractions of the legal theorists but as the 'bad man' looks at it. The bad man, Holmes wrote, 'does not care two straws for . . . axioms or deductions' (Holmes, 1897, p 460), but does want to know what conduct is likely to put him in jail or make him liable for damages.

This hard-headed focus on the consequences courts are likely to attach to our conduct led the realists to hold that we are under a legal duty if a court would enforce such a duty. The claim that 'it is the law that X is under a certain duty' is therefore equivalent to *predicting* that a court will enforce the duty. If the court does not enforce the duty, then the claim was false, because the '*law is what the courts say it is*'. There is, in other words, no law which pre-exists a court's decision on the matter.

Thus Llewellyn says: 'I should like to begin by distinguishing "real" rules and rights from paper rules and rights. The former are conceived in terms of behaviour; they are but other names, convenient shorthand symbols, for the remedies, the actions of the courts.' They are 'what the courts will do in a given case, and nothing more pretentious' (Llewellyn, 1930a, pp 447–8). Though Llewellyn calls these the real 'rules', he is clear that that they are not rules in the ordinary, normative or prescriptive sense of the word – the sense to which Hart calls attention – but are merely descriptive statements of the regular practices of the courts. He says:

> '[r]eal rules', . . . , if I had my way with words, would by legal scientists be called the practices of the courts, and not 'rules' at all. And for such scientists statements of 'rights' would be statements of likelihood that in a given situation a certain type of court action loomed in the offing. Factual terms. No more . . . They are . . . on the level of isness and not of oughtness.
>
> (Llewellyn, 1930, p 448)

Frank writes similarly:

> [f]or any particular lay person, the law, with respect to any particular set of facts, is a decision of a court with respect to those facts so far as that decision affects a particular person. Until a court has passed on those facts no law on that subject is yet in existence.
>
> (Frank, 1930, p 46)

It will be evident that, like Austin, the realists identify law with what the sovereign commands. The only difference is that Austin's sovereign law-maker is the legislature, whereas the realists' sovereign law-maker is the judiciary. This comes out very clearly in the writings of John Chipman Gray who made the paradoxical claim that statutes are 'sources of Law . . . not part of the Law itself' (Gray, 1972 edn, p 125). In support of this, he quoted from Bishop Hoadly who had said: '[w]hoever hath an *absolute authority* to *interpret* any written or spoken laws, it is *he* who is truly the *Law-giver* to all intents and purposes, and not the person who first wrote or spoke them' (Gray, 1972 edn, p 125, emphasis in original).

One objection to viewing statements about rights and duties as predictions about what the courts will do is that it leaves out the normativity of law – the fact that legal statements are accepted as guides to conduct, at least by legal officials.

Legal statements do not appear to be claims about what courts will *in fact* do, but statements about what individuals *ought* to do.

We have already seen that Hart criticised Austin's theory for missing this fact about law (see 1.2). And realism is very similar to the command theory in its focus on defining legal concepts in terms of facts about external, observable behaviour. Like Austin, the realists take a scientific approach to defining legal concepts – not in Langdell's sense of law as a closed system of logically related norms, but in the sense that they attempt to characterise law in a way which makes no reference to the mental states and attitudes of those who participate in legal institutions. Yet, as Hart says, laws do not function in the lives of individuals as the basis for predicting the decisions of courts, but rather as accepted legal standards of behaviour. Individuals do not confine themselves to the external point of view – 'recording and predicting the decisions of courts or the probable incidence of sanctions' – but 'continuously express in normative terms their shared acceptance of the law as a guide to conduct' (Hart, 1994, p 138).

Hart also has a further objection to defining the law as whatever the courts decide. He points out that this definition makes it unintelligible to say that a court has made a mistake about the law. Hart argues that realism confuses *finality* with *infallibility*. A court's decision is final when no appeal is possible from it. But this does not mean that there was no law on the matter save that which the court chose to apply. At least in those cases which fall under the central core of meaning of a rule, there are pre-existing standards of correct judicial decision which allow us to describe a particular judicial decision as mistaken, *even if it cannot be challenged within the legal system.*

Hart gives the analogy of a game. He notes that games can be played without an umpire. In such cases the players make an honest effort to determine who is winning in terms of the rules. What changes if we add an umpire to this picture? The umpire's determinations may be final but the *rules* do not change. It is not as if the umpire has *carte blanche* to choose the winner of the game: it is the umpire's duty to apply the rules as best as he or she can. Suppose that the umpire gives the game to someone who did not really win. Is the players' contrary view about who won the game a *prediction* about what the umpire would do – a prediction which turned out to be false? Clearly, says Hart, this is not the case. Rather, the players' view is a competing application of the rules which does not, unlike the umpire's views, have *official* status. The fact that the umpire's application of the rules has official status does not, however, guarantee that the rules have been *correctly* applied. And decisions of courts from which no appeal is possible are exactly, says Hart, like the decisions of umpires in games – final, but not necessarily infallible, and therefore not to be identified with the law on the matter.

4.3 Judicial behaviour

We have seen that, for the realists, legal doctrine is not the main factor in producing court decisions. How, then, do judges decide cases? And if law does not to any great extent influence or constrain judicial decision-making, how do we explain the fact that there are significant uniformities in judicial behaviour? To answer these questions, we need to turn to the realist account of judicial behaviour.

On the mainstream account of legal reasoning, as we know, legal reasons *justify* legal conclusions. Despite their differences, all the theorists we considered in the last chapter believe that interpretation of the law can and should be a *rational* and *principled* process. They hold that there are standards or norms of legal decision-making – that it is possible to provide good and convincing legal arguments for legal conclusions and that legal decisions can therefore be right or wrong.

Of course, mainstream theorists do not claim that, as a matter of fact, judges always decide according to the law. They are well aware that judges may, due to prejudice, bias or other legally irrelevant factors, fail to apply the law. Mainstream theorists say, however, that judges *can* apply the law and that they *should* do so – that judges who depart from the legal standards can be legitimately criticised for having gone wrong.

Realism offers a radically different account of adjudication. It holds that it is not *possible* to evaluate judicial decisions in the light of their justifiability in terms of legal standards. Judges cannot be criticised for departing from standards of correct decision-making because no such standards exist. Judicial decision-making is therefore not capable of being *rationally justified* but only *causally explained* in terms of *extra-legal* or *non-rational* factors operating, whether consciously or unconsciously, on the minds of judges. Once again, Holmes laid the foundation for this approach, saying:

> [t]he felt necessities of the time, the prevalent moral and political theories, intuitions of public policy, avowed or unconscious, even the prejudices which judges share with their fellow men, have had a good deal more to do than the syllogism in determining the rules by which men should be governed.
>
> (Holmes, 1923, p 1)

In explaining judicial decisions, some realists focus on facts about the psychology or personality of the individual judge, some on the social determinants of judicial decisions, and some on judicial views about policy. Frank, in elaborating on his fact-scepticism, stressed the effect of the prejudices of judges and jurors on their view of the facts of the case – for instance, in according credibility to the accounts of witnesses. Describing these prejudices, he said:

> in learning the facts with reference to which one forms an opinion...these more minute and personal biases are operating constantly...[The judge's] own past may have created plus or minus reactions to women, or blonde women, or men with beards, or Southerners, or Italians, or Englishmen, or plumbers, or ministers, or college graduates, or Democrats. A certain twang or cough or gesture may start up memories painful or pleasant.
>
> (Frank, 1930, p 106)

But, notwithstanding their differences of opinion about the exact nature of the extra-legal factors operating on judges, realists are united in seeing the real determinants of judicial behaviour as primarily non-legal. The key realist claim is that judges do not reason on the basis of abstract legal rules but respond at a gut level to the facts of the case on the basis of an array of non-legal influences. Judges do not, however, openly acknowledge the real causes of their decisions. Rather, taking advantage of the indeterminacy of the legal materials, they sift through the legal materials to find principles which support their instinctive view of the case. They invoke the law after the event, in other words, to rationalise a decision reached on non-legal grounds, misleadingly presenting it as if it were a deduction 'smoothly made from clear, pre-existing rules without intrusion of the judge's choice' (Hart, 1994, p 12).

The realists therefore tended to take an empirical approach to the law, being of the view that adjudication should be studied scientifically as a matter of observable behaviour. They had faith in the methods of the social sciences to uncover causal laws of judicial behaviour which would make it possible – so they thought – to predict how individual judges and courts would react to the facts of subsequent legal disputes.

Some of the realists adopted a rather crude stimulus-response model. They advocated the recording of regularities in judicial 'response' to the 'stimulus' of the facts of a case, in the same way that scientists record the reflex responses of laboratory animals to stimuli with which they are presented. In the 1960s, some behaviourist social scientists, influenced by this picture, tried to put it into practice. One of these was Glendon Schubert, a social scientist who thought it possible to predict judicial decision-making with mathematical exactitude on the basis of knowledge of such factors as the judge's religion and politics. In his book, *The Judicial Mind*, Schubert presents what he calls a 'model' of Supreme Court decision-making which is a 'logical consequence' of a theory of motivation, and which has a 'demonstrable capacity to serve as the basis for making predictions about the future behaviour of the justices'. Schubert claims that anyone who uses the model will make the same predictions, proving its 'scientific value' (Schubert, 1965, p 5). It is striking, in the light of the realists' reaction against the mechanical or mathematical jurisprudence of Langdell, that their views should turn judges into automata of another kind – that in place of a view of judges as mechanical *reasoners*, they should offer a mechanical view of judicial *behaviour*.

Though Llewellyn was initially sympathetic to a behaviourist approach, he took a rather different approach in *The Common Law Tradition*, in which he began to look on the institutional setting of judicial decision-making as a factor which 'helps doctrine out' so as to produce predictability (or what he called 'reckonability') in judicial decisions. Thus he discerned various 'steadying factors' in the institutional environment in which courts operate or factors which have a stabilising effect on judicial decision-making. One of the most important of these he called the 'period-style', which is the general way of going about the 'job' of judging at any particular time and place.

Llewellyn distinguished two styles which characterise the reasoning of common law judges: the Grand Style and the Formal Style. The former is more focused on achieving reasonable results which match contemporary needs; the latter is in thrall to the mechanical model of law and attempts to deduce the answers from pre-existing rules. The Grand Style is, according to Llewellyn, more likely to 'get the same results out of different judges' (Llewellyn, 1960, p 38). Another steadying factor is 'professional judicial office' or the expectations we have of the judicial role. This tradition 'grips [judges], shapes them, limits them, guides them; not for nothing do we speak of *ingrained* ways of work or thought, of men *experienced* or case-hardened, of *habits* of mind' (Llewellyn, 1960, p 53, Llewellyn's emphasis).

Whether Llewellyn's later work is compatible with the scientific aspirations of realism is debatable. It nevertheless remains true to say that, in general, with their emphasis on the social and psychological causes of judicial decisions, and on the 'law in action' as opposed to the 'law in the books', the realists wished to substitute the empirical observation, description and prediction of judicial behaviour, using the scientific model of cause and effect, for mainstream normative analysis of judicial reasoning in terms of legal reasons justifying judicial decisions.

4.4   The ideal judge

Since, for the realists, there is no pre-existing law which determines judicial decisions, it follows that there is no difference in character between the judicial task and the legislative task: both politicians and judges are in the business of making choices, unconstrained by law. Their activity is discretionary through and through, not just, as Hart thought, in 'hard cases'. Law is politics and cannot but be politics. Judges, though, are reluctant to admit this because it subverts the rule of law ideal that judges should be impartial and objective, deciding according to the law and nothing but the law. They therefore (whether consciously or unconsciously) conceal the influence of their own views by dressing up their subjective choices in the technical language of precedents and legal concepts – the so-called 'logic of the law'.

In place of this subterfuge, the realists tended to recommend that the essentially legislative nature of the judicial task should be both openly acknowledged and responsibly approached with the changing needs of society in mind. Thus, instead of pretending that it is possible to do justice 'according to law', judges should, they thought, approach the resolution of disputes in an 'instrumentalist' spirit. Judges should, in other words, focus on the *future* social and economic consequences of their decisions rather than on rights created by *past* precedents or even by statutory enactments. The realists therefore advocated an explicit focus on the policy dimensions of the choices judges need to make – choices which they believed should be informed by research in social scientific disciplines such as economics and sociology. In doing so they demonstrated great faith – some would say exaggerated faith – in the social sciences to yield objective and uncontroversial conclusions.

It is important to be clear on exactly what the realists were advocating. They did not deny that there can, on occasion, be reasons deriving from the *public interest* for judges to follow past judicial or legislative decisions. They conceded, for instance, that judges may legitimately choose to follow a past decision in the interests of predictability. They denied, however, that anyone has a *right* to have a past decision followed or that judges are *bound* as a matter of *principle* to follow past decisions. This follows from the realist insistence that law should be seen as a means to an end, not an end in itself, and evaluated solely in terms of its social effects. Thus, on the realist view, following a past decision may lead to the best social consequences in a particular case; but if it does not, there is no further, *principled* reason to follow the decision – no reason, that is, deriving from anyone's rights.

In order to appreciate the implications of this, let us return to Dworkin's example of the person who suffers emotional injury away from the scene of an accident (see 4.1) and let us see how a realist judge would decide the matter. In Dworkin's example, the law provides compensation if a close relative has suffered emotional injury at the scene of the accident but there is no direct precedent governing the situation where a close relative suffers emotional injury away from the accident.

Let us suppose that our realist judge happens to believe that even relatives who suffer emotional injury at the scene of the accident should not be compensated. This judge believes that the current state of the law is undesirable because it has bad social consequences. And let us also suppose that he or she concedes that there is no moral difference between suffering emotional injury at the scene of the accident and away from it. When confronted with a case in which a relative has suffered emotional injury at the scene of the accident, our realist judge will be obliged to award damages. The law is so clear on the matter that the public interest in predictable judicial decisions outweighs the undesirability of the rule. The realist judge can therefore do nothing about it. However, in the new case, where there is no direct precedent, and therefore no concern about predictability, the realist judge *can* do something about it. He or she can refuse to award compensation, *despite conceding that there is no moral difference between the two situations* and therefore despite the fact that his or her decision in the new case does not *cohere with the past decision*. This is because the realist judge is guided not by the need to give effect to pre-existing legal rights, but only by the need to make the decision with the best future consequences for the community (Dworkin, 1986, pp 161–3).

Dworkin, as one might expect, is highly critical of this results-oriented, policy-based approach to judging, which he labels 'pragmatism'. He describes it as taking 'the bracing view that [people] are never entitled to what would otherwise be worse for the community just because some legislature said so or a long string of judges decided other people were' (Dworkin, 1986, p 152). He argues that it does not fit our legal practices, which presuppose that we have legal rights which are capable of overriding community welfare, and, in rejecting the ideal of consistency in principle as valuable for its own sake, it does not provide a good justification for the exercise of political power. This is because – as we know from 3.9 – Dworkin thinks that legal decisions should exhibit integrity and coherence over time. He believes that to justify state coercion a conception of law must respect the equal status of citizens. And he argues that only the ideal of government acting in a coherent and principled manner by keeping faith with the principles which justify past political decisions affords such respect.

Thus if the law gives the right to compensation in certain circumstances, it should do so in all analogous circumstances, where 'analogous' circumstances are circumstances which are, despite their factual differences, not *morally* different from the original set of circumstances. They are circumstances which cannot be distinguished *in principle* from the circumstances in which the right was initially granted. Another way of putting this point is to say that, for Dworkin, if the law is to be justifiable it cannot be built on arbitrary distinctions. Realism, by contrast, rejects the need for principles and coherence in legal reasoning. Being focused only on the social consequences of judicial decisions, it sees nothing wrong with arbitrary distinctions.

Other critics of realism argue that it is an invitation to judicial dictatorship as well as deeply anti-democratic. Thus Geoffrey de Q Walker argues that once we allow judges to 'cast aside the restraining bonds of precedent' (Walker, 1988, p 174), and give effect to their own values, two unanswerable questions arise. First, why should we assume that the values which the realist judge injects into the law will be acceptable? After all, realism can be a vehicle for a variety of political agendas. Second, how can the realist grant of unlimited power to unaccountable judges be reconciled with democratic principles? Walker also observes that judges are not equipped to 'perform a feat of perfect social engineering on inadequate information in the individual case' (Walker, 1988, p 194). They do not have the expertise to assess social scientific evidence nor predict the social consequences of reforming the law in a particular direction. For these and related reasons, Walker goes so far as to call legal realism in its more extreme forms 'a form of judicial corruption' (Walker, 1988, p 197).

4.5   The economic analysis of law

The economic approach to law was developed in the United States in the 1960s and it continues to be very influential there, though it is not as prominent in other countries. Its roots lie in free market economic theory and it involves, as Richard Posner explains, 'the application of the theories and empirical methods of economics to the central institutions of the legal system' (Posner, 1975, p 759). It is now a complex and challenging area of theorising which accommodates different schools of thought. We will concentrate in what follows on some main themes, especially as found in the work of Posner, whose *Economic Analysis of Law* and *The Economics of Justice* are seminal in the field.

Like realism, the economic analysis of law is sceptical about the idea that legal doctrine is sufficiently determinate to justify legal outcomes and finds it more plausible to explain legal decisions in terms of external or non-legal factors. By contrast with realism, however, the focus of the economic analysis of law is *solely* on economic factors as the underlying explanatory (though not generally articulated) determinant of legal principles. Thus Posner says: 'the logic of the law is really economics' (Posner, 1975, p 764). This is a descriptive claim: economic principles explain common law decisions.

The economic analysis of law is also like realism in its instrumental or pragmatic approach to law, holding that the role of courts is not to do justice to individual litigants after the event, as theorists like Dworkin suppose. Instead, the economic analysis of law defends the desirability of making legal decisions with a view to their future consequences for society. It takes the view, in particular, that judges should choose legal rules which bring about an efficient allocation of resources – not only in commercial areas like contract law or tax law, but even in areas of law that do not seem to have an economic dimension, like criminal law and family law. This is a normative claim.

Posner is perhaps best known for this combination of descriptive and normative claims, for he argues both that the common law *is* best explained as a system for efficiently allocating resources and that judicial decisions *should* be guided by efficiency considerations – that, indeed, this is what *justice* (at least in the common law context) requires.

By 'efficiency', Posner means 'wealth maximisation'. Maximum social wealth obtains when all goods and resources are held by the individuals who value them most, as measured by their willingness to pay or – if they already own something – by what they demand in money to part with them. This concept can be illustrated by the following example. Let us suppose that A would be willing to pay up to $100 for a book of B's. This means that the book is worth $100 to A. Let us also suppose that B would be willing to sell the book to A for $90. If B then sells the book to A for $100, the wealth of society will have increased by $10, because A has a book worth $100 and B has $100, whereas prior to the transaction A had $100 and B had a book worth $90. Posner claims that judges do and should decide cases in such a way as to maximise social wealth.

4.6   Posner's normative claim

In order to understand Posner's claims we need to begin with a very influential article written by Ronald Coase in 1960 which provided the inspiration for much of the economic analysis of law. Coase argued that *in a situation of zero transaction costs, the rules chosen by courts will be irrelevant* because rational co-operative parties will trade their legal rights for more valued resources and will therefore always negotiate the solution which maximises wealth. (Examples of transaction costs are the costs in time and resources of getting together with the other party to trade, of drawing up documents, and of enforcing the bargain.)

Coase's claim can be illustrated using the following example, given by Dworkin. A candy manufacturer's machine is very noisy, making it more difficult for the doctor next door to run his practice. A court has to decide whether the doctor should be able to prevent the manufacturer from running the machine. Let us suppose that the court decides in favour of the doctor. Let us also suppose that this solution does not maximise social wealth because the candymaker will lose $10 by not running his machine but the doctor would lose only $9 if the machine were run. Coase's argument is that in a world of no transaction costs, the candy manufacturer would purchase the right to make a noise from the doctor for something over $9, because even after compensating the doctor for his lost practice he would still have money left over. In a world of no transaction costs, the initial distribution of legal rights would therefore not affect the final distribution of rights. If the court gives the right to the doctor, the manufacturer will buy it from him. If the court gives the right to the manufacturer, he will retain it because the doctor will not be willing to pay the $10 the manufacturer would demand to part with it. In either case, wealth will be maximised.

In real life, however, there are always transaction costs, such as the cost in time and money of getting together with the other party to negotiate an outcome. Let us suppose that in the situation of the doctor and the manufacturer the transaction costs would exceed $1. The consequence is that *if the court gives the right to the doctor, the transaction costs will prevent mutually beneficial trade in the right.* For the candy manufacturer will not pay more than $10 to purchase a right which is worth only $10 to him.

Given the transaction cost, the rule the court chooses is therefore of great importance. If the court gives the right to the doctor, the right will remain with the doctor and social wealth will not be maximised: the doctor will have $9 and the manufacturer will have nothing. This is the point at which Posner enters the picture. According to Posner, the court should in such situations try to *mimic* or *replicate* the market by producing the outcome that *would* have obtained *had* the transaction costs been zero and *had* the parties bargained freely. Posner argues, in other words, that when transaction costs are prohibitive, courts should choose legal rules that maximise social wealth: they should assign legal rights to those who would pay the most for them in a free market (Posner, 2003, pp 15–16).

Notice, however, that should the court impose this solution, as recommended by Posner, the doctor will not *actually* receive the amount over $9 that he would have received under the notional bargain. The compensation in question is purely *hypothetical*, not actual, as is the doctor's improvement in welfare. When the court chooses the wealth-maximising rule, the manufacturer has something worth $10 to him and the doctor has nothing. But this is the desirable outcome in Posner's view because it produces more wealth than the only *actual* alternative, *given the transaction cost*, which is that the doctor has $9 and the manufacturer has nothing (Dworkin, 1985, pp 239–40).

The court should therefore, according to Posner, give the candy manufacturer the right to make a noise because the increase in social wealth is large enough that the candy manufacturer *could* have compensated the doctor and still made a profit in a costless market and therefore *would* have secured the right to make a noise via negotiations in such a market; or because, alternatively, had the right originally been assigned to the manufacturer he would not have parted with it for the amount the doctor would have been willing to pay. The choice of a rule which gives the right to the manufacturer over a rule which gives the right to the doctor is efficient in this sense: that the candy manufacturer *could* compensate the doctor without either of them being worse off than under the alternative rule and with at least one of them being better off. This is known as Kaldor-Hicks efficiency. According to Posner, the increase in wealth to the community justifies the outcome, despite the fact that the doctor receives no actual compensation for his loss.

This obviously raises the question: *why* does it justify the outcome? Why should the law impose losses on the doctor in order to increase the size of the pie overall? What reason do we have for thinking this just? This question acquires extra force against the background of the fact that willingness to pay often depends on people's *ability* to pay. There are many goods for which poor people cannot afford to pay, including such necessities as medicine and food. Since their unwillingness to pay is related to their poverty, which in turn is a function of a distribution of wealth which many would argue is unjust (see Chapter 7), it can be asked why it is *just* for judges to allocate legal rights to those who have the resources which would enable them to purchase them in a free market. As CG Veljanovski says: '[t]he willingness-to-pay of individuals will depend on their wealth so that there is nothing sacrosanct about the fact that a law is Kaldor-Hicks efficient' (Veljanovski, 1982, p 42).

In response to points like these, Posner attempts to demonstrate that wealth maximisation is an ethically attractive principle. He relies on two arguments. First, he thinks that by comparison with notions like the fair distribution of wealth, which are indeterminate and subjective, it is relatively uncontroversial to allocate resources to those who are most willing to pay for them. What can be wrong with giving people what they value (as measured by how they choose to spend their time and money)? As Brian Bix says: '[i]f I sell you a book for $20, one would assume that I prefer the $20 to having the book, and you prefer the book to having the $20. If that were not the case, why would both of us go through with the transaction?' (Bix, 2003, p 192).

In 5.3 we will examine the moral theory of utilitarianism which is in important ways a precursor of the wealth-maximisation principle. Utilitarianism is the moral theory that in any situation the right thing to do is to maximise happiness. This theory also claims to be uncontroversial. After all, do we not all seek to be happy and to avoid unhappiness? If so, is it not rational to act in such a way as to achieve the greatest balance of happiness over unhappiness? Utilitarianism suffers from a number of problems, however. We will canvass some of these in 5.3 and 7.1, but for our immediate purposes it will be sufficient to note the difficulty of *measuring* people's happiness and unhappiness and therefore of *adding up* and *comparing* the amounts of happiness and unhappiness in different situations. Utilitarianism is therefore a 'spongy' (Posner, 1981, p 42) guide for legal decision-making. It is not a source of specific policies or guidelines (Posner, 1979, p 114).

Wealth maximisation is supposed to give us the attractions of utilitarianism (namely, the respect it shows for people's preferences) without this particular problem. It is said to provide more rigorous and more scientific guidance to judges. We determine how much people want something not by trying to measure the *happiness* they would derive by having it, but by looking at how much they are *willing to pay* for it. Posner says: '[t]he only kind of preference that counts in a system of wealth maximization is ... one that is backed up by money – in other words, that is registered in a market' (Posner, 1979, p 103). Money is therefore the easily measurable, common currency which allows us to make comparisons between different people and to calculate which course of action will yield the greatest total benefits.

In addition to arguing that wealth maximisation gives us the attractive features of utilitarianism without its defects, Posner also argues for the ethical attractiveness of wealth maximisation on the ground that it respects autonomy. In particular, Posner argues that the probability is that wealth maximisation will benefit everyone (or at least almost everyone) in the long run, including those who on occasion lose lawsuits decided on wealth-maximising grounds. Therefore everyone would have *consented* to the principle of maximising social wealth if asked in advance and the principle consequently respects their autonomy (Posner, 1981, pp 94–9).

Posner's critics do not find these arguments convincing. They argue that, whatever its other defects, at least the claim that happiness is a good makes sense. But the same is not true of social wealth. Thus Dworkin argues that social wealth divorced from happiness 'loses all plausibility as a component of value' (Dworkin, 1985, p 245) and 'makes no sense as a social goal, even as one among others' (Dworkin, 1985, p 264). He argues that individuals are not necessarily better off if they have more wealth. Improvements in wealth do not necessarily lead to improvements in happiness, and may sometimes even lead to a loss in happiness, because people may want things which are jeopardised by more wealth. Dworkin writes:

> [s]uppose ... that an individual faces a choice between a life that will make him happier (or more fulfilled, or more successful in his own lights, or whatever) and a life that will make him wealthier in money or the equivalent of money. It would be irrational of him to choose the latter. Nor, and this is the crux, does he lose or sacrifice anything of value in choosing the former. It is not that he should, on balance, prefer the former, recognizing that in the choice he sacrifices something of value in the latter. Money or its equivalent is useful so far as it enables someone to lead a more valuable, successful, happier, or more moral life. Anyone who counts it for more than that is a fetishist of little green paper.
>
> (Dworkin, 1985, pp 245–6)

Dworkin is equally critical of Posner's consent argument – the argument that wealth maximisation will benefit almost everyone in the long run, and therefore that everyone would have consented to the principle of maximising social wealth if asked in advance. Dworkin argues, among other things, that the mere fact that I *would* have consented to something had I been asked is not a good reason to enforce against me that to which I would have (but did not) consent (Dworkin, 1985, p 276). He is also doubtful about the claim that almost everyone is better off if judges decide common law cases according to wealth-maximising principles (Dworkin, 1985, pp 280–3).

4.7   Posner's descriptive claim

So far we have been discussing the normative aspects of Posner's theory. But Posner argues not only that courts should decide cases according to wealth-maximising principles but that they actually do so. He concedes that few judicial decisions explicitly make reference to economic concepts but he says that 'legal education consists primarily of learning to dig beneath the rhetorical surface to find [the true grounds of legal decisions], many of which turn out to have an economic character' (Posner, 2003, p 25). Digging beneath this surface, one finds that, whether consciously or not:

> [common law] doctrines form a system for inducing people to behave efficiently, not only in explicit markets, but across the whole range of social interactions. In settings in which the cost of voluntary transactions is low, common law doctrines create incentives for people to channel their transactions through the market...In settings in which the cost of allocating resources by voluntary transactions is prohibitively high making the market an infeasible method of allocating resources, the common law prices behaviour in such a way as to mimic the market. For example, the tort system allocated liability for accidents between railroad and farmer, driver and pedestrian, doctor and patient...in such a way as to bring about the allocation of resources to safety that the market would bring about if the market could be made to work.
>
> (Posner, 2003, pp 249–50)

To explain Posner's example a little more: accidents have social costs – the cost to the victim of the accident and the cost to the potential wrongdoer of taking action to prevent the accident. Posner's view is that the tort system is structured around rules of liability which minimise these costs. The tort system does not, for instance, insist that drivers of cars should drive at a snail's pace because if it were to do so the balance of costs over benefits would be greater than if, for instance, it were to hold drivers liable for negligent driving.

Posner's argument assumes that judges are able to work out what bargains would be struck by drivers and pedestrians if they were able to negotiate under Coasian conditions of zero transaction costs. Posner says: 'I believe that in many cases a court can make a reasonably accurate guess as to the allocation of resources that would maximise wealth' (Posner, 1981, p 62).

His critics, however, are sceptical. They also point out that the theory is almost impossible to test or refute because 'factors such as transaction costs or information costs may be used so loosely as to turn the whole exercise into tautology. At worst, evidence which might otherwise seem inconsistent with the theory is rationalized by invoking these immeasurable factors to make that evidence seem consistent with it' (Bottomley and Parker, 1997, p 341). Veljanovski makes the similar point that 'the law is rationalized as efficient by assuming a configuration of transaction (and other) costs that makes it so without any attempt to investigate whether these costs exist in practice' (Veljanovski, 1982, p 96). Furthermore, though Posner's critics are willing to concede that in areas like contract law many existing legal rules may be efficient, they are less convinced that Posner's analysis applies (or should apply) to non-market areas like criminal and family law.

It is worth emphasising, however, that though the critics of the economic analysis of law reject its more extreme claims and assumptions, and its single–minded focus on the collective value of efficiency at the cost of such individual values as rights (see Chapter 5) and justice (see Chapter 7), they do not deny that aspects of it have merit. For instance, as Stephen Bottomley and Stephen Parker point out, there are areas of the law, such as competition law and contract law, in which the answers may well depend on economic matters (Bottomley and Parker, 1997, p 365). Furthermore, the economic analysis of law enables us to assess the economic effects and efficiency costs of using the law to pursue valuable social goals, like the goal of creating a more just society or increasing average welfare. It thereby alerts us to the trade-offs these choices require, trade-offs which are easy to miss and difficult to quantify without the benefit of an economic methodology. Along the same lines, the economic analysis provides us with tools which enable us to choose the most cost-effective legal route to a given goal (Bottomley and Parker, 1997, p 296). For these and other reasons, Bottomley and Parker argue that it would be wrong to discount the positive contribution made by economics to law.

4.8   Critical Legal Studies and its intellectual roots

We turn now to the Critical Legal Studies movement (CLS), which emerged in the United States in the 1970s and included, among its adherents, Roberto Unger, Duncan Kennedy, Morton Horwitz, Mark Tushnet and Mark Kelman. Though in many ways the heir of realism, it combined realist themes with left-wing politics and a far-reaching critique of 'legal liberalism' which it sought to 'trash'. The critical legal scholars put great emphasis on the ideological nature of law – the social and economic interests to which it caters as well as its legitimising functions – and in so doing took realism's message that 'law is politics' more seriously than the realists themselves did. CLS as such is no longer very influential. It has, though, undoubtedly helped to inspire and inform more recent critical approaches to law, such as feminist legal theory (which we will explore in Chapter 8) and critical race theory (which is dealt with in 4.13).

The eclectic intellectual roots of CLS are essential to understanding it. Like the realists, the critical legal scholars (the 'crits') stress the indeterminacy of law – its inability to generate answers to legal problems and to constrain the decisions of judges who are therefore thrown back on political choices. Like the realists, they also claim that judges conceal the political nature of these choices by elaborate, post hoc, rationalising exercises in so-called 'objective legal reasoning'. And adherents of both movements think of the law as an instrument to advance political goals. But in the case of CLS, the indeterminacy thesis is embedded within a radical critique of the entire body of liberal legal theory, a critique which extends to all the theorists we have considered so far in this book and many more besides.

The crits wish to 'delegitimate' law, which they see as a tool of injustice. The realists, by contrast, were piecemeal reformists and liberals who thought that law should be used as an instrument to advance the values of American liberal democracy. Though their views might be thought to undermine the rule of law – in so far as the rule of law implies that government officials can and should be constrained by rules determinate in meaning announced in advance, and that independent judges can and should apply these rules regardless of whether they coincide with their own personal opinions – the realists seemed to think that social science could make good the deficiencies in legal doctrine and be a source of objective standards in judicial decision-making. Policy science could be the substitute for Langdell's legal science (Hutchinson, 1989, p 7). The crits, by contrast, have no such faith in the ability of social science to deliver a value-free balance of competing interests and they believe that the liberal notions of the rule of law and of legal rights which government officials and judges are duty-bound to respect are neither coherent nor desirable. Theirs is therefore a much more corrosive view than realism.

To understand their more radical – some say utopian – approach to these matters, we need to turn to the influence of Marxist theory on their thought, as well as that of postmodernist theory and deconstruction which were also an important influence on CLS, especially as the movement progressed. It should, though, be noted that the embrace of postmodernism and deconstruction has caused controversy within the movement, some of the crits preferring the more sociological, Marxist tradition of critique to the language-based approach which, as we will see, characterises postmodernism. Yet, the existence of these differences of opinion notwithstanding, there still remains, as Peter Fitzpatrick and Alan Hunt point out, a 'significant core of unity . . . in opposition to the dominant orthodoxies in legal scholarship and in agreement around a commitment to the necessity and possibility of social transformation' (Fitzpatrick and Hunt, 1987, p 2).

4.9   Postmodernism

Postmodernism is impossible to sum up in a few paragraphs. In part, this is because the writing of the postmodernists tends to be obscure and partly it is because there is considerable divergence among their views. Furthermore, in addition to writing about a wide sweep of phenomena – including 'low culture' phenomena not thought to be part of traditional academic territory, such as pop music and the mass media – postmodernists tend to identify with a range of intellectual disciplines, from literary theory to cultural studies, intellectual history and Continental philosophy. Important exponents of these ideas are Michel Foucault (1926–1984), Jean-François Lyotard (1924–1988) and Jacques Derrida (1930–2004).

This diversity nothwithstanding, some general, interconnected themes of specific relevance to CLS can be mentioned. First, in art, architecture and literature, where the term was first used, postmodernism was a reaction against modernism, the latter being understood to rest on the belief that art can transcend the particularities of social and historical context. Postmodernism in philosophy represents an analogous challenge to the rationalist or so-called 'Enlightenment' view that there are objective and universal standards of truth and justice discoverable by human reason. The Enlightenment is associated with eighteenth-century philosophers who believed in the power of human reason to advance knowledge and in the possibility of progress in history and social conditions. Postmodernists use the term the 'Enlightenment project' to describe the ideology these rationalist beliefs inspired – the ideology of liberal humanism which has dominated Western societies in modern times. Postmodernism, by contrast, inspired in part by the political horrors of the twentieth century and the failure of liberal humanism to deliver on its emancipatory promises, regards the idea of objective knowledge in science, morality and politics, and the associated ideas of order and social progress, as myths.

Postmodernism is therefore 'anti-foundationalist': it rejects the old certainties of what it calls 'grand theory' or 'grand narratives' (Lyotard, 1984, pp 15, 31–2). By these terms it means to refer to those theories, associated with philosophers such as Plato, Aristotle, Descartes, Kant and Marx, which claim to be able to explain everything or which claim to have found an absolute or certain foundation for knowledge and social institutions. Postmodernism rejects as authoritarian any such ambition to be in possession of the truth or to be able to provide criteria for truth. It wishes, in Lyotard's words, to 'wage a war on totality' (Lyotard, 1984, p 82), whether 'totalising narratives' take the form of God, science, or political theories like Marxism, whose account of the whole of human history is organised around a single, monolithic concept, that of class conflict. Postmodernism consequently constitutes a thoroughgoing attack on the mainstream, philosophical tradition which, though it has grappled with radical forms of scepticism and relativism, has rarely endorsed them.

Second, postmodernism stresses the socially conditioned nature of all thinking. It is, in fact, the socially conditioned or contextualised nature of knowledge that makes it impossible, according to postmodernists, to access 'reality' by transcending local or partial understandings of the world. There is no independent viewpoint on truth – no way of ensuring that theories mirror or accurately describe an external reality. Every viewpoint is an experienced viewpoint and experienced viewpoints always *construct* rather than *reflect* how things are. Every perception of the truth is therefore perspectival.

Third, this *epistemological* emphasis on difference, multiplicity and fragmentation in place of the Enlightenment ideals of unity and universality – the emphasis on situated viewpoints and the particular, subjective perspectives of individual subjects – is matched by a distinctive, postmodern *politics*. Postmodern politics focuses on the way in which those in power marginalise and oppress particular individuals and groups, such as blacks, women and gays, and it seeks the remedy in 'identity politics', a politics focused on the 'right to be different'.

Foucault's analysis of power represents an important inspiration for the development of this set of ideas. His work aims, in part, to expose established hierarchies and relationships of power as contingent, not natural; arbitrary, not rational. Foucault saw power and knowledge as opposite sides of the same coin. What we take to be objective knowledge is just the version of events authorised by those who have power. Though they give it the imprimatur of 'truth', it is merely their interpretation. Foucault uses the concept of 'genealogy' to describe the excavation of the historical and social origins of the claims which are treated as knowledge in different 'discourses'. Thus modern society has invented the concept of 'madness' – which is, in fact, the result of an historical process – just as it has invented the concept of what is 'normal' in sexual behaviour. Foucault traces these modern methods of social control through institutions like prisons and insane asylums, and practices like medicine, showing how difference is created by the powerful in order to marginalise and exclude groups like the insane and homosexuals.

Postmodern politics counters this marginalisation by attempting to give a voice to those who are different in terms of features like ethnicity, gender and sexual preference. Charles Taylor writes illuminatingly on the radical shift from a politics of 'universalism' to a politics of 'difference' that these developments reflect. The politics of universalism insists on an 'identical basket of rights and immunities' on the basis of our identical human worth and common human needs. The politics of difference, by contrast, asks us to recognise the unique identity of particular individuals or groups. It identifies discrimination and second-class citizenship not with *exclusion* from a *common* citizenship but rather with *assimilation*, uniformity and the ignoring of unique identities. It follows that if we are not to discriminate against vulnerable groups, we may have to treat them *differently*, rather than – as the politics of universalism would have it – identically (Taylor, 1994, pp 37–40). (For further discussion of these issues in so far as they affect women, see the discussion of difference feminism and postmodern feminism in 8.6, 8.7 and 8.9). But, once again, there is no claim to truth or objectivity and there are no absolutes. There are only different, situated interpretations. Thus terms such as 'justice' are used merely to express the particular viewpoint of particular groups in particular political contexts. They can be used only in a pragmatic way and judged only by pragmatic criteria.

Fourth, postmodernism builds on the 'turn towards language' – the idea that language constitutes or produces reality – that characterises much twentieth-century philosophical thought. The work of the Swiss structuralist linguist, Ferdinand de Saussure, was one important influence on the development of this approach towards language. Saussure saw language as a system of signs, a sign being a sound with a meaning. His view of language as a system or a structure led him to argue that no term has meaning in isolation from other terms: meaning is relational in the sense that it is a function of *differences* between concepts within a system. The concept of 'cat', for instance, has meaning only in relation to other concepts such as 'dog' and 'lion'. Hence words do not have meanings fixed by their relationship to objects and language cannot be used to describe the world objectively. On the contrary, different languages constitute different realities. At the same time, however, Saussure saw the system of signs which constitutes a particular language as stable by virtue of the rules which govern its operation.

Derrida, by contrast, rejects the idea of a stable system. For this reason he is often described as a 'poststructuralist'. He argues that meanings are inherently unstable and contingent and that texts have many, frequently conflicting meanings, none of which can be said to be more authoritative or more correct than any other. Not only is it the case, as Saussure argued, that the meaning of a word is a matter of its relation to other words within the language, rather than a matter of its relation to a non-linguistic reality to which it refers. Its meaning is also, for Derrida, a function of all the contexts of its use – past, present and future. The idea that the meaning of a text is that which the author intended – hence fixed to a given time – is decisively rejected. It is therefore impossible to achieve finality of interpretation: meaning is endlessly 'deferred' and incapable of being fully determined. Furthermore, the openness to change which the indeterminacy of meaning entails should be welcomed, not resisted. Once liberated from the idea that interpretations must conform to constraints to be found in the text, we, as readers, will be free to 'play', as we bring our own contexts to texts and in the process rewrite the texts we read.

If meaning is so unstable – always in the process of transformation – how, it might be wondered, can we communicate at all? Derrida argues that an illusion of stable meaning is created by binary oppositions. These are natural-seeming conceptual oppositions underlying mainstream philosophy – oppositions such as male/female, good/evil, reason/emotion, nature/culture, public/private, high culture/low culture. Derrida calls attention to the implicit hierarchy in the oppositions – the one term carrying positive connotations and the other negative – and the way in which the privileged term excludes and suppresses the 'other'. Thus men are what women are not. Yet, at the same time, Derrida says, maleness depends for its meaning on the meaning of femaleness to which it endeavours to define itself in opposition: its superiority is therefore built on sand. Seeing this allows us to 'deconstruct' the way in which the one term in the pair has been privileged and the other suppressed – the way in which one term is assumed objectively to be the norm while the other is assumed to be the exception or to be marginal. In destabilising in this way the dominant discourses and interpretations, exposing their contradictions and paradoxes, and subverting the traditional distinctions on which they rely, a space is created for excluded and marginal views. Thus Derrida writes:

> in a classical philosophical opposition we are not dealing with the peaceful existence of a *vis-à-vis*, but rather with a violent hierarchy. One of the two terms governs the other (axiologically, logically, etc) or has the upper hand. To deconstruct the opposition, first of all, is to overturn the hierarchy at a given moment.
>
> (Derrida, 1981, p 41)

Deconstruction therefore, as Ian Ward explains, 'uncovers the politics which underpins philosophy, and by concentrating on language reveals how this politics is secreted away' (Ward, 2004, p 168).

We will shortly see how the crits make use of these postmodernist ideas to argue that the legal materials can be interpreted in contradictory ways; that the incoherence of law has been concealed by the political context in which judges operate; and that exposure of the underlying contradictions and the suppressed alternative solutions will destroy the appearance of naturalness attaching to the dominant legal categories.

4.10 Marxism

In so far as Marxist theory is concerned, the important aspect of the work of Marx (1818–1883) for our purposes is his theory of history, which he called 'historical materialism'. According to historical materialism, changes in the economic system are the driver of all social change. Marx held that in any human society the 'forces of production' – the labour power, the materials, and the instruments and tools used in the process of production – are of fundamental importance in explaining everything else about that society, including law. The forces of production give rise, Marx said, to certain 'relations of production', these being class relationships or relationships of power and control. 'In acquiring new productive forces', Marx said,

> men change their mode of production; and in changing their mode of production, in changing their way of earning a living, they change all their social relations. The hand-mill gives you society with the feudal lord; the steam-mill society with the industrial capitalist.
>
> (Marx, 1847, p 166)

Just as the forces of production give rise to this network of social domination and exploitation, which Marx calls the 'base' of society, the base in turn gives rise to the 'superstructure'. The superstructure includes such social practices and institutions as politics, morality, religion, ideology, culture and, most importantly for our purposes, law. Marx says: 'legal relations . . . are to be grasped neither from themselves nor from the so called general development of the human mind, but rather have their roots in the material conditions of life' (Marx, 1859, p 362).

At the same time, though law and the other superstructural practices and institutions derive their character from the character of the base, Marx does not deny that they play an important social role. This is often misunderstood by those who think that Marx was a crude instrumentalist, who saw institutions like law as mere one-way reflections of the economy, having no causal efficacy of their own. On the contrary, Marx thought that legal, moral, religious and ideological beliefs influence the economy in very important ways. In particular, they help to sustain it by legitimising it. Thus, as GA Cohen shows in his book, *Karl Marx's Theory of History: A Defence*, the superstructure, for Marx, is not merely *explained by* but also *suits* or *sustains* the class relations which prevail in any particular society. It is functional for or helps to reproduce the economic relations of society. Thus particular superstructural institutions arise in order to serve the economic needs of society. Capitalism, for instance, could not survive without a legal system which services and legitimises the private ownership of the means of production (Cohen, 1978, pp 225–34).

Let us consider the function of law in more detail. Marx thought that the particular legal rules and doctrines which prevail in any particular society will be those broadly suited to the economic interests of the dominant class. But, as later Marxists like Antonio Gramsci (1891–1937) have been particularly concerned to emphasise, law involves more than coercion and repression. Law also papers over the cracks. Thus it does not *present* itself as the instrument of class exploitation and oppression. Instead, it presents itself as the impartial vehicle for everyone's interests.

Thus the law conceals the ugly facts of capitalism. In capitalist society, according to Marx, workers are forced to sell their labour-power but the legal 'fiction' of freedom of contract obscures this fact: though the wage-labourer 'is bound to his owner', this is by '*invisible* threads' (Marx, 1867, p 538, my emphasis). Social and economic inequalities are likewise disguised by the legal doctrine of equality. The doctrine makes it seem as if everyone enjoys the same rights, but what use is it to the homeless, for instance, that the rules governing the enjoyment and use of property apply to them in just the same way as they apply to capitalist entrepreneurs? Every equal right, says Marx, is 'a right of inequality in its content' (Marx, 1875, p 24). Yet another way in which law papers over the cracks is by making the status quo look natural or incapable of being changed by human action. The right to private property, for instance, appears inevitable and beyond challenge, whereas in reality, according to Marx, it is merely a contingent response to the economic needs of a dominant class at a particular time.

Marxists furthermore say that it is critical to law's effectiveness in serving ruling class interests that it should *not* present itself as skewed in favour of them. After all, if it were obvious to everyone that the main beneficiary of the law is the ruling class, the members of the exploited classes would be less likely to co-operate. But law, as we have seen, conceals this. It appears non-partisan. Indeed, on occasion, as Marxist scholars like EP Thompson point out, it *is* non-partisan, it being 'inherent in the very nature of the medium' that it cannot be 'reserved for the exclusive use only of [the ruling] class' (Thompson, 1975, p 264). In seeming thus to represent the requirements of justice, and on occasion by actually being just – by *not* being a *simple* or *straightforward* tool of the ruling class – law enhances the legitimacy of the status quo.

For Marxists law therefore has an extremely important ideological function, where the term 'ideological' refers to the ability of certain ideas to obscure and thereby maintain the exploitative relationships on which the society is based (Meyerson, 1991a, pp 2–4). '[I]n ideology', Marx said, 'men and their circumstances appear upside down' (Marx, 1846, p 36). CLS, as we will shortly see, is heavily influenced by the Marxist emphasis on the need to penetrate beneath the ideological surface – the mystified way in which things appear in legal doctrine – so as to reveal the underlying relationships of power and economic interests which the surface appearances disguise and, by disguising, serve.

In the light of this sketch of the intellectual currents on which CLS draws we can now turn to some of its key claims. I will concentrate in what follows on CLS views about legal doctrine and liberal thought, though it should be noted that the crits also devoted considerable critical energy to issues in legal education and the history of legal concepts.

4.11   Contradictions, incoherencies and law as ideology

A central element of the CLS project is to expose the contradictions and incoherencies in law which it claims lie beneath law's surface unity and its appearance of coherence – contradictions which run so deep that it is impossible to make coherent sense out of the legal materials. David Howarth summarises this central, deconstruction-influenced CLS claim as follows:

> [t]he Critical Legal Studies position is that the law is so full of contradictory values and so obviously the outcome of political conflict that judges can never make fully coherent sense out of it. They may try hard to remove inconsistencies, and to gloss over conflicts of value but, like jelly held in the fingers, the contradictions eventually ooze out somewhere.
>
> (Howarth, 1992, p 30)

Thus Duncan Kennedy argues in his early writings that the legal system exhibits contradictory commitments. One such contradiction is between a commitment to mechanically applicable rules as the correct way to resolve disputes, on the one hand, and a commitment to a situation-sensitive, ad hoc approach, on the other. Kennedy claims that this contradiction in turn reflects a more fundamental contradiction between the values of individualism or self-interest and altruism or sharing (Kennedy, 1976, p 1685). This more fundamental contradiction asserts itself, according to Kennedy, in many areas of the law.

In the law of contract, for instance, the concept of freedom of contract favours the individualistic right to drive a hard bargain at the expense of those whose vulnerability may be exploited, whereas concepts such as unconscionability and undue influence favour altruism or a concern for the welfare of the weaker party. Contract law is therefore internally contradictory, as are all the other branches of legal doctrine. Thus the existence of inconsistent legal outcomes equally supported by the legal materials, to which the realists first pointed, is, on the deconstruction-influenced CLS version of this theme, the reflection of much deeper and irreconcilable contradictions between competing social and political ideals in liberal legal thought and in society itself. Liberal legal thought contains, according to Mark Kelman, 'paired rhetorical arguments that both resolve cases in opposite, incompatible ways and correspond to distinct visions of human nature and human fulfilment' (Kelman, 1987, p 3). These 'deeply antagonistic ideologies' (Dworkin, 1986, p 272) are reflected within the law, leaving the law so contradictory that it is impossible to provide an interpretation which fits the bulk of it. (Contrast Dworkin: there is a single, coherent moral and political theory capable of justifying at least the bulk of the legal materials.)

If these contradictions are so pervasive in legal doctrine and liberal theory, how do the crits explain legal cases where the outcome appears to be entirely predictable? Again, they are influenced by the realists, especially the prominence the realists gave to the influence of extra-legal factors on judges, though in the case of the crits the extra-legal factors are seen through a more radical lens. They argue that the fact that judicial decisions can be predicted, and that judges often agree on the answer to legal questions, is an artefact of their shared political commitment to the status quo. Predictability in the law is therefore the consequence of ideological consensus among the powerful, not a function of the law's 'objective' requirements: '[t]he judicial emperor, clothed and coifed in appropriately legitimate and vogueish garb by the scholarly rag trader, chooses and acts to protect and preserve the propertied interests of vested white and male power' (Hutchinson, 1989, p 4).

Thus class and politics bias judges in favour of one of the sides to the political conflicts reflected in the legal materials, and they fail to notice that the 'repressed contradictory impulse' (Kelman, 1987, p 3) has as good a claim to resolve the dispute. Blind as they are to the way in which they privilege one of the conflicting interests and marginalise the other, it appears to them that there is just one option, pre-ordained by the law. But the appearance of legal coherence and consistency is an illusion. In fact, the outcome reflects an unreasoned, political affinity for one of the contradictory values, and is not made inevitable by the inherent logic of the law. To think otherwise – to attempt, as Dworkin does, a rational reconstruction of the law, in which 'the stuff of law [is presented] as tied together in a way that justifies most of it' (Unger, 1996, p 22) – is to be under the influence of what Unger calls a 'rationalising spell' (Unger, 1996, p 23).

If the law does not constrain judicial decision-making, what is its function? The answer most crits give to this question is heavily indebted to the Marxist view of law as ideology which was explained in the previous section: law legitimates the status quo. There is an appearance of naturalness or 'false necessity' attaching to the dominant legal categories, which makes the hierarchical power structures of the status quo invisible and gives them the appearance of neutrality and legitimacy. This mystifying facade of legitimacy therefore needs to be stripped off: liberal legal thought needs to be 'trashed' – its contradictions, chaoses, ideological biases, legitimating functions and injustices exposed – so as to enable us to recognise the contingent and oppressive nature of the choices which are contained in the law.

This will clear the way, the CLS movement promises, for alternative, more egalitarian ways of thinking about law and its role in society. The ultimate aim of the critical legal approach is therefore social transformation – though, as many critics have pointed out, the critical legal scholars tend to be vague about the nature of the future society they think desirable and how we might get there.

4.12   Rejecting liberal values

As Alan C Hutchinson explains, '[t]he CLS claims of indeterminacy do not simply penetrate legal doctrine and theorizing; they go to the very heart of liberal democratic politics' (Hutchinson, 1989, p 4). Prominent liberal notions which CLS scholars attack include rights, understood as protections for individual interests which the state is bound both to respect and safeguard (see 5.1), and the rule of law. In this they may once again have been influenced by Marx who launched a scathing attack on the idea of equal rights in a short piece called 'On the Jewish Question'. Marx thought that rights offer only what he called 'political emancipation', by contrast with real or 'human' emancipation. Rights, he said, exist only to protect those who are motivated by self-interest and who relate to other people in antagonistic ways – those who see others as a threat to themselves and their interests. Rights are therefore 'egoistic' rights – 'the rights of man separated from other men and from the community' – and the liberty they protect is the liberty of man viewed as an 'isolated monad, withdrawn into himself' (Marx, 1843, p 162). Rights therefore do not offer a genuinely co-operative society. They are, indeed, an obstacle to it.

Many of these notions resurface in CLS writings on rights. Some CLS writers argue that rights give undue prominence to individuals at the expense of our connections with others and the value of solidarity. They say that those who put their faith in the idea of rights see human beings as isolated individualists. Rights-theorists ignore our ties with the culture, traditions and conventions of the community to which we belong. This criticism derives from the 'communitarian' streak in CLS, where 'communitarianism' refers to the theory that we are essentially social creatures – creatures whose sense of identity and flourishing depends on a strong sense of connection with our own society and culture.

(For a more detailed discussion of communitarianism, see 5.7 and 7.7.) It is in this communitarian vein that Kennedy declares: '[t]he "freedom" of individualism is negative, alienated and arbitrary. It consists in the absence of restraint on the individual's choice of ends, and has no moral content whatever... We can achieve real freedom only collectively, through *group* self-determination' (Kennedy, 1976, p 1774, Kennedy's emphasis).

Other CLS writers claim that a focus on rights masks social and economic inequalities and leads to political paralysis:

> [t]his is the essence of the problem with rights discourse. People don't realize that what they are doing is recasting the real existential feelings that led them to become political people into an ideological framework that coopts them into adopting the very consciousness they want to transform. Without even knowing it, they start talking as if 'we' were rights-bearing citizens who are 'allowed' to do this or that by something called the 'state', which is a passivizing illusion – actually a hallucination which establishes the presumptive political legitimacy of the status quo.
>
> (Gabel and Kennedy, 1984, p 26)

The rule of law is dismissed for similar reasons. Morton Horwitz discusses EP Thompson's view that the rule of law, in so far as it imposes effective inhibitions on power and defends the citizen from 'power's all-intrusive claims', is 'an unqualified good' (Thompson, 1975, p 266, 267). Horwitz responds:

> I do not see how a Man of the Left can describe the rule of law as 'an unqualified human good'! It undoubtedly restrains power, but it also prevents power's benevolent exercise.... [I]t ratifies and legitimates an adversarial, competitive, and atomistic conception of human relations.
>
> (Horwitz, 1977, p 566)

4.13   CLS and critical race theory

Many commentators think that the CLS attack on rights and the rule of law is dangerous and demonstrates an unrealistic if touching faith in the belief that, as one CLS theorist puts it, 'people do not want just to be beastly to each other' (Singer, 1984, p 54). Included among these critics of CLS are theorists from minority groups – the so-called 'critical race theorists' – who seek to highlight the pervasive presence of racism in the legal system and to give voice to the 'outsider' perspectives on law of those who have been the victims of racial oppression. In developing such a race-conscious form of legal theory, the critical race theorists have explored, in part, the value of rights to those who have traditionally been denied them and who still suffer from oppression and discrimination. Included among these minority scholars are Mari Matsuda, Richard Delgado and Patricia Williams.

Williams, for one, points out that African American slaves were not regarded as legal subjects capable of enjoying rights. Now that that is no longer the case, it would be hard to persuade African Americans to surrender their rights on the basis of the theoretical reflections and experiences of mainly privileged white men, who can afford to take rights for granted. Williams writes: ' "[r]ights" feels so new in the mouths of most black people. It is still so deliciously empowering to say. It is a sign for and a gift of selfhood that is very hard to contemplate restructuring ... at this point in history' (Williams, 1987, p 431). Writing from the perspective of a black woman in the United States, Williams therefore refuses to turn her back on such 'reformist' and liberal notions as rights and the rule of law in the hope of more far-reaching but vaguely described forms of social transformation.

Delgado argues along similar lines that:

> [o]ne explanation for the CLS position on rights may be that the average Crit, a white male teaching at a major law school, has little use for rights. Those with whom he comes in contact in his daily life – landlords, employers, public authorities – generally treat him with respect and deference. Rarely is he the victim of coercion, revilement, or contempt.
>
> (Delgado, 1987, pp 305–6)

4.14 Other criticisms of CLS

One important criticism of CLS relates to the issue of fundamental contradictions in the law. Dworkin argues that the crits confuse *contradictory* principles with *competing* principles (Dworkin, 1986, p 268). He says that the fact that there are competing principles to be found within the law is hardly surprising. It would, in fact, be a symptom of failure in a legal system, and more generally in political thought, if they did not recognise at the level of abstract principle that, for instance, both individual interests and the welfare of others are worth protecting. Such recognition of the complexity of the world does not, Dworkin says, support the thesis of thoroughgoing indeterminacy and incoherence within the law (Dworkin, 1986, pp 441–4).

The crits tend to assume that when principles pull in opposite directions they must be equally weighty, and that the choice between them must therefore be resolved arbitrarily or on political grounds. But this overlooks the fact that when principles come into conflict with one another it is usually possible to argue that one principle is, in the circumstances, more powerful. Dworkin, it will be remembered, argues that a principle can be *relevant* to a situation but not necessarily *decisive* of the answer (see 3.7). For instance, though our law respects the principle that no-one should profit from their own wrongdoing, there are cases in which other principles are more important. In cases where one applicable principle can be shown to be more important than another, any conflict between them will have been *rationally* resolved and it will be false to say that the law is incoherent or makes no sense (Meyerson, 1991, pp 443–5).

Second, it is worth pointing out that there are parts of the CLS picture which are not necessarily inconsistent with mainstream views. Consider the key claims of positivism. As we have seen, positivists hold that the criteria of legal validity in any society are conventional and that there is no necessary connection between law and morality. In so far as legal reasoning is concerned, positivists believe that legal rules have a core of clear meaning and the resolution of a case which falls within that central core is unambiguously dictated by the law. They say that judges can in such cases apply the law according to its clearly applicable meaning without regard to their own personal views as to what it ought to be. Positivists therefore believe that at least on some occasions – namely, where the language of the legal rule is clear – there are standards or norms of legal decision-making and that it is possible to provide good and convincing legal arguments for legal conclusions.

There is nothing in the positivist picture which suggests that it regards law as necessarily just or benign or neutral, in the sense of 'serving everyone's interests'. When positivists say that legal reasons *justify* legal conclusions they do not mean that they *morally* justify the conclusions, but only that the conclusions are *based on legal arguments*. They say that there are normative standards of legal argumentation and that there is therefore such a thing as a convincing legal argument. But law and morality are separable – they say – and therefore a convincing legal argument may or may not be a convincing moral argument. Thus when positivists claim that it is possible for judges to *apply* the law neutrally (that is, in accordance with its clear meaning), this does not commit them to the view that the laws *themselves* are neutral. Positivists can also accept that legal concepts may serve to legitimate the injustices of the status quo and that judges are, in fact, often biased by their class position and make political decisions which serve the interests of the powerful. They therefore do not deny that there can be external influences on judicial decisions nor that judges may abuse their power.

Hart is quite clear on all of this. As we saw in 1.6, Hart thinks that a system of law may well be more unjust than a system of primary rules, for when the primary rules are unjust and exploitative, law may make things worse by providing for more efficient forms of exploitation and oppression. 'In an extreme case', he says, 'only officials might accept and use the system's criteria of legal validity. The society in which this was so might be deplorably sheeplike; the sheep might end in the slaughterhouse. But there is little reason for thinking that it could not exist or for denying it the title of a legal system' (Hart, 1994, p 117). This claim leads Jeremy Waldron to describe Hart's vision of law as 'somber and foreboding' (Waldron, 1999, p 186), and in this respect Hart's picture is rather like that of the crits.

This is not to say that there are no differences between positivists and the crits. The main claim on which they are in essential disagreement is on the indeterminacy of law. Positivists believe that the rules of law are at least sometimes determinate and that, however non-neutral and unjust they may be in their *content* and *effects*, they can at least sometimes be impartially or neutrally *applied* (applied, that is, without recourse to the judge's personal political beliefs). For the crits this is, of course, impossible. In their view judges cannot but make subjective, political choices.

Chapter 5

Rights

Having considered the nature of law and legal reasoning in some detail, we turn in the remaining chapters of this book to explore some normative issues about the shape the law *should* take – the standards, in other words, which *good* law should meet. And in this chapter we deal, in particular, with the concept of moral rights, both as limits on the exercise of governmental power and as the source of positive obligations on government to assist its citizens.

You should be familiar with the following areas:

- The distinction between civil and political rights and socio-economic rights
- Utilitarianism
- Rights as constraints on utilitarian reasoning
- The Kantian justification for rights
- Critiques of rights
- Bills of Rights

5.1 The concept of moral rights against the government

It is obvious that we enjoy legal rights. Legal rights are those rights, enforceable through the courts, which are granted us by statute, common law and constitutional provisions. But do we enjoy *moral rights against the government*? Such rights – if they exist – are claims which we are justified in making regardless of whether the legal system recognises these claims and even if it denies them. They therefore serve as the basis for criticising governments which fail to respect them. Thus if people have a moral right not to suffer racial discrimination they have this right independently of the law, and a society like apartheid South Africa, in which the legal system was built on systematic racial discrimination, violated this right on a daily basis.

Moral rights against the government are asserted as a means of protecting very fundamental interests – interests which are essential to the leading of a worthwhile life. In earlier centuries, moral rights of this kind were often called 'natural rights' – meaning by this rights we have simply by virtue of our nature as human beings, or rights we have in a 'state of nature', or rights conferred on us by the 'law of nature'. Now it is more usual to refer to rights of this kind as 'human rights'. Human rights are rights of fundamental importance which all humans possess whatever legal system they live under and regardless of whether or not the law respects their rights. They tell us not how political power is used but how it *ought* to be used – not how states do treat their citizens, but how they should.

Although the idea of human rights is currently very popular, as evidenced by the growing number of international, regional and domestic human rights instruments, it is not uncontroversial, and there are many theorists who believe that the human rights movement is not as progressive and universal as it proclaims itself to be. In this chapter we will discuss the concept of moral rights against the government; the arguments in favour of and against the idea that we possess such rights; and the particular rights we might be thought to have. We will also consider the mechanisms for giving such rights legal force.

5.2   Which rights are claimed as human rights?

If there are interests which are essential to the leading of a worthwhile life, and which our government is morally obliged to respect and protect, which interests might these be? The best-known attempt to formulate a list of such interests is the Universal Declaration of Human Rights which was adopted by the General Assembly of the United Nations in 1948 as a response to the atrocities committed during the Second World War. This is not to say that the 1948 Declaration should be regarded as the be-all and end-all on the matter. For one thing, the world has subsequently seen the emergence of many other international covenants and treaties as well as domestic bills of rights. Second, the generality of the language used in the Declaration leaves the scope and limits of the rights it mentions very open-ended. It nevertheless remains useful in picking out a number of rights which are commonly claimed as human rights. The most important of these are the ones mentioned in the following paragraphs.

Most obviously, the Declaration mentions the rights to life, liberty and security of the person. Particular liberties are also more specifically mentioned: these include the right not to be enslaved; the right to freedom of thought, conscience and religion; the right to freedom of opinion and expression; and the right to freedom of peaceful assembly and association. The Declaration contains a number of rights arising out of the administration of the legal system. These include the right not to be tortured or subjected to cruel, inhuman or degrading treatment or punishment; the right to the equal protection of the law; the right not to be subjected to arbitrary arrest, detention or exile; the right of access to court; and the right to be presumed innocent until proven guilty. There are also rights of political participation, including the right to take part in the government of one's country. The right to property also figures, as does the right to non-discrimination, to privacy, to marry, and to form and join trade unions.

In addition to the rights mentioned in the previous paragraph, which are usually called 'civil and political rights', the Declaration also contains rights which are connected with material well-being. This represents a significant reconceptualisation of the content of human rights and of the state's duties towards its citizens in the twentieth century. It was previously generally assumed that the function of rights is only to safeguard human freedom or human liberty, such as the freedom to practise one's religion or express one's views. But most contemporary defenders of human rights believe that some degree of welfare is as essential to the leading of a worthwhile life as the protection of our liberties, and that rights therefore have just as important a role to play in protecting material well-being as in protecting freedom. Hence they argue for so-called 'socio-economic rights', these being rights which safeguard the satisfaction of our basic needs or welfare. The rights to health care, to education and to housing are examples of socio-economic rights. Contemporary defenders of human rights generally also believe that we enjoy 'cultural rights' or rights to respect for our cultural practices, and nowadays attention is also frequently paid to the rights of the world's indigenous people.

The Declaration follows this path in including such rights as the right 'to just and favourable conditions of work and to protection against unemployment'; to 'rest and leisure'; 'to education'; and to 'a standard of living adequate for the health and well-being' of oneself and one's family, 'including food, clothing, housing and medical care and necessary social services'.

5.3 Rights as constraints on the general interest

In order to understand the concept of a moral right, and the distinctive and controversial role that rights play in moral and political thought, we need to begin with the moral theory of utilitarianism, to which rights-theory is fundamentally opposed. Suppose we are faced with a conflict of interests between different individuals. Whatever we do, some individuals will gain and others will lose. How should we resolve the conflict?

Utilitarianism tells us that we should always act so as to produce the greatest balance of happiness over unhappiness, both in our personal lives, and in social decision-making. It is the latter which is our concern in this chapter. The early utilitarians tended to understand happiness as a pleasurable state of mind, whereas contemporary utilitarians tend to see it more as a matter of satisfied preferences or desires – getting what one wants, regardless of whether that is accompanied by the experience of pleasure. I will ignore these complexities here, and talk interchangeably about 'happiness' and 'preference satisfaction'. I will also use the word 'welfare' as a catch-all word to describe what utilitarians believe to be the basis of morality.

Bentham, one of the earliest utilitarians, put the utilitarian approach like this: '[a]n action may be said to be conformable to the principle of utility . . . when the tendency it has to augment the happiness of the community is greater than any which it has to diminish it' (Bentham, 1789, p 127). Utilitarianism is therefore a *consequentialist* theory: it measures the rightness or wrongness of our actions solely by reference to their consequences, and by reference to one set of consequences in particular – their effect on the balance of human happiness over human unhappiness. Whether our actions are intrinsically right or wrong – right or wrong independent of their consequences – is of no concern. Utilitarianism is also, in one sense of the word, an *egalitarian* theory: the happiness of *everyone* affected by our conduct must be weighed in the scales when deciding what to do. One person's happiness is just as important as another's and therefore 'everyone is to count for one, nobody for more than one.'

It will be remembered from 2.6 that Bentham, though insisting on the separability of law and morality, believed that morality *should* inform law, and it is precisely utilitarian morality which he thought ought to be the basis of all legislative activity and legal institutions.

On the face of it, utilitarianism looks an attractive and plausible theory. What could be wrong, after all, with a concern for human happiness? The answer to this is that there might be something wrong with treating human happiness as the *only* moral value. In particular, many philosophers have objected to utilitarianism on the ground that the goal of maximising happiness may violate individuals' *rights*, the protection of which is another, competing source of value.

Some, like Robert Nozick, go further, as we will see in 7.10. Nozick argues that the goal of maximising happiness *always* violates rights and that individuals' interests should *never* be sacrificed to collective goals. He believes, in other words, that utilitarian considerations play no role at all in morality. But in what follows I will concentrate on the more plausible view that maximum happiness can be a legitimate goal for governments to pursue, provided that this is not at the expense of individuals' rights.

Consider the following examples which are often used to show the importance of rights. Suppose the police have captured a terrorist who has planted a bomb in a sports stadium packed to capacity. Let us suppose that there are 100,000 people in the stadium. The terrorist refuses to disclose the location of the bomb and the police know it is about to explode. The terrorist is immune to torture but the police have also captured his small child and they know that if they torture the child the terrorist will disclose the location of the bomb. Clearly, the welfare that can be brought to the 100,000 people who will be saved from a painful death as well as to their relatives and friends far outweighs the suffering and even the death of the innocent child. Utilitarianism therefore seems to instruct us to torture the child – something which most people would regard as abhorrent and precluded by the child's right not to be tortured.

The second example involves the punishment of an innocent person. Suppose that a terrible crime has been committed in a small town and the population is in an inflamed state. They believe that a particular man is responsible for the crime although the sheriff knows he is innocent. The sheriff also knows, however, that unless the man is arrested and executed thousands of people will be killed in rioting. Utilitarianism seems to tell the sheriff to make a scapegoat of the innocent man so as to prevent the loss of many lives. After all, the unhappiness caused to the innocent man will be far outweighed by the benefits to all the other inhabitants of the town.

The third example involves satisfying illegitimate or reprehensible preferences. Suppose the majority in a society are racists who strongly dislike and wish to persecute a racial minority. Because utilitarians treat all preferences as on a par regardless of their content, they will be in favour of allowing the majority to oppress the minority if the satisfaction this brings the majority outweighs the harm done to the minority.

It is against the background of examples like these that we are able to understand the claims made by those who believe in rights. As we have seen, utilitarians are concerned solely with maximising welfare. As a result, they believe that all interests should be balanced against each other in calculating which course of action will bring maximum happiness. They take all preferences into account, being indifferent to what it is that people want and to the nature of the harm that may need to be imposed on some people in order to satisfy the preferences of others. They approach all moral questions as a matter merely of a 'cost-benefit' analysis.

Rights-theorists, by contrast, believe that some preferences are *illegitimate* and should not be taken into account in deciding what to do, no matter how intensely felt or widely shared these preferences may be. Thus they argue that it is not *appropriate* to balance some people's racist preferences against other people's interest in not being discriminated against, racist preferences having *no weight at all* from the perspective of morality.

Rights-theorists say that while it is reasonable to balance *some* interests against others in a utilitarian way, accepting losses for some people in return for benefits for others, this is not true of our *important* interests – interests the satisfaction of which is essential to the leading of a worthwhile life. Such interests, they argue, are too important to be left to the mercy of a cost-benefit utilitarian exercise. In the case of our more everyday interests, all we can say is that we would *like* them to be satisfied. But in the case of our important interests, what we are *entitled* to *insist on* as a matter of *justice* enters the picture.

Rights-theorists argue that our important interests therefore deserve *special* protection from the demands of others and that we should recognise this by granting these interests the status of 'rights' – the function of rights being precisely to protect individuals from having to sacrifice their fundamental interests merely on the ground that their loss will be outweighed by gains to others. Rights therefore serve as markers for those basic interests which individuals cannot be expected to sacrifice on the basis of a routine utilitarian calculation. Dworkin uses the metaphor of a 'trump' to explain this idea, a trump being a playing card of a suit that outranks the other suits. Dworkin says:

> [i]ndividual rights are political trumps held by individuals. Individuals have rights when, for some reason, a collective goal is not a sufficient justification for denying them what they wish, as individuals, to have or to do, or not a sufficient justification for imposing some loss or injury on them.
>
> (Dworkin, 1977a, p xi)

Collective goals can, by contrast, justify the invasion of lesser interests. Dworkin gives the example of a law which forbids motorists to drive up Lexington Avenue:

> though the New York government needs a justification for forbidding motorists to drive up Lexington Avenue, it is sufficient justification if the proper officials believe, on sound evidence, that the gain to the many will outweigh the inconvenience to the few.
>
> (Dworkin, 1977a, p 191)

But rights are a card of a stronger suit than the general interest and '[i]f someone has a right to something, then it is wrong for the government to deny it to him even though it would be in the general interest to do so' (Dworkin, 1977a, p 269).

Another way of putting this point is to say that rights-theorists see rights as moral 'constraints' on what governments may do to individuals. Though governments may legitimately pursue the general welfare, there are certain matters – such as protecting people against being tortured or killed or discriminated against – which take priority over collective goals. Rights are therefore moral considerations of a distinctive kind. They are a way of preventing the government from trading off our most important interests against the public interest. Whereas the public interest focuses on the *total* or *average* amount of welfare, rights give priority to the basic interests of *individuals* even at the expense of society. (For further discussion of individualism, see 8.5.)

This is not necessarily to say that utilitarian considerations can *never* justify the violation of a right. Though some rights-theorists take this view, they do not all do so. For Nozick, as we will see in 7.8, rights are absolute and may never be violated for utilitarian reasons. Finnis likewise believes that there are absolute human rights (Finnis, 1980, p 225). But Dworkin allows for the possibility that rights may be violated in really exceptional circumstances. For him, rights serve to give certain interests *substantially* more protection than other interests, *largely* but not *entirely* immunising them against being overridden in the public interest. Rights, for Dworkin, therefore cannot be overridden merely because to do so would benefit the community to some, perhaps small, degree. However, where there is a sufficiently grave and demonstrated threat to society, rights may justifiably be infringed. For instance, freedom of speech might be justifiably infringed during wartime in order to avoid defeat.

One person's rights may, of course, also come into conflict with the rights of someone else and rights may therefore need, on occasion, to be balanced against *other rights*. The right to freedom of speech, for instance, may need to be balanced against someone else's right not to be defamed. But weighing up the relative *importance* of two individuals' competing rights is much less problematic from the moral point of view than overriding a right in order to maximise happiness. A clash of rights involves a clash between the fundamental interests of separate, identifiable individuals. Contrast a clash between an individual and society – a group of people whose demands have been added up or combined so as *cumulatively* or *numerically* to outweigh the individual's claims, despite the fact that the interests of each member of the group, considered one by one, may be trivial when compared to the interests of the individual who is sacrificed to the group, or even reprehensible.

5.4   The idea of human dignity

We turn now to the question whether we *should* recognise rights. The need to address this question may not be obvious because many people assume that the only people who reject rights are tyrants and dictators (Waldron, 1992, p 93). But this assumption is not correct. As we have seen, rights constrain utilitarian reasoning. But this means that they act as a constraint on the pursuit of even *meritorious* social goals, preventing measures which would, in the absence of the right, be perfectly legitimate.

Consider, for instance, the right to freedom of speech. Speech can cause harm in all sorts of ways. It can be used to deceive, to insult, to harass, to threaten, to offend, to provoke violence and to persuade other people to act in undesirable ways. But if we recognise a *right* to freedom of speech we expect the public to put up with these harms to a much greater extent than in the case of other kinds of conduct which cause similar harms. A right such as the right to freedom of speech therefore has social costs. And even rights which prevent the innocent from being tortured and punished will appear from the utilitarian perspective as indefensible. After all, in particular circumstances, such as the torture and scapegoating cases described earlier, rights will lead us to choose what JCC Smart calls the 'greater misery, perhaps the *very much* greater misery, such as that of hundreds of people suffering painful deaths' (Smart and Williams, 1973, p 72, Smart's emphasis).

Rights therefore come at a considerable price, making the question about their justification urgent. As Dworkin observes:

> [t]he institution of rights against the Government is not a gift of God, or an ancient ritual, or a national sport. It is a complex and troublesome practice that makes the Government's job of securing the general benefit more difficult and more expensive, and it would be a frivolous and wrongful practice unless it served some point.
>
> (Dworkin, 1977a, p 198)

In explaining the point of rights, many rights-theorists are influenced by the moral philosophy of Kant. Kant thought that there is something uniquely precious about human beings, a characteristic that makes us uniquely valuable and confers dignity on us. This is our capacity for rational choice. Kant argued that this capacity gives rise to a special moral status that separates human beings from all other creatures and by virtue of which we are owed a special kind of respect. In particular, we should always be treated as ends in ourselves, and never be used in an instrumental way for someone else's or society's benefit – never be used, as he said, as a mere means to someone else's ends. Thus Kant wrote that each rational being 'should treat himself and all others, *never merely as a means*, but always *at the same time as an end in himself*' (Kant, 1785, p 95, Kant's emphasis).

Rights-theorists like Dworkin and John Rawls (1921–2002) are heavily influenced by these Kantian ideas. They argue that invading someone's fundamental interests for the good of society denies that person the respect they are owed in virtue of their humanity. Jeremy Waldron explains their perspective as follows:

> [o]ne possible view is that our convictions [about rights] are based on a deep ethical view about the respect we owe to one another in virtue of our common humanity, and in virtue of our potential to act morally ... [W]e believe that people have got to be able to retain their dignity, their self-esteem, and at least the basic capacity to make a life for themselves ... Human dignity is violated when someone is tortured, their home-life thrown open to surveillance, their culture denigrated, their political voice taken away, or their needs treated with indifference. You cannot do that to people and expect them to retain the basis of self-esteem that they must have in order to live a human life. If the price of prosperity, security, or social utility is that we deprive some people of this basic respect, then prosperity, security and utility cost too much.
>
> (Waldron, 1992, p 97)

Rawls puts the point in a nutshell, saying: '[e]ach person possesses an inviolability founded on justice that even the welfare of society as a whole cannot override' (Rawls, 1971, p 3).

In assessing the plausibility of the Kantian argument for rights we need, of course, to consider the counter-arguments. We have already touched on some of these in discussing the CLS critique of liberal values (see 4.12), but it is now necessary to consider the matter in more detail. I will address the arguments under four headings, though there is considerable overlap between the various claims and the headings should therefore not be seen as watertight. The four headings are: rights are selfish; rights function to protect those who wield power; rights are incompatible with the value and importance of community; and rights are ethnocentric. Finally, in Chapter 8 we will view this topic through one last lens, when we consider the feminist view that instead of making adversarial claims of rights we should be working with a model of care, co-operation and affection (see 8.13).

5.5   Are rights selfish?

Bentham was deeply hostile to the notion of moral or natural rights, as his scathing attack on the 1789 French Declaration of the Rights of Man and the Citizen demonstrates. Bentham's hostility rested in part on the fact that he thought it impossible to demonstrate that we have natural rights, or what their content might be, and he concluded from this that the only rights are legal rights. He said that no-one can be said to enjoy a right unless someone else is liable to suffer a legal sanction for failing to respect that right. In the absence of a sanction, according to Bentham, claims of right are mere wishful thinking. And just as 'hunger is not bread', so 'a reason for wishing that a certain right were established, is not that right' (Bentham, 1795, p 330).

It is hard to understand why Bentham took this position. He did not take the same view of other moral concepts like 'duty' and 'obligation' which exist, according to him, independently of legal recognition. But in the case of rights he was adamant that there are no rights without law or rights which law can be said to violate. Thus Bentham pronounced the idea of natural rights 'simple nonsense'. Natural and imprescriptible rights were, he quipped, 'rhetorical nonsense, nonsense upon stilts' (Bentham, 1795, p 330).

Bentham's hostility to the notion of natural rights was also a function of his utilitarianism. This led him to argue that those who are not willing to sacrifice themselves without limit to the general good are egoistic or selfish. Thus he argued that natural rights were not merely 'nonsense' but 'dangerous nonsense', for they 'add force' to the 'selfish and dissocial passions' which are the 'great enemies of public peace'. 'Society is held together', Bentham remarked,

> only by the sacrifices that men can be induced to make of the gratifications they demand: to obtain these sacrifices is the great difficulty, the great task of government. What has been the object, the perpetual and palpable object, of this Declaration of Pretended rights [the Declaration of the Rights of Man and the Citizen]? To add as much force as possible to these passions, already but too strong: to burst the cords that hold them in: to say to the selfish passions, there – everywhere, is your prey: to the angry passions, there, everywhere, is your enemy. Such is the morality of this celebrated composition.
> (Bentham, 1795, p 321)

This passage shows that Bentham was opposed to the idea of moral rights precisely because they give priority to individual interests over collective interests, in defiance of the utilitarian injunction to focus only on maximum happiness.

Rights-theorists respond to the utilitarian critique by pointing out that rights do not protect *all* of our interests but only those of our interests which are essential to the leading of a worthwhile life – our interests, for instance, in bodily integrity, freedom from discrimination, religious freedom and adequate health care. They also point out that selfishness is discreditable (Waldron, 1987, p 209). To be selfish is to care about one's own interests more than one should. But is it really discreditable to refuse to surrender one's entire self to society and the interests of other people? Is it, for instance, selfish to ask that one not be called upon to sacrifice one's *life* for the general good? And is it selfish to claim a right not to be tortured? Or a right to practise one's religion? Or a right to health care? Rights-theorists argue that it is not.

Many rights-theorists also take the view that we do not necessarily discharge all of our moral obligations merely by respecting other people's rights. Nozick is an exception: he thinks, as we will see in 7.10, that rights exhaust morality. But most rights-theorists think that rights are merely *one part* of morality. They say that we are bound to respect rights, but once that baseline is secured we should also care about the general good and collective goals. There is therefore plenty of scope for altruism and co-operation which is nevertheless consistent with setting limits on the kinds of sacrifices people can legitimately be asked to make in the public interest. Indeed, it may be unrealistic to expect people to act altruistically and out of a concern for the community *unless* their basic interests are first secured (Waldron, 1987, pp 206–7).

5.6 Do rights cater only to the interests of the powerful?

Marx is perhaps the best-known defender of the view that rights are a way of serving the interests of the capitalist class and that the promise of freedom and emancipation which they offer is a sham. We already know from 4.12 that he attacked rights in his early essay, 'On the Jewish Question'. In this essay he argued that rights are a 'bourgeois' notion which create an illusion of freedom and equality while in reality serving the interests of the dominant, property-owning class by guaranteeing its unhindered acquisitive activity. Marx also believed that rights will not be necessary in a socialist society, in which the private ownership of the means of production will have been eliminated and class divisions will, according to him, have disappeared. In such a society, Marx suggested, guarantees that our interests will be protected will be unnecessary.

Many commentators have found this picture rather simplistic both in its understanding of the interests protected by rights and in its view of the circumstances that make rights necessary. Thus Steven Lukes, in his book *Marxism and Morality*, argues that Marx had a 'narrow and impoverished' view of human rights (Lukes, 1985, p 63) and that he was too quick to think that they are dispensable.

This may seem obvious about the rights which are commonly regarded as human rights today. Nowadays, as we have seen, there is a growing emphasis on the importance of socio-economic rights in addition to the traditional rights to liberty. Though Marx's arguments might seem cogent when applied to an absolute right to private property, such as that argued for by Nozick (see 7.9 and 7.10), it is more difficult to see why rights which serve our basic needs – such as the right to health care, to education and to housing – should be thought to cater only to the self-serving interests of the capitalist class. Furthermore, though socio-economic rights are the most obvious examples of rights which serve more universal interests, Lukes argues that even the eighteenth-century conception of rights – which was, of course, the conception attacked by Marx – included rights which have little do to with serving the egoistic interests of the capitalist class but are valuable to everyone, no matter what their class. Lukes mentions, for instance, the rights to freedom of speech, to be presumed innocent until proven guilty and not to be arbitrarily arrested. To this list one could add the democratic rights enshrined in such documents as the French Declaration.

In so far as the dispensability of rights is concerned, Allen Buchanan argues that even if a society existed in which there were no class conflicts and no class interests, there would still be a need for rights. For even in such a society, it would, for instance, be necessary to protect individual liberties against paternalistic interference, prevent the common good being pursued in unacceptable ways, and specify the nature of our obligations to provide or preserve resources for future generations (Buchanan, 1982, p 165).

5.7   Rights and community

A contemporary critique of rights can be found in the work of communitarians such as Michael Sandel, Charles Taylor, Michael Walzer and Alasdair MacIntyre. They argue that liberal rights-theory assumes a false, individualistic view of the self and wrongly puts individual interests ahead of identification with and participation in community.

We will return to the communitarian critique of the liberal conception of the self in 7.7. For the moment it is enough to note the following. Though liberals do not, contrary to some popular conventional stereotypes, believe that human beings can exist outside society, they do believe that we are able to stand back from our social roles and social practices, subject them to critical scrutiny and reject them if found wanting. Communitarians take issue with this view. They believe that our identity is constituted by the community in which we find ourselves and that we can be obliged to pursue ends we have not chosen.

This philosophical view about the nature of the self has normative implications which bear on the topic of rights. In particular, it leads communitarians to the view that the good for human beings consists in identification with a 'common form of life', an identification which is in tension with the idea of rights. For, as Taylor says, 'I cannot be too willing to trump the collective decision in the name of individual rights if I haven't already moved some distance from the community which makes these decisions' (Taylor, 1985, p 211).

In place of rights, with their individualistic focus, communitarians would have us substitute a politics of the common good based on shared objectives. They argue that this will make it possible to enjoy certain communal goods, such as solidarity, fraternity and a sense of belonging, which we will be shut out from if we persist in focusing on what is good for individuals.

Rights-theorists respond by pointing out that, historically, shared social practices have operated to exclude certain groups: groups such as women, blacks and gays have played little part in defining the common good of the community and, indeed, these groups have typically been oppressed at the hands of those who define the shared communal goals. Thus Will Kymlicka writes:

> [c]ommunitarians like to say that political theory should pay more attention to the history of each culture. But it is remarkable how rarely communitarians themselves undertake such an examination of our culture. They wish to use the ends and practices of our cultural tradition as the basis for a politics of the common good, but they do not mention that these practices were defined by a small segment of the population.
>
> (Kymlicka, 1990, p 228)

Rights-theorists conclude that members of marginalised and disadvantaged social groups are better served by rights which protect them from forced identification with cultural practices than by a politics of the common good.

5.8   Are rights ethnocentric?

As we have seen, those who defend human rights believe that they represent universal goods to which all people in all social circumstances are entitled. However, many critics of rights are sceptical of such claims to universality. The idea that there are universal principles of political morality is strikingly expressed by Rawls at the end of *A Theory of Justice*. He writes:

> [t]hus to see our place in society from the perspective of this position is to see it *sub specie aeternitatis*: it is to regard the human condition not only from all social but also from all temporal points of view. The perspective of eternity is not a perspective from a certain place beyond the world, nor the point of view of a transcendent being; rather it is a form of thought and feeling that rational persons can adopt within the world. And having done so, they can, whatever their generation, bring together in one scheme all individual perspectives and arrive together at regulative principles that can be affirmed by everyone as he lives by them, each from his own standpoint.
>
> (Rawls, 1971, p 587)

As we might expect, the idea that we are able to adopt the 'perspective of eternity' is rejected by communitarians, with their emphasis on the importance of culture and shared understandings in constituting social identity. If what is good for people arises not out of universal needs and interests but out of their particular way of life – their society and its practices – it is a mistake to attempt to evaluate such ways of life by reference to external standards which make no sense in the context of particular, local practices. Communitarians argue that the attempt to impose human rights on those who do not understand them represents just such a mistaken attempt to evaluate societies from the outside.

Furthermore, this mistake is compounded by the fact that the external standpoint rights-theorists seek to impose is not, after all, a supra-cultural standpoint but – according to the communitarians – a merely Western standpoint. Human rights therefore do not represent universal values, according to communitarians. They merely represent the local practices of contemporary Western societies. Those who deny this are guilty of 'cultural imperialism' or 'ethnocentrism'.

Thus Walzer argues that questions of justice can only be debated within the context of particular communities and their particular traditions. He writes:

> [w]e are (all of us) culture-producing creatures; we make and inhabit meaningful worlds. Since there is no way to rank and order these worlds with regard to their understanding of social goods, we do justice to actual men and women by respecting their particular creations. And they claim justice, and resist tyranny, by insisting on the meaning of social goods among themselves. Justice is rooted in the distinct understandings of places, honors, jobs, things of all sorts, that constitute a shared way of life. To override those understandings is (always) to act unjustly.
>
> (Walzer, 1983, p 314)

Rights-theorists respond to these charges in a number of ways. First, they reply that they are alive to the dangers of assuming that Western values are the correct values. But, they say, this does not imply that 'anything goes' and that everything is 'relative'. Instead, it should alert us to the possibility of bias in our judgments and lead us to be cautious in making moral judgments about other societies.

Second, they point out that rights set only 'minimum goals'; they do not purport to provide a 'complete social programme' (Waldron, 1987, p 173). Those who defend rights believe that all human beings are of equal moral value and therefore that all governments are obliged to provide their citizens with minimum standards of protection, particularly in so far as their freedom, security and welfare are concerned. This leaves plenty of room for diversity in cultural practices and moral beliefs once the minimum is secured. Hart, as we will see in 6.5, distinguishes between moral rules that are essential to any society's existence – such as prohibitions against murder, deceit and violence – and moral rules which are a function of particular cultural practices – such as food taboos and religious practices. Rights-theorists do not deny that the latter rules legitimately differ from society to society. It is only *rights* which, according to them, apply in all cultures.

Rights-theorists also question why these minimum standards should apply only to those in Western societies. Why – Joel Feinberg rhetorically asks – should people living in Western societies be so privileged (Feinberg, 1990, p 335)? Furthermore, do those who are denied their human rights in totalitarian societies or discriminatory societies take the view that rights are just a Western invention?

Thomas Scanlon challenges the argument that rights are ethnocentric along just these lines, saying:

> this argument rests on the attribution to 'them' of a unanimity that does not in fact exist. 'They' are said to be different from us and to live by different rules. Such stereotypes are seldom accurate, and the attribution of unanimity is particularly implausible in the case of human rights violations. These actions have victims who generally resent what is done to them and who would rarely concede that, because such behaviour is common in their country, their tormentors are acting quite properly.
>
> (quoted in Feinberg, 1990, p 336)

5.9   Translating moral rights against the government into law

Supposing one believes in rights against the government, how, if at all, should they be translated into legal institutions? It may come as a surprise, but those who believe that the government ought to respect and protect human rights do not necessarily believe that courts should be given the power to strike down legislation which is incompatible with human rights (Waldron, 1999a, p 212). To many this stance may look paradoxical. If someone believes that human rights should be respected and protected, surely they will also be in favour of a judicially enforceable bill of rights. Is it not, after all, the very point of rights to trump majoritarian decision-making?

Justice Jackson expressed this point of view when he stated in the US case of *West Virginia State Board of Education v Barnette* (1943):

> [t]he very purpose of a Bill of Rights was to withdraw certain subjects from the vicissitudes of political controversy, to place them beyond the reach of majorities and officials and to establish them as legal principles to be applied by the courts. One's right to life, liberty, and property, to free speech, a free press, freedom of worship and assembly, and other fundamental rights may not be submitted to vote; they depend on the outcome of no elections.
>
> (at 638)

But not all defenders of human rights agree with Justice Jackson that the purpose of a bill of rights is to place limits on the legislative power of parliaments.

When rights are contained in a constitution – 'constitutionalised' – the idea of rights as moral claims which can be asserted against the government is given legal force. The best-known example of such a constitutionally entrenched bill of rights is the US Bill of Rights which gives power to the Supreme Court of the United States to strike down legislation, regardless of the extent of its popular support, which is in breach of any of the rights protected by the Bill of Rights. The effect in such cases is 'counter-majoritarian': the majority is prevented from passing laws which are inconsistent with human rights.

It is exactly for this reason that some theorists object to constitutionally entrenched bills of rights. They point out that rights issues are often highly controversial. For instance, can abortion be legitimately restricted? Should voluntary euthanasia be allowed? Should pornography be censored? According to the critics of the US model, such controversial, essentially political decisions should be made through the democratic political process, not handed over to a handful of unelected judges who are not responsible to the community for the decisions they make. They argue that constitutionally entrenched bills of rights give too much power to judges to impose their own personal opinions on the public, leading to the unwelcome politicisation of the judiciary and a decline in public confidence in the objectivity and impartiality of judges. These theorists also tend to worry about the ability of the courts to make good decisions about rights, while simultaneously arguing against the low opinion many have of legislatures. Thus Waldron believes there is little need to fear the 'tyranny of the majority', for 'people's votes and opinions are not always the reflex of their interests'. 'Citizens and representatives', he says, 'often do vote on the basis of good faith and relatively impartial opinions about justice, rights, and the common good' (Waldron, 1999a, p 14).

Many are convinced by this critique of judicially enforceable bills of rights, and therefore argue, to use Thomas Campbell's words, for 'the importance of finding an institutional way of emphasising and facilitating the democratic expression of human rights which does not involve major judicial input, an institutionalisation which preserves the idea of fundamental rights but reclaims it for democracy' (Campbell, 1994, p 211).

One commonly proposed mechanism for 'reclaiming' human rights for democracy is a statutory bill of rights. Such bills can be amended or repealed like any other statute and therefore any rights protection they grant can subsequently be taken away either in whole or in part. Typically, they direct courts and tribunals to interpret law (sometimes only statutory law, sometimes both statutory law and the common law) in a manner that is consistent with the human rights protected by the bill, but only if it is 'possible' to do so. Some statutory bills of rights also allow courts to make a 'declaration of incompatibility', such a declaration being to the effect that a challenged law is not consistent with a protected right. The offending legislation remains valid, however, and must be applied to the case at hand, it being left up to the government and parliament whether to change it or not.

The upshot is that a statutory bill of rights does not empower courts to invalidate democratically passed legislation. A declaration of incompatibility may put *political* pressure on the government, but the majority is not *legally* prevented from passing laws which are inconsistent with human rights. The principle of parliamentary sovereignty therefore remains intact. Statutory bills of rights do not, in other words, give legal effect to the idea of rights as moral claims which place limits on and direct the exercise of state power. Instead, they are merely *interpretative* instruments which attempt to achieve a compromise between the values of parliamentary sovereignty and judicial supervision of human rights. The underlying philosophy is said to be one of 'dialogue' between the different branches of government – striking a balance between the powers of the legislature and the judiciary by allowing each to express its own view as to what human rights require – rather than one of giving the unelected judiciary the 'monopoly' or 'final say' over human rights issues, a philosophy which, as we have seen, some view as undemocratic, divisive and a threat to public confidence in the judiciary.

The Human Rights Act 1998 (UK) ('the HRA') is a statutory bill of rights. It incorporates into domestic law the main rights under the European Convention on Human Rights 1950 as well as various articles from the First and Sixth Protocols to the European Convention. The so-called 'Convention rights' are: the right to life; protection from torture and from inhuman or degrading treatment or punishment; the prohibition of slavery and forced labour; the right to liberty and security; the right to a fair trial; the right to no punishment without law; the right to respect for private and family life; freedom of thought, conscience and religion; freedom of expression; freedom of assembly and association; the right to marry; the prohibition of discrimination; the protection of property; the right to education; the right to free elections; the abolition of the death penalty; and the provision for the use of the death penalty in time of war.

The HRA provides that so far as it is possible to do so, primary and subordinate legislation must be read and given effect in a way which is compatible with the Convention rights. It also provides a court at (or above) the level of the High Court with the power to make a declaration of incompatibility where it is satisfied that a provision is incompatible with a Convention right. Such a declaration does not, however, affect the validity, continuing operation or enforcement of the provision and the government is not obliged to introduce legislation which removes the incompatibility. The Act also provides for a fast track procedure to allow amendment to primary legislation. In particular, if a minister considers that there are compelling reasons for so proceeding, he or she may amend the legislation by a remedial order.

It will be clear that the HRA represents an attempt to protect human rights while simultaneously safeguarding traditional views about the judicial function. It is, though, still an open question as to how desirable and effective this model will prove to be.

Chapter 6

Public and private

In this chapter we consider whether there are any moral limits on the use of the law, particularly the criminal law. Clearly, the threats and punishments imposed by the criminal law restrict our freedom – something which, without further justification, is a bad thing. We therefore need to investigate the grounds on which the law may *justifiably* prohibit us from acting as we please. Is it justifiable to use the criminal law to outlaw prostitution, for instance? Or homosexuality? Or trading on Sundays? Or euthanasia? Is society justified in punishing *any* behaviour which it considers immoral? Or is there an area of conduct which is 'private' and therefore beyond the law's rightful reach? And if there is an area which is private in this sense – an area in which we should be left free to make our own choices – what kind of conduct falls within it? Of course, if there is such an area, we would be entitled to claim a *right* to act free of state interference in it, which means, as we now know from our discussion of the trumping character of rights, that any public interest in regulating our conduct would necessarily take a back seat.

You should be familiar with the following areas:

- Mill's harm principle
- The idea of the neutral state
- Devlin's critique of Mill
- The relevance of the philosophical debate about the existence of a private realm to the issues of pornography, abortion and euthanasia

6.1   Getting clear on the issue

Most of the examples in this area revolve around the so-called 'offences against morals' and the issue is therefore sometimes described as one of 'law and morality.' We need, however, to be careful here. We should not confuse the issue currently under consideration with the issue discussed in Chapter 2. There we asked whether there is a necessary connection between the *concepts* of law and morality. We investigated whether it is *possible* for there to be law which is unjust or which is not identified using moral criteria. Now we are asking a very different question, a question about the law's *legitimate reach*: is there an area of human conduct which should be immune from legal interference even if the majority has moral objections to the conduct in question?

Another possible source of confusion stems from the fact that the issue is sometimes dealt with under the heading of 'the legal enforcement of morality'. This way of describing it suggests that the debate is between those who believe that the law should enforce moral standards and those who do not. But, of course, very few people (with the exception, perhaps, of anarchists) believe that the law should not enforce society's moral standards *at all*. Almost everyone agrees that, for example, the law should prevent people killing one another or cheating one another. The debate is rather between those who think that *all* of a majority's moral beliefs are, in principle, legitimately translatable into law and those who think that only a *sub-class* of the behaviour of which the majority disapproves can be rightfully subjected to punishment. It is between those who think there are *theoretical* limits to the law's enforcement of morality and those who think that there are at most *practical* limits.

Notice, also, that our question is a *normative* question. We are not aiming to describe the *actual* uses to which *actual* societies put the criminal law. We are *evaluating* the uses to which the criminal law may be put, asking whether some of these are *illegitimate* – that is, not a *proper* or *justifiable* or *morally permissible* use of the criminal law. Our concern is with whether the law *ought* to respect our freedom of choice in certain areas of life, not with its actual record on these matters. We are, in other words, concerned with what the law ought to be, not what it is.

6.2   A liberal approach

John Stuart Mill (1806–1873) made an influential contribution to our understanding of these matters in his book, *On Liberty*. He asked: '[w]hat is the rightful limit to the sovereignty of the individual over himself? Where does the authority of society begin? How much of human life should be assigned to individuality, and how much to society?' (Mill, 1859, p 92). And he answered this question in terms of his 'harm' principle. He said that there are definite limits to the power which can be legitimately exercised by society over adult citizens. In particular, 'the only purpose for which power can be rightfully exercised over any member of a civilized community, against his will, is to prevent harm to others. His own good, either physical or moral, is not a sufficient warrant' (Mill, 1859, p 15).

It is important to understand that Mill uses the word 'harm' in a much *narrower* way than we ordinarily use it, in the process giving real bite to his harm principle. Mill concedes that virtually everything we do has the potential to harm someone else in the *ordinary* sense of the word. Some people, for instance, take objection to gays expressing affection for each other in public. But Mill did not intend his harm principle to justify the punishment of *this* kind of harmful behaviour – offensive behaviour – because he wanted to ensure a space for individual freedom of action insulated from the public's prejudices and bigotries.

For Mill, however offensive conduct may be, and however much the majority may disapprove of it, in the absence of any tangible injury it does not cause 'harm' in his sense of the term. This is because, for him, causing harm involves the violation of a *distinct and assignable obligation to a definite person or persons* and this can take only two forms: either *infringing or putting at real risk the rights* of another person or *failing in one's duty to benefit others*.

The rights Mill has in mind are moral rights, not legal rights. Moral rights are a *narrow* sub-class of interests, as we saw in 5.2. They protect only our most fundamental interests. Murder, rape, assault and theft are obvious examples of the infringements of rights. Moral duties to benefit others are similarly narrowly confined. Certainly, they do not coincide with everything which it would be good of us to do for others. An example of a duty to benefit others is the duty to pay one's taxes. Giving large amounts of money to charity, on the other hand, though good to do, is not something we are under an obligation to do and that is why we describe someone who is particularly generous as having 'gone beyond the call of duty'.

Someone who is guilty of infringing rights or of failing in their duty to benefit others can, according to Mill, justifiably be punished or compelled to perform the beneficial act. But if someone is not guilty of such a violation, then – however objectionable other members of society may find their conduct – they should enjoy perfect freedom to do as they please. Thus, 'no person ought to be punished simply for being drunk; but a soldier or a policeman should be punished for being drunk on duty' (Mill, 1859, p 100).

Mill also puts this point by saying that the law may legitimately take an interest in our '*other-regarding*' but not our '*self-regarding*' behaviour. He defines self-regarding behaviour as behaviour which affects only oneself or other adults who have voluntarily consented to be affected. As with harm, he uses the notion of 'affecting' in a special way. Clearly, in the ordinary sense of the word, all of our behaviour has the capacity to affect others in some or other way. But, for Mill, behaviour only affects others if it violates an obligation to a definite individual or individuals. If it does not amount to such a violation, then it is self-regarding and there should be perfect freedom to engage in the conduct.

Mill gives a number of examples of illegitimate interference with self-regarding or harmless conduct (in his sense of these words). Though some of these are rather old-fashioned, the point he is making is quite clear. His examples include laws preventing people from eating certain foods for religious reasons; laws prohibiting 'public amusements', such as music, dancing and the theatre; laws prohibiting the sale of alcohol; laws preventing people from working or amusing themselves as they please on Sundays; and laws preventing the Mormons from practising polygamy.

Mill's harm principle is therefore highly protective of human liberty. Its effect is to carve out a substantial private area in which we are entitled to act freely, immune from government interference. The public sphere, in which state interference is justifiable, is correspondingly cut down: conduct is public only if rights have been infringed (or are likely to be infringed) or if a duty to perform a beneficial act has been evaded. Contrast a utilitarian approach to this matter, which would simply weigh up the majority's distaste for certain conduct against the desire of a minority to indulge in it: the majority's desires would almost invariably win out.

It should perhaps be stressed that the private and public spheres, defined as Mill defines them, do not coincide with the sphere of what takes place *in* private and what takes place *in* public. Conduct which takes place behind closed doors may violate another person's rights, while conduct which takes place in full public view may violate no rights.

It is also important to understand that the reason why Mill defends a private sphere of freedom of action is *not* because he believes that people will always use their liberty well. On the contrary, he believes that harmless conduct may well be morally wrong. Thus he says: '[t]here is a degree of folly, and a degree of what may be called... lowness or depravation of taste, which, though it cannot justify doing harm to the person who manifests it, renders him necessarily and properly a subject of distaste, or, in extreme cases, even of contempt' (Mill, 1859, p 95).

So the reason why the law may not interfere in harmless conduct is not because there is nothing *wrong* with such conduct. Rather, Mill's harm principle announces, in effect, that if our conduct does not violate the rights of others, we are *entitled* to do as we please, however immoral our conduct may be or be thought to be by the majority. Though Mill does not speak in these terms, the harm principle therefore gives us what amounts to a right to freedom of action in personal decisions, a right which 'trumps' the majority's wish to restrict our conduct, to use Dworkin's phrase (see 5.3).

How does Mill defend the harm principle? He gives an *indirect utilitarian* argument for it. He says that the general welfare will be served if the state restricts liberty only in order to prevent harm to others. This may look paradoxical. After all, as we have seen, the harm principle will undoubtedly frustrate the majority's wishes on occasions and it therefore appears to be in *conflict* with the general welfare. How then can Mill say that it is *required by* the general welfare?

Mill thinks that it is only on the surface that the harm principle conflicts with the general welfare. He believes that if we look more closely we will see that following the harm principle will overall and in the long run serve the end of maximum happiness. This is because, according to Mill, if we allow the majority to curtail liberty on *utilitarian* grounds, rather than on the basis of the harm principle, the majority will quite often make *mistakes* as to what will be in the public interest. Mill writes: 'the odds are that [the public] interferes wrongly, and in the wrong place' (Mill, 1859, p 102). For, '[i]n its interferences with personal conduct it is seldom thinking of anything but the enormity of acting or feeling differently from itself' and it therefore ignores 'the pleasure or convenience of those whose conduct [it] censure[s]' (Mill, 1859, p 103). On such matters, its opinion is therefore 'quite as likely to be wrong as right' (Mill, 1859, p 103). Since the majority's prejudices will prevent it from being able accurately to weigh up the costs and benefits of interference, the only way to maximise human happiness is to disable the majority from acting on its views in this area, in effect granting a right to freedom of action in self-regarding matters.

6.3   The neutral state

Many contemporary liberals take an approach which is broadly similar to Mill's but instead of using the concepts of harmful and harmless conduct, they rely on the contrast between the 'right' and the 'good'. In particular, instead of arguing that the state is not entitled to prevent harmless conduct, liberals like Rawls and Dworkin argue that the state should not attempt to force a particular view of the good life on its citizens.

A view of the good life is a view about what goals it is worthwhile to pursue and about what ways of life it is inherently good to lead. The state should be, these liberals say, 'neutral' (in the sense of 'not take sides') on the inherently controversial question of what kind of life its citizens should lead (Rawls, 1993, pp 190–5). Of course, these liberals do not say that the state should be neutral on *all* questions of value. Just as Mill argued that the state must prevent harmful conduct, contemporary liberals argue that the state must insist on the protection of rights and punish those who violate them. The protection of rights is a justifiable aim of the state, they say, because, being in everyone's interests, it is uncontroversial. Rights represent shared moral values, unlike conceptions of the good. Neutralist liberals therefore conclude that if individuals are not violating anyone's rights, they should be left free to pursue their own conceptions of the good.

6.4   A conservative challenge

In an essay entitled 'Morals and the Criminal Law', Lord Justice Devlin attacked the liberal view of the function of criminal law. His target was the Wolfenden Report, presented to the British government in 1957, which concluded that prostitution should not be made illegal and that homosexuality should be decriminalised. The Report clearly adopted the liberal position, stating that a decisive consideration was the importance of individual freedom of choice and action. For this reason, sin should not be equated with crime, and 'there must remain a realm of private morality and immorality which is ... not the law's business' (Wolfenden Report, 1957, para 61).

Devlin disagrees. He argues that society has the right to use the criminal law to enforce whatever moral standards are conventionally accepted. There may be various practical reasons why in particular circumstances it should not do so, but there are no theoretical reasons preventing society from using the law to punish 'sin' or immorality as such. For there is no *principled* distinction – such as the one Mill sought to draw, using the criterion of harm, or such as the one drawn by

Rawls between the right and the good – dividing the private from the public sphere. 'It is not possible', Devlin says, 'to define inflexibly areas of morality into which the law is in no circumstances to be allowed to enter' (Devlin, 1965, p 13). The private–public distinction is therefore incoherent.

Devlin begins by pointing out that the criminal law as it stands does not observe Mill's harm principle. Consider the situation of a doctor who gives a lethal injection to a terminally ill person at that person's request. In terms of Mill's definition of harm, the doctor's conduct is harmless. After all, the patient has voluntarily consented to be killed. No-one else has been done a tangible injury. But the law does not accept consent as a defence to a charge of murder. The doctor will be found guilty of murder, the patient's consent notwithstanding.

It follows that the criminal law punishes some activity which is harmless in Mill's sense. It prohibits euthanasia not because it violates anyone's rights but because it is 'an offence against society' (Devlin, 1965, p 6) – because it threatens 'one of the great moral principles upon which society is based, that is, the sanctity of human life' (Devlin, 1965, p 6). In this situation, Devlin concludes, the function of the criminal law is simply to enforce a moral principle, no less and no more.

Devlin next argues that society has the *right* to pass judgment on the personal conduct of its members, irrespective of whether their behaviour is harmful in Mill's sense. This is because shared moral beliefs are what hold society together: 'a recognized morality is as necessary to society as . . . a recognized government' (Devlin, 1965, p 11). Furthermore, since morality is essential to society's existence, it follows that any immorality is capable of 'affecting society injuriously' (Devlin, 1965, p 15), and therefore that society not only has the right to pass *judgment* on such matters but also the right to use the law to *enforce* its judgments. Immorality is potentially as threatening to society's survival as treason and therefore '[t]he suppression of vice is as much the law's business as the suppression of subversive activities' (Devlin, 1965, pp 13–14).

Of course, having told us that society has the right to punish immorality as such, regardless of whether the immoral conduct violates anyone's rights, Devlin needs to tell us how we go about ascertaining what kind of conduct is immoral. He gives a distinctive answer to this question. He says that immorality is what the 'reasonable man' considers to be immoral. This reasonable man should not, however, be confused with the 'rational man'. For the reasonable man 'is not expected to reason about anything and the judgement may be largely a matter of feeling' (Devlin, 1965, p 15). The reasonable man's judgments are the judgments of 'common sense' (Devlin, 1965, p 17).

It is important to understand that some theorists agree with Devlin that society has the right to punish immorality while understanding the notion of immorality in very different terms. For Devlin, the morality which society is entitled to enforce is whatever morality happens to be current in a particular society. He does not ask whether the moral judgments of the reasonable man in that society are *acceptable* or can be *rationally defended*. By contrast, philosophers like Aristotle and Aquinas, who agree with Devlin that no conduct in principle falls outside the criminal law, nevertheless believe that conduct must be *objectively* wrong in order to be justifiably forbidden by law. They say that conduct must be *really* wicked before it is prohibited, not merely *widely believed* to be wicked (George, 1993, p 6). They wish to use the law to make men virtuous. For this reason they are sometimes called 'perfectionists', because they think that it is legitimate to use the law to encourage us to lead lives which are *intrinsically* worthy and to discourage us from leading lives which are intrinsically unworthy. (Contrast the view, discussed in 6.3, that the state should be neutral on matters of the good life.) But this, as we have seen, is not Devlin's view at all. He does not inquire into the rational basis of the judgments of the reasonable man.

Having argued that society has the right to use the weapon of the law to enforce the moral 'feelings' of the reasonable man and to prohibit any kind of immorality, Devlin turns at the end of his essay to discuss the circumstances in which society should exercise its right. His view is that the legislature should weigh the interests of the individual in freedom of choice against the interests of society. He concedes that certain considerations may sometimes speak in favour of the former.

The legislature should not, for instance, punish private immorality if the reasonable man does not feel a 'real feeling of reprobation', amounting to 'intolerance, indignation and disgust' (Devlin, 1965, p 17). (On the other hand, if a vice is regarded as 'so abominable that its mere presence is an offence' (Devlin, 1965, p 17), then society should eradicate it.) If the conduct is consensual and takes place in private, this may be another relevant factor, for the interest in privacy may on occasion outweigh the public interest in the moral order. Furthermore, the standards to which the law holds us are necessarily less demanding than the standards to which morality holds us.

But these are merely *relevant*, not *decisive*, factors according to Devlin. There are no hard and fast principles circumscribing what the legislature may legitimately do, and there is certainly no *right* to be left alone in the area of personal conduct. The issue is a *practical* one, demanding a pragmatic judgment in each case which takes into account all the relevant factors. For instance, although adultery is just as harmful to the social fabric as bigamy, it would be too difficult to enforce a law which made adultery a crime. Adultery should therefore be tolerated, while bigamy should be prohibited. 'There is,' Devlin says, 'no logic to be found in this... The fact that adultery, fornication and lesbianism are untouched by the criminal law does not prove that homosexuality ought not to be touched' (Devlin, 1965, p 22). There is, in other words, no *principle* which serves to separate crime from sin. Rather, it may merely in certain circumstances be *impractical* to punish sin, namely, when the costs of doing so are greater than the benefits. (Contrast Dworkin: the law should be coherent. If certain conduct is outside the law, then all analogous or morally indistinguishable conduct should be outside the law.)

6.5   Some criticisms of Devlin

Joel Feinberg points out the dubious relevance of Devlin's first argument – that there are circumstances in which the criminal law refuses to accept consent as a defence to a criminal charge, and that the criminal law as it stands therefore does not conform to Mill's harm principle. It may be true that the criminal law punishes harmless conduct, but, as Feinberg says, the liberal view aims to tell us not what the law *does* prohibit but what it *should* and *should not* prohibit. Though Devlin is right that the law may not *in fact* always reflect liberal principles, this does not prove that the liberal principles are wrong (Feinberg, 1990, p 165).

Furthermore, Feinberg goes on to argue, there are occasions on which the law's refusal to accept consent as a defence can be explained on *liberal* grounds, that is, without recourse to the idea that the law is enforcing a moral principle. Consider a case in which someone consents to their own maiming or disfigurement for the purposes of defrauding an insurance company. There are reasons perfectly consistent with Mill's approach for not accepting their consent as a defence, namely, that the conduct *harms an identifiable third party*. Or again, consider a case where someone in a psychotic state consents to be maimed or disfigured. Again, there are acceptable liberal reasons for not accepting their consent as a defence, namely, that the consent is not *genuinely voluntary*. But if someone in sound mind and without intent to perpetrate a fraud consents to be maimed, then Feinberg thinks that the law *should* accept their consent as a defence. He gives the example of someone who sells one of their kidneys. Provided that the bargain is not exploitative, Feinberg thinks that this is a private choice with which the law should not interfere (Feinberg, 1990, pp 170–1).

Hart attacks other aspects of Devlin's argument. One focus of his attack is Devlin's conception of morality – namely, popular reactions regardless of whether they have a rational foundation. Hart points out that most opponents of the liberal point of view have been objectivists about morality. Believing that morality has a rational foundation (by contrast with the non-cognitivists about morality discussed in 2.6), they see nothing wrong with using the state to enforce it. As we have seen, this was how perfectionists like Aristotle and Aquinas argued. At least this makes a certain sense, says Hart. (Though, as we know from our discussion of Mill, objectivists about morality are not *bound* to take the perfectionist view. They may, as Mill himself did, regard morality as having a rational foundation but nevertheless believe that there are reasons for the state not to enforce the whole of it.)

But Devlin, as we have seen, is not an objectivist about morality. He wishes to translate not *reasoned judgments* about morality into law but rather *gut feelings* of indignation, intolerance and disgust. And Hart argues that when we bear in mind 'all the misery which criminal punishment entails' (Hart, 1977, p 84), there is no justification for turning feelings of this kind into criminal law without subjecting them to 'critical scrutiny' (Hart, 1977, p 87). For the disgust may be based on ignorance, superstition or prejudice. After all, many women used to be burnt because the majority thought they were witches and many people used to be (and some still are) outraged by those who associate with those of a different race.

Hart also takes issue with Devlin's view that a shared morality is essential to society and with his related comparison between sexual immorality and treason, a comparison which Hart finds 'absurd' (Hart, 1977, p 86). Hart argues that offences against 'decency' do not threaten the very fabric of society. He says that there must

be a consensus of moral opinion on *certain* matters if society is no
into anarchy. Thus it would not be worth living in a society in whic'
agree that murder and theft are morally wrong. But morality/
seamless web and it is not the case, according to Hart, that *all* of *i*
beliefs are of equal importance to social stability – that deviating from ᵕ
moral code in *any* respect will lead to its disintegration. On the contrary, Hart says,
'we have ample evidence for believing that people … will not think any better of
murder, cruelty and dishonesty, merely because some private sexual practice which
they abominate is not punished by the law' (Hart, 1977, p 86).

6.6 Pornography

Having examined the theoretical considerations relevant to deciding whether
there should be a private sphere of freedom of action protected against state
invasion, we are now in a position to apply our reflections to some controversial
topical issues. Let us begin with the issue of pornography.

If we look at the law governing the availability of sexually explicit materials
(so-called 'obscene' materials) in a number of common law jurisdictions it is
possible to discern two main bases on which the law has traditionally sought to
prohibit their dissemination: either it relies on the idea of offence caused by
explicit depictions of sexuality to community standards of decency (the US and
Australian approach) or it relies on the tendency of the materials to deprave and
corrupt their users (the English approach). (I am here assuming that children are
neither exposed to the materials nor used in their production. Everyone will agree
that the making of child pornography should be a crime. It is adult pornography
which raises the more difficult issues.)

It will be obvious that neither of the legal aims I have mentioned would pass
Mill's test, since the materials are prohibited not on the grounds that an identifiable
individual's rights have been infringed. Rather, they are prohibited on the
moralistic grounds of their offensiveness to the community or of their tendency to
cause 'moral harm' to their users (a harm which does not, of course, fall under
Mill's definition of harm). The first is an aim that Devlin would endorse, the
second an aim that perfectionists would endorse. It seems to follow that if one
takes a liberal approach to these matters, insisting that harm in Mill's sense is
the only legitimate basis for criminalising conduct, the enjoyment of sexually
explicit materials should be regarded as a private matter, outside the legitimate
reach of the law.

But before we come to this conclusion we need to examine an important
contemporary argument made by certain feminists. This argument calls for the
suppression of certain sexually explicit materials not – so it is claimed – on the
traditional moralistic grounds just described, but rather on grounds which even
someone like Mill could apparently endorse.

The feminists in question distinguish erotica from pornography. They define
erotica as the explicit depiction of sex between equals and they take the view that

adults who wish to consume erotica should be free to do so. Pornography, by contrast, on their view, depicts sexual violence towards women or depicts women in a degrading or dehumanising way, as sexual objects. Pornography therefore *harms* women. It sends the message that women are inferior and encourages discriminatory and violent acts against them. It infringes women's rights to equality and non-discrimination and can therefore legitimately be suppressed.

It will be obvious that the feminist attack on pornography presents itself as very different from the conservative approach of thinkers like Devlin. It claims that its aim is not to prevent offence or 'moral harm'. After all, it is not – it claims – against the explicit depiction of sex as such. Its stated aim is rather to protect women's rights to equality and non-discrimination, which is a legitimate and non-moralistic concern. Hence the title of Catharine MacKinnon's article on this matter: 'Not a Moral Issue' (MacKinnon, 1987, p 146).

This view informed the Canadian case of *R v Butler* (1992) which upheld the constitutionality of the obscenity provisions of the Canadian Criminal Code in the face of a freedom of speech challenge. The majority – apparently endorsing Mill's approach – said that deviations from society's morals should not be punished if they cause no harm. If the obscenity provisions had aimed to prevent 'dirt for dirt's sake' (at 476) they would therefore have been invalid. But the majority found that this was not the case. On the contrary, the provisions were justified by the need to prevent harm to women and to protect women's right to equality, because sexually explicit materials which depict sex with violence, or which depict sex which is degrading and dehumanising, reinforce male–female stereotypes and make anti-social and unlawful acts against women more likely.

But is this reasoning really an accurate application of Mill's approach? Would someone who takes Mill's harm principle seriously really accept this argument? It would all depend on the facts. Violence and sexual inequality are major social problems, and if exposure to pornography makes violent and discriminatory acts against women probable, the harm principle would certainly require its suppression. On the other hand, some social scientists point out that in many countries where pornography is banned there is more violence and discrimination against women than in countries where it is openly available.

Furthermore, three national commissions which reported on the matter – the 1970 Report of the Commission on Obscenity and Pornography in the United States, the 1979 report of the Williams Commission in the United Kingdom, and the 1985 Special Committee Report on Pornography and Prostitution in Canada – found that there was no causal link between the consumption of pornography and criminal or anti-social acts. These commissions supported the view that the causes of violent personality lie in childhood, long before any exposure to pornography, and that the desire to consume violent pornography is a symptom of a violent personality rather than a cause of it.

Even the findings of the Ronald Reagan-appointed Meese Commission, which are regarded as supporting the feminist position on pornography, are, in truth, very weak. The Meese Commission found that sexually violent materials (but not degrading or dehumanising materials) raise the probability of sexually violent behaviour to some extent – an extent which may, however, be so small that sexual violence would still be unlikely even in the presence of exposure to the materials. The Commission further found that the evidence for even this weak claim was problematic and that it could not be relied on in circumstances where we require great confidence in our empirical findings (Schauer, 1987, p 753, 767).

But if the risk to women's rights created by even the most objectionable pornographic materials is as speculative as it seems to be, then it seems that the harm principle would not, after all, support their suppression and that the attempt to invoke it in this context may be misplaced. Of course, women's rights may be violated in the course of producing pornography. Women may, for example, be coerced or tricked into making pornography, or assaulted while making it, and the harm principle would certainly demand the criminalisation of such conduct. Furthermore, the harm principle arguably supports regulations which restrict access to pornography – for instance, by confining its sale to specialised sex shops – on the ground that people have a right not to have pornography thrust on their attention against their will. But Mill is clear that the harm principle is only applicable where there is *strong evidence* of a *real risk* to people's rights – that, as we have seen, is what makes his principle so robust – and it does not seem that even the worst kind of pornographic materials create such a danger. If so, the harm principle cannot be used to justify their outright prohibition.

Furthermore, it should also be noted that though some restrictions on access to pornography may be compatible with the harm principle, the principle would prevent these restrictions from being excessive. The harm principle is inconsistent, for instance, with the reasoning of the majority of the Supreme Court of the United States in *Paris Adult Theatre I v Slaton* (1973). This case involved the showing of obscene films by a cinema which refused admission to minors, gave due warning of the nature of the films and did not employ any offensive external advertising. Chief Justice Burger, who wrote the majority opinion, nevertheless held that the films could be banned, saying that the idea of a privacy right and a place of public accommodation were, in this context, mutually exclusive. In this connection, he quoted Professor Bickel's remark that 'what is commonly read and seen and heard and done intrudes upon us all, want it or not' (at 59). Chief Justice Burger then went on to describe as 'morally neutral' the view that the exhibition of obscene material in a public theatre jeopardises the majority's 'right to maintain a decent society' (at 69).

Mill would not agree. For Mill, the fact that conduct occurs *in a place of 'public accommodation'* would not automatically make it *public conduct*, in the sense of conduct with which the law may legitimately interfere. Likewise, the fact that the showing of obscene films 'intrudes' on people would not, in itself, convince Mill that the films should be banned. Virtually all activity 'intrudes', for 'no-one is an island', as Mill himself conceded. The question, for Mill, would be whether the intrusion violates a right in the sense of a distinct and assignable obligation owed to a definite individual or individuals. Given the fact that the films were inoffensively advertised, that minors were excluded, and that the audience was forewarned, it is hard to find any such violation. Certainly, Mill would not agree with Chief Justice Burger that there is any such thing as 'a *right* to maintain a decent society'.

6.7   Abortion

Abortion is another issue which can usefully be approached in the light of our discussion of the private–public distinction. Do anti-abortion laws represent an attempt to enforce the moral principles of the majority in matters of personal conduct – in which case a liberal would be bound to regard them as an illegitimate attempt to interfere with private choices – or can they be justified on harm-based grounds?

Much depends in answering this question on how we conceive of the moral status of the foetus. (I will use the word 'foetus' to refer to the unborn child from the beginning of pregnancy until its end.) What kind of creature is it from the moral point of view? Scientific evidence about conception does not help us to answer this question. We know that within approximately 24 hours after the sperm has penetrated the ovum the 46 chromosomes which go to make up a person's unique genetic identity are present. But what *moral* significance should we attach to the start of a new genetic identity? How should we *treat* it? Science cannot answer this question. It is a *philosophical* question and we therefore need to canvass different philosophical answers to it.

At one extreme is the view that the foetus is, from the moment of conception, morally speaking just like a baby: it has interests of its own from the moment of conception; it enjoys all the rights which a baby enjoys; and it is entitled to be treated in exactly the same way in which we treat babies.

If this view is correct, everyone – not only conservatives and perfectionists but also liberals – will agree that the state is entitled to prevent abortion. After all, if the foetus from the moment of conception has the same rights as a baby, destroying it would violate its right to life and be as serious as murder. There would therefore be a straightforward rights-based or harm-based justification for anti-abortion laws. Indeed, if this view is correct, it would follow that the state not only may but that it *must* prohibit abortion: the state would have a responsibility to forbid all abortions, just as it has a responsibility to forbid the murder of babies. Dworkin calls this a 'derivative' justification for anti-abortion laws because it is derived from rights and interests that it assumes foetuses have (Dworkin, 1993, p 11).

But not everyone agrees that the foetus has, from the moment of conception, the same moral status as a baby. At the other extreme from the derivative view is the view that the foetus has no moral status at all – that, at least in the early stages of pregnancy, it is just a bit of human tissue, comparable to something like the appendix, and that its destruction has no moral significance whatsoever.

There is also a view which is intermediate between the two extremes. The intermediate view rejects the idea that the destruction of a foetus raises no moral issues at all but it also rejects the idea that the foetus has the same moral status as a baby. The basis of this intermediate view is the idea of 'intrinsic value'.

Those who hold this view see the foetus as a living human organism which has 'sacred' or intrinsic value from the moment of its conception, meaning by this that its destruction is always an intrinsically bad thing. (They see the foetus, Dworkin explains, in somewhat the same way that we see art works, or species diversity – as having value in themselves. If a species disappears we see that as objectively bad – bad because the world has been diminished, not because humans suffer as a result.) At the same time, those who hold this view believe that the foetus acquires rights and interests only late in pregnancy – at about the time of viability – and until that point is reached, abortion is not the destruction of something which enjoys the right to life.

Dworkin calls this a 'detached' argument against abortion because it is detached from the view that a foetus has rights and interests (Dworkin, 1993, p 11). It takes the view that human life has intrinsic moral significance and that abortion is therefore always, in itself, a waste of something valuable, but it does not equate abortion with murder. Unlike the derivative view it is therefore not committed to the view that abortion is *absolutely* morally impermissible. On the contrary, it opens the door to balancing the value of foetal life against other considerations – considerations which may serve to *outweigh* the badness of abortion in certain circumstances. If such circumstances obtain, abortion will not be *overall* or *all-things-considered* wrong; it will be the lesser of two evils and therefore morally justifiable.

Which of these views is right? Dworkin argues that the detached view is more plausible than the derivative view. He reasons as follows. First, he argues that although many people espouse the derivative view, they do so only as a matter of rhetoric, and virtually everyone, in reality, holds the detached view. He points out that most of those who claim to hold the derivative view believe that abortion is morally permissible in certain circumstances. They are likely to believe, for instance, that abortion is permissible to save the mother's life, or to terminate a pregnancy which is the result of rape, or even in cases of severe foetal abnormality. But reasons of this kind would never justify the killing of a baby. The same people would undoubtedly regard it as murder if a doctor were to kill a new-born baby in order to save its mother's life. And they would say the same about the killing of a baby which was conceived as the result of a rape, or of a severely disabled baby. A baby does not forfeit its rights because its mother was raped or because it is severely disabled.

The fact, therefore, that most of those who claim that a foetus has the same moral status as a baby are nevertheless willing to countenance abortion for reasons that would never justify the killing of a baby shows that they do not *really* believe that the foetus has the same moral status as a baby. Dworkin gives the example of President Bush and Vice-President Quayle – both avowed 'pro-lifers' – who in the 1992 presidential campaign said they would support their own daughters if they wished to have an abortion. As Dworkin points out, they would surely not do that if they really thought that abortion meant the murder of their grandchildren (Dworkin, 1993, p 20). The real reason why they are against abortion, according to Dworkin, is because they hold the detached view: they are against abortion because it is a waste of human life.

Dworkin's reasoning also reveals the flaws in the frequently made argument that, though the foetus has a right to life, this right is outweighed by the mother's rights to sexual and reproductive autonomy. If it were *really* true that the foetus has a right to life, it would be *impossible* for that right to be outweighed by the mother's rights: in any competition of rights between mother and foetus, the foetus would have to win. After all, important as women's rights are, we do not think them capable of justifying the killing of a baby; and if a foetus really has the same moral status as a baby, then women's rights could not justify the killing of a foetus. Those who think that women's rights justify abortion therefore *cannot* believe that the foetus has a right to life; and if women *do* have a right to abortion, it cannot be true that the foetus has a right to life.

Having argued that most people do not believe in foetal rights, Dworkin goes on to argue that they are correct. He argues that it is incoherent to ascribe to an early foetus an interest in not being destroyed (and therefore a right not to be destroyed) because something has interests of its own only when it has some form of mental life – when it can suffer pain and have experiences. Since scientists have shown that the neurological developments which make mental life possible take place only late in pregnancy, abortions in the first two trimesters of pregnancy are not against the interests of the foetuses whose lives they take away. Dworkin concludes that the derivative objection to such abortions does not make sense: it is not possible to object to abortion in the first two trimesters on the basis of the value of its life *to* a foetus, but only on the detached basis that there is intrinsic value in human life.

Dworkin's view of the debate about abortion implies that the opposing camps are not as far apart from each other as they think. According to Dworkin, most pro-lifers do not really believe that abortion is murder and most pro-choicers do not think that the destruction of a foetus is a trivial matter. Most members of both camps agree that human life has inherent value. Where, then, do they differ? They differ, according to Dworkin, only in how they understand the intrinsic worth of human life and therefore in their views as to what justifies its destruction: their disagreement comes down to a disagreement about when and why abortion amounts to a wrongful failure to respect human life.

Some people value human life primarily because of the biological marvel that it represents, whether they trace this to evolution or God. Others put the emphasis on the way in which human beings consciously confer value on themselves. They emphasise the creative investment humans make in their lives. Those who assign greater importance to the human investment in life will in most circumstances find the destruction of a foetus less of an evil than the frustration of a woman's attempt to determine her own fate. They are the pro-choicers. By contrast, those who emphasise nature's investment believe that the best way to respect the value of human life is to allow abortion only in the most exceptional of circumstances. They are the pro-lifers. They believe that there are very few circumstances in which abortion is morally justifiable. Their disagreement is therefore about the correct balance to be assigned to the biological and the human in the value we place on human life.

If this is the nature of their *moral* disagreement, what attitude should the *law* take to the matter? May the state justifiably prohibit abortions before viability if Dworkin is correct that early foetal life has no personal value to the foetus and that the only justification for such laws is therefore to protect the intrinsic value of foetal life? Are such laws compatible with the kind of robust respect for an area of 'sovereignty over personal decisions' (Dworkin, 1993, p 53) which we find in liberal thinkers like Mill? Dworkin puts the question like this: '[s]hould any state... have [the] power, as a matter of justice and decent government' to 'decide for everyone that abortion insults the intrinsic value of human life and to prohibit it on that ground?' (Dworkin, 1993, p 154).

Dworkin's answer is that no state should have that power. As we have seen, people are deeply divided about the circumstances in which abortion is a wrongful failure to respect human life. Furthermore, Dworkin claims that convictions of this kind – about how and why human life has importance and how best to respect its inherent value – are fundamental to our moral personalities, 'touching the ultimate purpose and value of human life itself' (Dworkin, 1993, p 158). Indeed, Dworkin argues that our disagreements on this matter are so fundamental that they are akin to religious disagreements. Most people will agree that the state should not impose a preferred religious view. Dworkin thinks it is just as unacceptable to force people to conform to the majority's controversial understanding of what respect for the intrinsic value of human life requires. Just as we have the right to confront religious questions for ourselves, decisions about abortion in the initial stages of pregnancy should be seen as a matter of a woman's private choice rather than be made the subject of majoritarian determinations.

In the US case of *Roe v Wade* (1973), Justice Rehnquist said that abortion cannot be a private matter because it involves an operation by a physician (at 172). It will be clear that he misses the liberal point, just as Chief Justice Burger did in *Paris Adult Theatre I.* When liberals call a decision 'private', they mean that it is a decision which individuals are entitled to make for themselves; the fact that they may need the assistance of others in implementing their choices does not make it any the less private.

Dworkin thinks that even early abortion is often an ethical mistake (Dworkin, 1996, p 36). He believes, nevertheless, that the state is not entitled to prevent *even morally impermissible abortions* because no-one's rights are at stake in the initial stages of pregnancy – only a detached value is under threat – and so a pregnant woman has the right to make her own moral decisions in this area of life.

In a passage which is strongly reminiscent of Mill, Dworkin describes a pregnant woman's right to freedom of choice in the following terms: '[o]thers... may disapprove, and they might be right, morally, to do so... But the state in the end must let her decide for herself; it must not impose other people's moral convictions upon her' (Dworkin, 1993, pp 33–4). Seen in this light, the law ought to make abortion in the initial stages of pregnancy available on demand, as a matter of a woman's *rights*. And a law such as the Abortion Act 1967 (UK), which makes access to abortion contingent on the opinion of two doctors that certain specified grounds for an abortion exist, clearly falls short of this requirement.

6.8   Euthanasia

We have discussed the question whether there are any moral limits on the state's authority to prohibit killing at the one end of life – life in the womb. Now we turn to the question whether there are any moral limits on its authority at the other end of life – when people are terminally ill or in an irreversible coma or incurably demented.

In discussing the issues raised by euthanasia, a distinction is commonly made between voluntary and non-voluntary euthanasia. Voluntary euthanasia is euthanasia which is carried out at the request of an adult person of sound mind who wishes to die. Non-voluntary euthanasia is performed on someone who is not capable of understanding the choice between life and death. Such a person might, for instance, be permanently comatose and they might not have expressed a preference before they became comatose about what they would like to happen to them in such circumstances.

Non-voluntary euthanasia raises issues which are not relevant to this chapter. We are concerned in this chapter only with delineating the area in which adults should be free to make their own choices and its focus will therefore be on voluntary euthanasia – the extent to which the law should respect the wish to die. Do we have the right to make decisions about death for ourselves? If so, what sort of assistance in dying should we be able to request? Should we be allowed to refuse life-prolonging treatment? Should doctors be permitted to kill us at our request?

We need to begin with a distinction between passive euthanasia and active euthanasia. Passive euthanasia involves letting someone die by intentionally failing to treat them in a way that would prolong their life. For instance, if a doctor accedes to a terminally ill person's request not to be put on a respirator, as a result of which they die from respiratory failure, that would be passive voluntary euthanasia. By contrast, if the same person were to request that the doctor give them a lethal injection, that would be a request for active euthanasia. The doctor would *actively* be the cause of death, whereas in the respirator case the doctor merely *omits* to keep the patient alive. In the respirator case, it is 'nature' or the person's disease which is the cause of death.

Under English law, adults who are in full command of their mental capacities have the right in principle to refuse life-sustaining treatment. But they cannot ask to be actively killed and anyone who acquiesced in such a request would be held criminally liable. Nor can they ask their doctor for a prescription for lethal drugs, because assisting a suicide is also a crime in terms of s 2 of the Suicide Act 1961 (UK). The interesting question for the purposes of this chapter is whether the law on this matter sufficiently respects the personal autonomy of those who wish to die.

Let us begin with the refusal of life-sustaining treatment. Liberal views would support the right to refuse medical treatment because withholding one's consent to medical treatment is an obvious example of harmless or self-regarding conduct in Mill's sense of the term. It may be morally wrong to want to die, as Kant, for instance, thought, but refusing treatment violates no-one's rights. On a liberal view the state is therefore not entitled to force us to accept medical treatment. The majority may believe that it is wrong to choose a premature death, but to use the law to enforce a moral principle of this kind – one which does not seek to prevent harm – would be to intrude impermissibly into an area of private choice.

The fact that the law allows us to refuse medical treatment even though we will die without it therefore demonstrates a clear endorsement of the liberal line of reasoning we find in thinkers like Mill: personal autonomy trumps official views about the sanctity of life. But the very same line of reasoning seems to argue in favour of legal acceptance of assisted suicide and active voluntary euthanasia. After all, if people are prevented from being assisted to die in these ways, the damage done them is as serious as treating them against their wishes. Furthermore, like refusing life-prolonging treatment, assisted suicide and active voluntary euthanasia seem to violate no-one's rights, and it therefore appears that they can be forbidden only on the illiberal or moralistic basis that they are an insult to the intrinsic importance of human life.

Dworkin argues along these lines, lines which parallel his reasoning in the abortion context. He points out that when the state seeks to prolong human life against the contrary wishes of those who wish to die, the aim is not to protect anyone's rights or interests. The aim is 'detached' (Dworkin, 1993, p 198). It is to protect the intrinsic worth of human life according to the majority's understanding of that value. Dworkin also points out that many people do not share the majority's understanding. They believe that choosing premature death, whether by way of assistance in suicide or voluntary euthanasia, is *not* an insult to the value of life. They believe, in fact, that respect for the intrinsic value of human life speaks in *favour* of allowing people to choose to die. They think that 'the character of [their] whole life would be compromised' (Dworkin, 1993, p 228) if they were not able to hasten their death in certain circumstances, should they so choose.

On this argument, when the law is used to forbid us from making our own decisions as to when and how we die, the majority relies on deeply contested assumptions about how best to respect the intrinsic value of human life. When taken in combination with the fact that the making of such choices violates no-one's rights, Dworkin concludes that the majority does not have the right to impose its judgment on such 'spiritual' or life-defining matters. He says: '[m]aking someone die in a way that others approve, but he believes a horrifying contradiction of his life, is a devastating, odious form of tyranny' (Dworkin, 1993, p 217). It follows from this line of reasoning that the law on end-of-life decisions is incoherent – liberal in so far as it allows us to refuse life-prolonging treatment but illiberal when it comes to active euthanasia and assisted suicide.

One possible response to this criticism is to argue that legalising active euthanasia and assisted suicide would *not*, in fact, be harmless. Legalising such conduct, it is often said, would present a serious risk of harm because it might lead to vulnerable people being killed against their wishes. Ill people who feel themselves a burden on their relatives might ask to be killed, or might be pressurised into making such a request, or might make such a choice when they are in a depressed state of mind. For these and similar reasons – so the argument continues – the law's prohibition of active voluntary euthanasia and assisted suicide does *not* represent an illegitimate intrusion into the realm of private choice and is perfectly justifiable on *liberal* grounds: the state has a legitimate, harm-based interest in preventing people's lives being ended against their wishes and the legalisation of active euthanasia would create a risk of such unjustified killings.

How would liberals respond to this argument? I think they would take very seriously the risks which legalising active euthanasia and assisted suicide poses but they would not agree that total prohibition is the best way to avoid these risks. They would argue that we can protect vulnerable people against abuse while still accommodating the right to die. Liberals are likely to point out that there are analogous risks in allowing people to refuse treatment. Patients may, for instance, become depressed and ask for their life-sustaining machinery to be switched off or be pressurised by others into asking for it to be withdrawn. But the law does not treat *these* risks as a reason to force people to accept medical treatment against their wishes. It deals with the problem by building safeguards into the system: it makes sure that refusals of treatment are fully voluntary, fully informed and made by people in full command of their mental faculties.

Liberals will point out that a similar approach could be taken to active euthanasia and assisted suicide. In this way, the risk of harm could be averted without undue intrusion on private choices. Since the risks do not speak in favour of total prohibition, the law's prohibitory attitude can therefore be explained only on the basis that its real objection to active euthanasia and assisted suicide is that they are immoral – an objection which liberals will argue is not legitimately translatable into law. They will say that we have a right to personal autonomy in such matters which the law has failed to respect.

Chapter 7

Justice

In this chapter we are concerned with issues of social and economic justice. A striking feature of our society is its vast disparities in wealth, power and status. Are these disparities just? What moral principles should we use as the basis for our choice of legal institutions and arrangements to deal with social and economic inequality? Is it a legitimate goal of government to reduce poverty, using measures like progressive income and wealth taxes to redistribute resources from the wealthier to the poorer members of society? Or is it the case that there is a right to economic freedom which trumps all social goals, including the creation of a more just society, in which case any interference with economic freedom to reduce poverty would be difficult to justify or might not even be justifiable at all?

We will examine three important contemporary answers to these questions: utilitarianism; John Rawls's contractarian theory as expounded in *A Theory of Justice* and *Political Liberalism*; and Robert Nozick's 'minimal state' theory contained in his book, *Anarchy, State and Utopia*.

You should be familiar with the following areas:

- The utilitarian approach to social and economic justice
- Rawls's two principles of justice and his contractarian argument for them
- Rawls's theory of political liberalism
- Nozick's theory of justice as entitlements

7.1   Utilitarianism

We have already encountered utilitarianism in 5.3. It is the theory that we should always act in such a way as to bring about the greatest net balance of human welfare. In so far as questions of economic justice are concerned, utilitarians therefore believe that goods and resources should be distributed in whatever way conduces to maximum welfare. This may require the reduction of poverty, depending on the factual circumstances. On the other hand, it may require vast social and economic inequality. If inequalities do increase the net balance of human welfare, then they cannot be said to be unjust or unfair, for there is, according to utilitarians, no *independent* measure of justice in the distribution of goods and resources: the just distribution is merely whatever distribution happens to achieve the greatest total welfare. As JJC Smart explains:

> [t]he concept of justice as a fundamental ethical concept is really quite foreign to utilitarianism... [A utilitarian] is concerned with the maximization of happiness and not with the distribution of it... [I]t does not matter in what way happiness is distributed among different persons, provided that the total amount of happiness is maximized.
>
> (Smart, 1978, p 104)

Thus utilitarians offered a choice between the following two societies would pick society II:

Society I

Individuals	Units of welfare
A	10
B	10
C	10
D	10

Society II

Individuals	Units of welfare
A	1
B	1
C	1
D	100

In Society I, welfare is distributed equally and the total amount of welfare is 40 units. In Society II, welfare is distributed very unequally but the total amount is much larger – 103 units. Utilitarians would therefore be bound to say that Society II is more just than Society I, despite the fact that the gains in welfare to D which make Society II desirable from the perspective of maximum happiness are bought at the cost of the suffering of A, B and C. For the way in which the gains and costs are distributed is irrelevant from the utilitarian point of view.

Rawls objects to this conception of justice on the Kantian grounds that, in treating A, B and C as mere pawns whose interests can be sacrificed in order to achieve maximum happiness, it ignores their 'separateness' as persons. Rawls takes issue with a passage from Smart in which he says:

> if it is rational for me to choose the pain of a visit to the dentist in order to prevent the pain of toothache, why is it not rational of me to choose a pain for Jones, similar to that of my visit to the dentist, if that is the only way in which I can prevent a pain, equal to that of my toothache, for Robinson?
>
> (Smart, 1961, p 26)

Building on Kant's views about human dignity and the need to respect persons as ends in themselves (see 5.4), Rawls argues that this is *not* rational – that it is wrong to extend a form of decision-making which is rational for individuals to society as a whole. We do not think it matters how one person distributes their satisfactions over time. That is why we regard it as rational to put up with the pain of the dentist today in order to benefit from healthy teeth in later life. But Smart's analogy treats the differences between different *persons* as of no more moral significance than the differences between different *times* within *one* person's life. The effect is to treat the desires and interests of different people as if they were the desires and interests of a 'mass person' whose overall good can be maximised by sacrifices of some of its constituent parts.

Though Nozick and Rawls have very little else in common, Nozick agrees with Rawls on this point. He says: 'there is no social entity with a good that undergoes that sacrifice for its own good' (Nozick, 1974, pp 32–3). For Rawls and Nozick, individuals are of intrinsic importance – they are of importance *in their own right*, not merely as interchangeable vessels for happiness – and their interests therefore cannot be sacrificed without limit. As we will see, their rejection of utilitarianism is central to both theorists' conceptions of justice.

7.2 Rawls's principles of justice

In his classic work, *A Theory of Justice*, Rawls argues for two principles of justice to govern the basic structure of society, the basic structure being 'the way in which the major social institutions distribute fundamental rights and duties and determine the division of advantages from social cooperation' (Rawls, 1971, p 7). The first principle concerns rights and liberties, while the second concerns income, wealth and power.

The first principle states that '[e]ach person is to have an equal right to the most extensive total system of equal basic liberties, compatible with a similar system of liberty for all' (Rawls, 1971, p 302). The second principle states that '[s]ocial and economic inequalities are to be arranged so that they are both: (a) to the greatest benefit of the least advantaged, consistent with the just savings principle, and (b) attached to offices and positions open to all under conditions of fair equality of opportunity' (Rawls, 1971, p 302). (The 'just savings principle' is the principle that resources must be left for future generations and 'fair equality of opportunity' means that there must be equal opportunities of education for all, to the extent that this is achievable given the ongoing existence of the family as a social institution.)

It is clear from the first principle that Rawls believes that a just society will respect rights as moral constraints on what government may do to individuals. Rawls puts this by saying that the 'right' is prior to the 'good'. He believes that in a just society the right will take priority over the good in two ways. First, in any competition between rights and the claims of the *general good*, rights will be more important. (This view of the function of rights as constraints on utilitarian reasoning will be familiar from 5.3.) Second, in a just society, rights will not be sacrificed for *perfectionist values* or values derived from the belief that a particular way of life is intrinsically superior or inferior to other ways of life. (The notion of perfectionism will be recalled from 6.4.)

Rawls does not exactly specify the content of the rights or 'basic liberties' which are protected by his first principle, though he does say that they include political liberty (the right to vote and to be eligible for public office); freedom of speech and assembly; liberty of conscience and freedom of thought; freedom of the person; the right to hold personal property; and freedom from arbitrary arrest and seizure as defined by the concept of the rule of law (Rawls, 1971, p 61). Rawls says that the principles of justice are compatible with both private and state ownership of the means of production (Rawls, 1971, pp 273–4), thereby making quite clear that the right to own the means of production is not a basic liberty and is therefore not protected by the first principle.

The most important part of the second principle for our purposes is the principle that social and economic inequalities are just only if they improve the situation of the least advantaged members of society. Rawls calls this the 'difference principle'. In order to understand the implications of the difference principle, let us suppose we are asked which of three societies is most just. The three societies distribute economic resources between the same four individuals (who are average representatives of the different classes in the three societies) in different ways. (By contrast with utilitarians, Rawls believes that distributive justice is concerned with the *resources* to which individuals have access, not the *welfare* or *satisfaction* derived from their use of resources.) The three societies are as follows:

Society 1

Individuals	Resources
A	10
B	10
C	10
D	10

Society II

Individuals	Resources
A	20
B	30
C	40
D	50

Society III

Individuals	Resources
A	1
B	1,000
C	2,000
D	3,000

Someone who believes that justice requires strict equality would choose Society I because everybody gets the same. A utilitarian, who believes that justice is synonymous with maximising happiness, would choose Society III because Society III offers the greatest average and total happiness (on the assumption that resources translate into happiness). Rawls, who believes that a just society must satisfy the Difference Principle, would think Society II is most just, because A, who is the representative of the worst off class in society, does best in Society II. The inequalities in Society II make *everyone* better off than they would be in a society of pure equality. By contrast, the inequalities in Society III are not to the advantage of the worst off members of society. The difference principle is therefore a strongly egalitarian principle, requiring redistribution from the advantaged to the disadvantaged until the point is reached at which any further equalisation would harm the prospects of even the worst off class. It reduces social inequality to the greatest extent possible.

How might inequalities make everyone better off? Rawls explains that this would be so if incentives are needed to encourage people of ability to develop their talents and exert themselves in socially valuable ways. Thus he says:

> the greater expectations allowed to entrepreneurs encourages them to do things which raise the long-term prospects of laboring class. Their better prospects act as incentives so that the economic process is more efficient, innovation proceeds at a better pace, and so on. Eventually the resulting material benefits spread throughout the system and to the least advantaged.
>
> (Rawls, 1971, p 78)

Rawls does not express any opinion as to whether these empirical claims are true. He says merely: '[t]he point is that something of this kind must be argued if these inequalities are to be just by the difference principle' (Rawls, 1971, p 78).

Notice that it does not seem likely that the inequalities which we find in *our* society are to the advantage of the worst off individuals and could therefore be justified in terms of Rawlsian principles. As David Lyons points out, in our society:

> [t]he occupants of some social positions receive enormous shares of primary goods without performing any useful social functions at all. And, while some of the special benefits enjoyed by those in the highly paid professions, such as law and medicine, may be needed to attract competent individuals to those jobs, it is arguable that the benefits actually received exceed the level required to ensure that those tasks are performed well. Such inequalities as these that flow from basic institutions could not be justified under the difference principle. Our system also seems to require that there be a permanent pool of unemployed as well as low-paid laborers, and individuals within these groups may well be worse off than they would be under egalitarian arrangements. That too would violate the difference principle.
>
> (Lyons, 1984, p 134)

7.3   The veil of ignorance

We now know what a just society would look like, according to Rawls: it would respect our basic rights and liberties and it would allow only those inequalities which benefit the worst off individuals. But why does he think this? What are his arguments? At the heart of *A Theory of Justice* is a simple idea, namely, that justice is a matter of what people would choose if they did not know facts about their own particular situation which would bias them to make a choice in their own interests. If a child is given a cake and told to share it fairly with her sister and she wants to know what is fair, we might answer: cut it on the assumption that you could end up with either piece.

Rawls argues that if we want to arrive at principles of justice to govern the basic structure of society we should reason similarly. We should ask ourselves what principles people would agree to if they were placed in an imaginary situation which Rawls calls the 'original position'. In this position they are behind a 'veil of ignorance'. They are, for instance, ignorant of such features of themselves as their social class and their natural talents and abilities. They do not know whether their family circumstances are privileged or impoverished. They do not know how intelligent, or strong, or talented they are. Nor do they know the probability of finding themselves in any particular social position. Furthermore, though they know that they have a conception of the good life – they know, for instance, that they have views about religion, politics and philosophy – they do not know what actual beliefs they hold and they therefore do not know what their particular conception of the good life is. They may be atheists or fundamentalist Christians. They may be ascetic in their tastes or consumerist.

They are therefore required to choose principles to govern their own future life-prospects, and the rights and liberties they will enjoy, knowing nothing about what distinguishes them in real life from other individuals. They must make a choice which will be of most advantage to themselves, but they do not know what social position they will occupy, or what natural abilities they will have, or what conception of the good they will hold. Their choice will therefore not be influenced by their *particular* situation and their *personal* conception of the good life. They will have no reason to make a choice which is biased in favour of a particular social position because they will not know whether such a choice will benefit them.

Of course, in order to make such a choice, they must have *some* information and they must know *something* about what matters to them. Rawls says the choice must be made on the assumption that they are concerned only to advance their own interests and therefore that they wish neither harm nor good to others. Furthermore, they know 'the general facts about human society' (Rawls, 1971, p 137). They understand, for instance, political affairs and the principles of economic theory. They also know that they want what Rawls calls the primary goods. Primary goods include goods such as rights and liberties, powers and opportunities, income and wealth, and a sense of one's worth (Rawls, 1971, p 62). According to Rawls, these are things that everyone wants, because whatever our goals and ambitions may happen to be, we are more likely to achieve them if we enjoy more of the primary goods rather than less. Since a just society is a stable society, the people in the original position also know that they must make a choice which they would be prepared to honour in real life, not one which they would immediately want to renege on when it comes to be implemented. Rawls calls this last condition the 'strains of commitment': the parties cannot enter into agreements that may have consequences they cannot accept. Thus 'they must weigh with care whether they will be able to stick by their commitment in all circumstances' (Rawls, 1971, p 176).

Rawls thinks that if individuals were to be placed in the original position and asked to choose principles of justice to govern their society they would choose the principles set out in 7.2. First, if they know nothing about their conception of the good, they will choose a society which does not take sides on what kind of life it is worthwhile to lead but leaves its citizens maximally free to pursue their own goals, provided they do not interfere with the similar freedom of others. People would not choose a society in which, say, socialists are not tolerated, because when the veil is removed they might find that they themselves embrace socialism. Hence they will choose a society which respects the basic liberties.

Second, if they know nothing about their natural talents and social position, nor the probability of finding themselves in a particular social position, Rawls thinks that they will choose the Difference Principle to govern the distribution of wealth in their society. It is worth examining in a little more detail the reasoning which leads, according to Rawls, to the choice of the Difference Principle. Let us return to the three societies described in 7.2. According to Rawls, individuals behind the veil of ignorance, not knowing whether they will be A, B, C or D, nor the probability of finding themselves in these social positions, would choose to 'maximin', that is, to maximise what they will receive should they land up in the minimum (worst off) position, namely that of A. They will therefore choose Society II.

They will not choose Society I, the society of pure equality, because everyone is worse off in that society than in Society II. And they will not make the utilitarian choice of Society III because Rawls thinks that behind the veil of ignorance no-one would choose to risk lower prospects of life for themselves in order to make it possible for others to be better off. This is because it would be irrational to gamble with something so important as one's life-prospects, forgoing the guarantee of a satisfactory minimum and taking the chance of an intolerable outcome in the hope of finding oneself in one of the better off classes. There are also the strains of commitment to be taken into account – the fact that the parties must make a choice they could live with in real life, whatever position they subsequently find themselves in. Since the choice of Society III would be very difficult to live with should they turn out to be A, it is not a choice the parties would make.

For all these reasons, according to Rawls, parties behind the veil of ignorance would not choose Society III. They would not take the view that A's sacrifice in Society III is compensated for by the greater sum of benefits enjoyed by B, C and D. Instead, they would allow inequalities only if they make *everyone* better off than they would be in a society of pure equality. They would, in other words, choose the Difference Principle. In effect, as Rawls explains, the parties in the original position would agree 'to regard the distribution of talents as a common asset and to share in the benefits of this distribution whatever it turns out to be' (Rawls, 1971, p 101).

The last point to note in so far as the choice of principles is concerned is that Rawls argues that the parties in the original position would want the first principle to take priority over the second, except in societies where economic development is at a very low level. By 'taking priority' he means that they would not sacrifice their basic rights and liberties for an increase in income, wealth or power. They would, in other words, permit no exchanges between basic liberties and social and economic gains (Rawls, 1971, p 63). This is because they know that they are most likely to be able to pursue their personal goals and ambitions in a society which respects their basic liberties. Thus they would not accept an authoritarian society, even if everyone would be economically better off in such a society than in a free society.

7.4 Contractarianism

Rawls's approach to matters of justice is 'contractarian'. The contractarian tradition in political philosophy seeks to derive the legitimacy of government from the consent or voluntary agreement of the governed. There is, however, an important difference between the early social contract theories of the seventeenth and eighteenth centuries, like those of Hobbes, Locke and Rousseau, and Rawls's theory.

The early contract theorists tended to treat the contract as an actual contract, whereby individuals in a pre-political 'state of nature' negotiated the terms of their obedience to the state. This supposition is open to the obvious objection that no such state of nature has ever existed or actual contract ever taken place. But Rawls's contract is not undermined by this criticism because his contract is not actual.

Rawls argues that certain principles are principles of justice not because anyone has actually chosen them but because they *would* be chosen by rational individuals concerned to advance their own interests if they were forced to deliberate impartially and without personal bias in a situation in which differences in bargaining power have been negated. It is the *fairness of the conditions under which the principles would be chosen* which, according to Rawls, guarantees their justice. For this reason he calls his conception of justice 'justice as fairness'. Hence Rawls's is a hypothetical contract whose role is merely to *model* or *make vivid* a situation of impartial deliberation that is fair to all the parties and neutralises or filters out the influence of personal bias. Criticisms to the effect that such a contract is 'fantastic', or that people are not like this in 'real life', or that we care about other people as well as ourselves therefore miss the point. The point of the contract is merely to get us to think about justice from a genuinely impartial perspective which is not biased by our own interests.

Of course, this puts the onus on Rawls to explain *why* the veil of ignorance is fair to all the parties. Why should anyone who wishes to occupy the standpoint of justice put themselves behind the veil of ignorance? Rawls justifies putting the parties behind the veil of ignorance in the following way. He points out that children born to wealthier parents have access to better education and greater resources, both of which give them a head-start in the competition for society's rewards. Likewise, those who have talents and skills which are in social demand have better life-prospects than those who do not have such skills and talents. But, Rawls argues, no-one *deserves* to be born to wealthy parents or deserves their greater natural abilities, any more than anyone deserves to be born to poor parents or to be born disabled. One's social position and natural abilities are a mere matter of *luck*. These characteristics are, as Rawls puts it, 'morally arbitrary'. Hence if we want to deliberate impartially about principles of justice we should do so in ignorance of our social position and natural talents, so that we are not tempted to make a choice tailored to our interests as someone holding a particular, undeserved ticket in the natural and social lottery of life.

Notice that although the Difference Principle allows the socially and naturally advantaged to profit from their good luck – at least in circumstances in which incentives are required to encourage people of ability to develop their talents and exert themselves in socially useful ways – those who are advantaged profit only on terms that benefit everyone. They are therefore not being rewarded on the basis that their talent and hard work give them a *right* to be rewarded, which would, according to Rawls, be unfair. Instead, they are being rewarded only in order to improve the situation of the least advantaged.

In so far as the parties are ignorant of their particular conceptions of the good, once again Rawls argues that this is required if they are to deliberate impartially. He says they should choose principles of justice in ignorance of their conceptions of the good so as to prevent the influence of 'arbitrary contingencies' (Rawls, 1971, p 141). If the people in the original position knew their conception of the good, they would be tempted to 'win for themselves a greater liberty or larger distributive shares on the grounds that their activities are of more intrinsic value' (Rawls, 1971, p 329).

7.5   Are the conditions of the original position fair?

In evaluating Rawls's argument, one matter to consider is whether the conditions of the original position *are* the appropriate conditions under which to choose principles of justice. Accepting that the choice of principles of justice must be impartial and not geared to the self-interest of any particular group in society, is it necessary to ignore *all* the differences between individuals if we wish to make such an impartial choice? As we have seen, Rawls uses the veil of ignorance as a way of supposedly ensuring that no-one is advantaged or disadvantaged in the choice of principles by factors which are arbitrary from the moral point of view. But are the factors which he regards as morally arbitrary *really* morally arbitrary? And what about the motivation of the parties in the original position? Must individuals really have the motivations Rawls ascribes to them if they are to make an impartial choice of principles of justice?

Consider, for instance, the fact that the parties in the original position know that they want more rather than less of the primary goods. According to Rawls, this element of the original position is fair because, whatever else individuals may want in life, everyone wants the primary goods. But critics of Rawls have objected to this assumption. Jonathan Wolff describes the criticism like this:

> it has been said that these goods are not neutral. These goods are particularly suitable for life in modern capitalist economies, built on profit, wages, and exchange. Yet surely there could be non-commercial, more communal forms of existence, and hence conceptions of the good in which wealth and income – even liberty and opportunity – have lesser roles to play. So, runs the criticism, Rawls's original position is biased in favour of a commercial, individualist, organization of society, ignoring the importance that non-commercial, communal goods could have in people's lives.
>
> (Wolff, 1996, p 188)

Consider, also, Rawls's claim that if we are to reason impartially about justice we should imagine we do not know our natural talents and our family circumstances. This leads the parties in the original position, as we have seen, to regard any inequality as unfair unless everyone can be shown to benefit from it. In effect, the veil of ignorance leads them to treat natural and social advantages as collective assets which are available to be exploited for the good of everyone. Rawls believes that this aspect of the veil of ignorance is justified because social and natural advantages are arbitrary from the moral point of view. But is this line of reasoning cogent?

Nozick argues that it is not. He concedes that our natural talents are arbitrary from the moral point of view and that we therefore do not *deserve* them. But this does not mean, he says, that we do not have the *right to benefit* from our use of them and that we should therefore be kept ignorant of them when asked to choose principles to govern the distribution of wealth – an ignorance which, as we have seen, makes it rational for the more talented to refrain from demanding larger shares. He writes:

> [i]t is not true, for example, that a person earns Y (a right to keep a painting he's made, [for instance]...) only if he's earned (or otherwise *deserves*) whatever he used (including natural assets) in the process of earning Y. Some of the things he uses he just may *have*, not illegitimately. It needn't be that the foundations underlying desert are themselves deserved, *all the way down*.
> (Nozick, 1974, p 225, Nozick's emphasis)

Nozick gives the analogy of a group of students who have taken an examination but not yet received their grades. If the students had to decide unanimously on a particular distribution of grades not knowing what grade they have actually received, no doubt they would agree that each person should receive the same grade. But this is absurd, says Nozick, because it ignores the fact that grades do not fall out of the sky. Those who have earned a high grade have a *right* to the grade, even if they do not deserve the intelligence which is part of the reason why they were able to earn it.

The same applies to wealth, according to Nozick. Rawls deprives the contractors of knowledge of their natural advantages, leading them to treat wealth as 'falling from heaven like manna' (Nozick, 1974, p 198), and therefore available to be divided up in a way which benefits everyone. But wealth, according to Nozick, is not a social pie which comes into the world unencumbered by prior claims. Wealth comes into the world already *belonging* to particular individuals by virtue of the fact that they created it using their natural talents. And it is therefore as unfair to expect individuals to choose principles for the distribution of wealth in ignorance of their talents as to ask students to agree on a distribution of grades in ignorance of the grades they have received and to which they are entitled.

7.6 Would Rawls's principles be chosen in the original position?

Let us now pursue a different line of criticism and assume, for the sake of argument, that the original position *is* a fair position from which to make choices about the basic structure of society, and ask whether Rawls is right that his principles *would* be chosen in the original position as the basis for distributing the benefits and burdens of social co-operation.

Arguably, the first principle is more likely to be chosen than the second. We know that behind the veil of ignorance the contractors do not know their particular conception of the good life. If they do not know their conception of the good life, it is plausible to suppose that they will choose a society which tolerates maximum freedom of choice. They are hardly likely to choose a society which, for instance, persecutes certain religious minorities if they do not know whether they will be a member of one of these minorities. They are much more likely to choose a neutral state which does not attempt to force a particular religion or any other conception of the good life on its citizens (see 6.3).

But would it be rational to choose the Difference Principle in the original position? After all, the Difference Principle represents a very cautious, risk-averse choice. It focuses only on improving the position of the worst off. The implication is that even a massive increase in the resources of the more advantaged is ruled out if the position of the least advantaged deteriorates by the smallest amount. Rawls does not build risk-aversion into the psychology of the parties in the original position, as some of his critics suggest. Instead, he attempts to justify the choice of the Difference Principle by saying that it would be *rational* to be very cautious in the special circumstances of the original position, given the fact that the parties are making an irreversible choice of principles to govern their entire life-prospects. But *would* it be rational?

Rawls may be right that *utilitarianism* (Society III in our earlier example) might appear too risky to the parties in the original position, since if they end up in A's position, they will have to make *intolerable* sacrifices in order to maximise overall welfare. But is there not, perhaps, a strategy which is less risk-averse than the Difference Principle but not as risky as utilitarianism? RM Hare suggests that there is such a strategy. He calls it an 'insurance strategy'.

In order to understand the insurance strategy, let us add a fourth society to the three societies described previously in 7.2. In this society, resources are distributed in the following way:

Society IV

Individuals	Resources
A	9
B	100
C	200
D	300

Let us suppose that the situation of A in Society IV, though not quite as good as in Society II or even Society I, is nevertheless tolerable. By contrast, the situation of A in Society III is intolerable. Hare concedes that people in the original position might not be willing to take the risks inherent in choosing Society III. But he suggests that they might well choose Society IV over Society II.

In Society IV the *average* position is much better than in Society II and no-one is in *intolerable* circumstances. Hare's suggestion is therefore that individuals in the original position might be inclined to insure against calamity, by fixing a social minimum or safety-net below which no-one in their society should be allowed to fall, thus ruling out the choice of Society III. But, provided that everyone enjoys the minimum, they might well be prepared to trade off some losses for the disadvantaged for great gains for the more advantaged (Hare, 1975, pp 104–6).

Dworkin has a different objection to the Difference Principle. He argues that the morally arbitrary factors of social circumstance and natural endowment are not the only causes of unequal success in life. There is also a *non-arbitrary* source of social and economic inequality, namely, people's *choices* (Dworkin, 1981, pp 302–3). Will Kymlicka illustrates Dworkin's point with the following example. Consider two people who are *alike in their social background and their natural talents* and who start off with equal resources. One chooses to live a life of leisure, whereas the other becomes a successful entrepreneur. Soon their initial equality in resources will be replaced by striking inequality. Does justice now demand that the state redistribute from the entrepreneur to the person who has chosen the life of leisure (Kymlicka, 1990, pp 73–5)?

Dworkin argues that it does not. He argues that though a redistributive scheme should be 'endowment-insensitive', it should be 'ambition-sensitive' (Dworkin, 1981, p 311). It should, in other words, distribute benefits and burdens in a way which compensates for *involuntary* disadvantages, like impoverished family circumstances or lack of talent, while holding us responsible for our *choices*. Yet Dworkin concedes the difficulty, in practice, of working out whether a person's prosperity is due to the influence of choice or chance.

Rawls would in any event not be swayed by Dworkin's argument, because he is sceptical about the very idea of free choice. He says:

> [n]o one deserves his place in the distribution of natural endowment...The assertion that a man deserves the superior character that enables him to make the effort to cultivate his abilities is equally problematic; for his character depends in large part upon fortunate family and social circumstances for which he can claim no credit. The notion of desert seems not to apply to these cases.
>
> (Rawls, 1971, p104)

7.7 Political Liberalism

In the three decades that followed the publication of *A Theory of Justice*, Rawls significantly restated his views, mostly in response to criticisms originating from communitarian theorists. This shift in his approach is documented in most detail in his 1993 book, *Political Liberalism*.

In *A Theory of Justice*, as we have seen, the parties in the original position choose principles of justice in ignorance of the ends which they think worthwhile to pursue. They seek only to maximise their share of the primary goods, because these are, according to Rawls, all-purpose means to any goals. This leads the contractors to choose a framework of rights which is anti-perfectionist – that is to say, neutral on matters of the good – and which therefore gives maximum freedom for the contractors to pursue their ends, whatever these may turn out to be.

In *A Theory of Justice*, Rawls justifies this aspect of the original position by saying that 'it is not our aims that primarily reveal our nature', for 'the self is prior to the ends which are affirmed by it' (Rawls, 1971, p 560). It is therefore, for Rawls, our nature as 'free and equal rational beings' (Rawls, 1971, p 574), with the capacity for choosing our own ends and for changing our minds about what sort of life we find ultimately worthwhile, that ultimately explains why a just society must be neutral on what ends it is worthwhile to choose. It must be neutral *in order to respect our capacity for choice* – the fact that 'a moral person is a subject with ends he has chosen' (Rawls, 1971, p 561).

This view has affinities with a view which has come to be known as 'cosmopolitanism', and particularly with 'cosmopolitanism about culture', which, as Samuel Scheffler explains, is a view which 'emphasizes the fluidity of individual identity, people's remarkable capacity to forge new identities using materials from diverse cultural sources, and to flourish while so doing' (Scheffler, 1999, p 257). The term 'cosmopolitanism' is used in deference to the Stoics who thought that we are citizens of the world – that, as the Stoics put it, the *cosmos* is more important than the *polis*. For those who are cosmopolitans about culture, world citizenship means that 'individuals have the capacity to flourish by forging idiosyncratic identities from heterogeneous cultural sources, and are not to be thought of as constituted or defined by ascriptive ties to a particular culture, community or tradition' (Scheffler, 1999, p 258).

Communitarians reject this picture of our affiliations and loyalties as things we *choose*. They argue that the self is not 'unencumbered' but is rather 'embedded' or 'situated' in existing social practices from which it cannot detach itself but which it must accept as setting the parameters for its choices. The self is therefore not prior to the ends which it affirms. On the contrary, our ends – our reasons for action – are at least in part a function of the social context in which we find ourselves: our attachments to families, religious groups, ethnic affiliations and so on. Thus Michael Sandel writes:

> [c]ertain moral and political obligations that we commonly recognize – such as obligations of solidarity, for example, or religious duties – may claim us for reasons unrelated to a choice. Such obligations are ... difficult to account for if we understand ourselves as free and independent selves, unbound by moral ties we have not chosen.
>
> (Sandel, 1994, p 1770)

Communitarians conclude that Rawls's liberalism reflects a controversial philosophical conception of the self which is deeply flawed and that there is therefore no reason to accept the anti-perfectionist view about justice to which it leads – the view that a just society does not promote or discourage any particular version of the good but is neutral about such matters. Why, they ask, 'should we not base the principles of justice... on our best understanding of the highest human ends?' (Sandel, 1994, p 1773).

In *Political Liberalism*, Rawls responds not by retracting his views about justice but by arguing that they do not rest on the controversial philosophical claims about the self to which he was apparently committed in *A Theory of Justice*. He now gives up the idea of deliberating about justice *sub specie aeternitatis* – from the perspective of eternity (see 5.8) – and says that his theory is not a 'moral doctrine of justice' but 'a strictly political' conception' or a conception 'limited to the domain of the political' (Rawls, 1993, p xv).

In the course of explaining the notion of a political conception of justice, Rawls says that his earlier work was not sufficiently mindful of the fact that modern democratic societies are characterised by the permanent fact of 'reasonable pluralism' (Rawls, 1993, p 36). This is the fact, according to Rawls, that in modern democratic societies there is a diversity of reasonable but irreconcilable religious, moral and philosophical doctrines about such issues as the meaning of life and the nature of the self. Rawls calls all such doctrines 'comprehensive', saying that a comprehensive doctrine is one which 'includes conceptions of what is of value in human life, and ideals of personal character, as well as ideals of friendship and of familial and associational relationships, and much else that is to inform our conduct, and in the limit to our life as a whole' (Rawls, 1993, p 13). Rawls now believes that reasonable people cannot be expected to affirm the same views on these comprehensive matters or matters of ultimate significance and that this is the 'normal result' of a democratic society's 'culture of free institutions' (Rawls, 1997, p 766).

Clearly, given the fact of reasonable pluralism, no comprehensive doctrine is capable of serving as the basis of agreement about the principles which should govern the structure of society and any attempt to found political community on such a doctrine could only be maintained by oppression (Rawls, 1993, p 37). How, then, is a just and stable democratic society possible? (Notice the distance between this question, with its essentially *practical* focus on achieving consensus, as well as its starting-point within the tradition of democratic societies, and the search for philosophical and universal foundations for a theory of justice which characterised *A Theory of Justice*.)

Rawls's answer to this question is to say that the route to social unity in a democratic regime is a conception of justice which:

> is framed to apply solely to the basic structure of society, its main political, social, and economic institutions as a unified scheme of social cooperation; ... is presented independently of any wider comprehensive religious or philosophical doctrine; and ... is elaborated in terms of fundamental political ideas viewed as implicit in the public political culture of a democratic society.
>
> (Rawls, 1993, p 223)

Such a conception of justice would be a political conception of justice. Utilitarianism, Marxism, the liberal views of thinkers like Mill and Kant, and even the form of liberalism espoused in *A Theory of Justice* are not political conceptions of justice. By comparison with the more modest conception of justice to be found in *Political Liberalism*, which tries to elaborate a conception of justice for the basic structure alone, the views of these other theorists about justice are a consequence of more general moral commitments.

Furthermore, a political conception of justice is, unlike these other conceptions of justice, 'publicly justifiable' (Rawls, 1993, p 12). This is because it is not derived from any comprehensive doctrine and does not take sides on the controversial issues which divide the different comprehensive doctrines. Instead, it can be presented by drawing only on certain shared, uncontroversial moral ideas which are implicit in the public political culture of contemporary democracies. At the same time, Rawls believes that a political conception of justice is compatible with all reasonable comprehensive doctrines and can therefore be affirmed by these doctrines from within their own perspectives. A political conception of justice can therefore gain the support of what Rawls calls an 'overlapping consensus'. An overlapping consensus 'consists of all the reasonable opposing religious, philosophical and moral doctrines likely to persist over generations and to gain a sizable body of adherents in a more or less just constitutional regime' (Rawls, 1993, p 15).

In elaborating on this account, Rawls argues that the dualism between 'the point of view of the political conception' and 'the many points of view of comprehensive doctrines' (Rawls, 1993, p xxi) has its origins in democratic political culture. He claims that in modern democratic societies citizens draw a distinction between their *public* identity and their *personal* identity. When reasoning about matters of justice, they reason as public selves, detaching themselves from their controversial moral, religious and philosophical beliefs, and confining themselves to principles which could be endorsed by everyone as the basis for fair co-operation between them. Though they may have 'affections, devotions, and loyalties that they believe they would not, indeed could and should not, stand apart from and evaluate objectively' (Raws, 1993, p 31), they regard themselves differently 'in a democratic society when questions of political justice arise' (Rawls, 1993, p 33). For our conception of democratic citizenship is incompatible with 'the zeal to embody the whole truth in politics' (Rawls, 1997, p 767).

By contrast with the conception of the person which we find in *A Theory of Justice*, which aims to capture the *essential* nature of a person by reference to the capacity to choose free of all prior commitments, this is a purely 'political conception of the person' (Rawls, 1993, p 29). The political conception conceives of persons as free to affirm whatever ends they please for *political purposes only*. It is a merely political idea, rather than a metaphysical idea, where 'political' in this context means 'implicit in the political culture of a democratic society'.

Likewise, though citizens in a democratic society reason on the basis that they want more primary goods rather than less, this is not because the primary goods are essential all-purpose means for any way of life. That, as we saw in 7.5, and as

Rawls now concedes, is a controversial philosophical view. Rather, Rawls now says that he is offering a conception of human needs *for political purposes only*: the primary goods specify our needs '*as citizens*' – that is, our needs in a democratic society when questions of justice arise (Rawls, 1993, p 188).

Rawls, it should be emphasised, does not deny that our particular conceptions of the good will be central to our sense of ourselves in our *non-public* lives. He is therefore no longer committed to the claim that the reason why we should abstract from our conceptions of the good in reasoning about justice is because we are free and rational beings who can choose our ends without limit. This would be to assume a comprehensive philosophical view about the self with which reasonable people might disagree. It is merely to say that *when we deliberate about principles to govern the basic structure of a democratic society*, we should not be influenced by our conception of the good. The rationale of the veil of ignorance is merely to sensitise us to this requirement, thereby enabling us to elaborate a political conception of justice which can constitute common ground in a society characterised by the fact of reasonable pluralism. As Rawls now makes quite clear, 'the original position is simply a device of representation: it describes the parties, each of whom is responsible for the interests of a free and equal citizen, as fairly situated and as reaching an agreement subject to conditions that appropriately limit what they can put forward as good reasons' (Rawls, 1993, p 25). The conditions of the original position, in other words, are designed to reflect our antecedent belief that in a democratic society a conception of justice cannot be justified by reference to comprehensive doctrines but only by reference to shared standards. Rawls then goes on to argue that his two principles of justice, as contained in *A Theory of Justice*, are principles which would be endorsed by everyone as the basis for fair co-operation and are capable of gaining the support of an overlapping consensus.

7.8   Nozick's theory of entitlements

We turn now to Nozick's very different view of economic justice which represents a significant challenge to Rawls's views. Where Rawls is on the left of the liberal spectrum, Nozick is on the right, at least in so far as matters of economic justice are concerned. (In so far as matters of personal freedom are concerned, Nozick is extremely permissive.)

For Nozick, justice is a matter of *how* people come to be in possession of what he calls their 'holdings', not a matter of imposing a particular *pattern* of distribution in benefits and burdens. For Nozick, liberty is the most important value, not equality. This leads him to defend the free market and to oppose taxation for the purposes of redistributing wealth and resources. It is important to understand, though, that Nozick defends the free market not on the grounds that it maximises a society's wealth but because it is the only *just* system. As far as Nozick is concerned, even if the market were grossly inefficient, it would still be required as a matter of justice.

According to Nozick, justice should not be seen as a matter of carving up a social pie over which no-one has any antecedent claims. Justice is rather a matter of *entitlement*: a distribution is just if individuals are entitled to the holdings they possess under the distribution.

Three principles govern whether individuals are entitled to their holdings under a distribution. The 'principle of just acquisition' states that holdings over something which was previously unowned must have been acquired in a just way. This condition will be fulfilled if the position of others no longer at liberty to use the thing – since it now has an owner – is not thereby worsened (Nozick, 1974, p 178). Nozick believes that this condition is easy to fulfil. For even though appropriation of previously unowned resources leaves less of that resource for others, they are likely to benefit in other ways. If, for instance, they work for those who have appropriated the resource they will probably be better off financially than they were when the resource was not privately owned.

Thus Nozick asks: '[i]s the situation of persons who are unable to appropriate (there being no more accessible and useful unowned objects) worsened by a system allowing appropriation and permanent property?' And he answers: '[h]ere enter the various familiar social considerations favoring private property' (Nozick, 1974, p 177). Among these, according to Nozick, are the fact that private property 'increases the social product by putting means of production in the hands of those who can use them most efficiently (profitably)'; that private property encourages 'experimentation'; and that it 'enables people to decide on the pattern and types of risks they wish to bear' (Nozick, 1974, p 177).

Nozick's second principle, the 'principle of transfer', describes how holdings can be justly transferred from one person to another, namely, for Nozick, by the exercise of free choice. Thus donating property, bequeathing it or selling it are all examples of just transfer. The third principle, the 'principle of rectification', states that if individuals acquire property unjustly – by force or fraud, for instance – then the property can be taken from them and returned to the rightful owner. In short, if a distribution is the consequence of the free transfer of justly acquired resources, people are entitled to their holdings under the distribution and the distribution is just.

Furthermore, their right to their holdings is an *unqualified* right, according to Nozick. Provided they respect the rights of others to their holdings, they may do with their holdings exactly as they please, using them and disposing of them as they see fit. Such unrestrained capitalism will no doubt lead to massive inequalities in society, as the talented and those born to privileged families prosper, while those who lack skills and are born to poor families suffer, but taxation to relieve poverty or to provide goods such as public education or public health care would violate people's rights over their property and is therefore unjust. The only legitimate use of tax money is to protect individuals in the enjoyment of their rights and the state's role is therefore confined to that of 'night-watchman' – ensuring that there is no force, theft, fraud or breach of contract. Thus tax money may be used to provide goods such as a defence force, a police force and a legal system but any more extensive, welfarist state is morally illegitimate.

7.9   The Wilt Chamberlain argument

How does Nozick argue for this seemingly implausible conclusion? One of his arguments – the so-called 'Wilt Chamberlain' argument – is intended to show that all patterned conceptions of justice can only be maintained by intolerable, continual interference with people's liberty. A patterned conception of justice assesses the justice of a distribution in terms of its conformity to a particular pattern. It allocates resources to particular individuals on the basis of some or other of their characteristics. Thus someone, for instance, who believes that distributive shares should be related to *need* holds a patterned conception of justice. Other examples of patterned conceptions are: to each according to their *contribution to society*, or to each according to their *moral merit*. Rawls's Difference Principle is another example of a patterned conception of justice.

Nozick's conception of justice, by contrast, is unpatterned. It says that *whatever* distribution of holdings results from the free transfer of justly acquired resources is just. It is irrelevant who gets what and how much they get. Justice is solely a measure of a distribution's having come about in the right way (namely, in a way which satisfies the principles of just acquisition, transfer and rectification). There is no pattern to which the distribution must conform.

Nozick asks the defenders of a patterned conception of justice to imagine that their favoured pattern has been realised. Perhaps these persons believe that everyone should have an equal share of society's resources. They are therefore to imagine that they are living in a society in which everyone has been given an equal share. Call this distribution D1. Now suppose that all the people in this society very much want to watch Wilt Chamberlain play basketball and are prepared to pay $1 each to do so. At the end of the season, the pattern will have been disrupted. Resources will no longer be distributed equally: Wilt will be a multi-millionaire and everyone else will be $1 poorer. Call this distribution D2. Nozick argues that any attempt to maintain D1, the favoured pattern, would involve either forbidding people to transfer money to Wilt Chamberlain or reversing their free choices by forcing Wilt to pay the money back. It would have to 'forbid capitalist acts between consenting adults' (Nozick, 1974, p 163). All patterned conceptions of justice are therefore paradoxical in giving people property and then forbidding them to use it in ways they would like to.

Critics of this argument argue that it assumes that we have absolute rights to use and dispose of our property as we wish and therefore begs the very question at issue. Thus Thomas Nagel argues that the fact that the defenders of D1 would tax Chamberlain is a problem only on the assumption that D1 was intended to specify a distribution of absolute entitlements of the kind Nozick believes in. 'But', Nagel points out:

> absolute entitlement to property is not what would be allocated to people under a partially egalitarian distribution. Possession would confer the kind of qualified entitlement that exists in a system under which taxes and other

conditions are arranged to preserve certain features of the distribution, while permitting choice, use, and exchange of property compatible with it. What someone holds under such a system will not be *his property* in the unqualified sense of Nozick's system of entitlement.

(Nagel, 1981, p 201, Nagel's emphasis)

A system which confers qualified property entitlements of this kind is not, contrary to Nozick's claims, a system which *forbids* free choice. Though it does not allow *unrestricted* free choice, it does allow individuals to make choices within the legal parameters set by the state.

7.10 The self-ownership argument

It seems, therefore, that the Wilt Chamberlain argument does not provide support for the view that our holdings over our property are absolute. But Nozick has an additional argument for this conclusion. He argues that all other conceptions of justice are not only incompatible with liberty but are also *unjust*.

Like Rawls, Nozick emphasises the Kantian principle that we are all ends in ourselves – separate individuals, leading separate lives – and that we therefore have rights which protect us against being asked to make sacrifices for the general good. But, unlike Rawls, he thinks that this principle prevents the wealthy from being forced to contribute to the welfare of the poor. This is because the Kantian principle implies, according to Nozick, that we have rights over ourselves – rights of self-ownership – by contrast with slaves, in whom other people have rights. But if we own our selves, then, Nozick says, we must own our talents. And, as Kymlicka explains in a summary of Nozick's argument: 'if I own my talents, then I own whatever I produce with my self-owned talents. Just as owning a piece of land means that I own what is produced by the land, so owning my talents means that I own what is produced by my talents' (Kymlicka, 1990, p 105). Rawls's theory of justice, which treats talents as a collective resource to be used for the benefit of everyone therefore, according to Nozick, violates the principle of self-ownership and fails to respect the distinctness of individuals.

Nozick writes:

> [s]eizing the results of someone's labor is equivalent to seizing hours from him and directing him to carry on various activities. If people force you to do certain work, or unrewarded work, for a certain period of time, they decide what you are to do and what purposes your work is to serve apart from your decisions. This process...makes them a *part-owner* of you; it gives them a property right in you.
>
> (Nozick, 1974, p 172, Nozick's emphasis)

Taxation of earnings from labour is therefore the equivalent of forced labour. It is like 'forcing unemployed hippies to work for the benefit of the needy' (Nozick, 1974, p 169).

If talents are a collective resource to be used for the benefit of everyone, surely – Nozick goes on to ask – the logic of this approach also requires that we should treat bodily organs in the same way. If one person has two healthy kidneys why should we not force her to give up one of them to someone who is in kidney failure? After all, she does not *deserve* to have two healthy kidneys. It is a matter of mere good luck. If we object to this idea because we believe we are not resources for the benefit of others, then we should also object, according to Nozick, to the idea of using people's *talents* as resources for the benefit of others.

Nozick concludes that if we are to respect the distinctness of individuals, we need to recognise absolute rights over property, which means, in turn, that any redistribution from the wealthy to the needy is totally illegitimate. The needy cannot claim that they have a 'right' to assistance because '[n]o one has a right to something whose realization requires certain uses of things and activities that other people have rights and entitlements over' (Nozick, 1974, p 238).

Nozick's critics disagree. They do not think that requiring some people to sacrifice some of their income in order to assist others violates those people or ignores their separateness as persons. Hart points out that Nozick assumes that the only alternative to recognising an absolute right to liberty, free of all state interference, is unrestricted utilitarianism which respects no rights at all and countenances unlimited interference with individuals. But there is, in fact, another option, namely, the immunising of *certain* of our liberties, though not *all* of them, against the claims of the general good. Thus Hart argues that not all restrictions on liberty are equally grave. Some restrictions on liberty violate people and deprive their lives of meaning. Others, like taxation, do not have this effect. 'How can it be right to lump together, and ban as equally illegitimate', Hart asks,

> things so different in their impact on individual life as taking some of a man's income to save others from great suffering and killing him or taking one of his vital organs for the same purpose?...Is taxing a man's earnings or income which leaves him free to choose whether to work and to choose what work to do not altogether different in terms of the burden it imposes from forcing him to labour?
>
> (Hart, 1983, p 206)

In their book, *The Myth of Ownership: Taxes and Justice*, Liam Murphy and Thomas Nagel make a similar point. They say that we should, of course, be allowed to hold personal property with discretion to do what we want to do with it. But this is a far cry from saying, as Nozick does, that market liberties, such as the liberty to contract and freely to dispose of one's property, belong with 'the basic human rights as part of the authority that each of us ought to retain over our own lives' (Murphy and Nagel, 2002, p 64). There is, Murphy and Nagel say:

> no moral similarity between the right to speak one's mind, to practice one's religion, or to act on one's sexual inclinations, and the right to enter into a labor contract or a sale of property unencumbered by a tax bite. Denying the

latter... is just not the kind of interference with autonomy that centrally threatens people's control over their lives.

(Murphy and Nagel, 2002, p 65)

Though there are limits to the authority of the state over us, as Mill argued and rights-theorists affirm, Nozick has therefore not, according to his critics, shown that market freedoms contribute to the setting of these limits.

Chapter 8

Feminist jurisprudence

Like Critical Legal Studies and critical race theory, feminist legal theory offers a critical perspective on the law. In the case of feminism the starting-point is law as seen through the lens of women's experiences and the objective of the critique is to demonstrate that women are subordinated through the law – that, though it may pretend otherwise, the law is not neutral or impartial in its treatment of men and women. Instead, it systematically reflects, maintains and legitimates 'patriarchy', which is the phenomenon of power being in male hands. Mainstream law is 'malestream' law. In addition to its analysis of law as reflecting and perpetuating male values and male interests, feminism is also, of course, a political movement which aims to challenge male power and eliminate women's subordination.

These shared beliefs and political commitments do not, however, lead all feminists to adopt the same theoretical approach. In fact, feminist legal scholarship is characterised by a diversity of theoretical views about, for instance, the causes of women's inequality and the best strategies for addressing it; the significance that should be attached to the differences between men and women; and the possibility and desirability of theorising about the position of women as such. There are different ways of categorising the different 'feminisms', but one frequently used set of categories distinguishes four broad schools of feminist thought: liberal feminism, cultural or difference feminism, radical feminism and postmodern feminism. This chapter will explain their different approaches. It will also explore feminist views about issues previously canvassed in this book, such as rights, the private–public divide, adjudication and justice.

You should be familiar with the following areas:

- The formal equality model
- The feminist attack on liberalism
- Difference or cultural feminism
- MacKinnon's radical feminism
- Postmodern feminism
- The feminist critique of the public–private distinction
- Feminist views about rights
- Feminism and adjudication

8.1   Liberal feminism

It is only in about the last hundred years that women have had the right to vote, to the same educational opportunities as men, to own and manage property on marriage and to be admitted to the professions such as medicine and law. The law took even longer to recognise women's right to be paid the same as men for doing the same job. These benefits and opportunities were withheld from women on the basis of stereotyped beliefs about their innate differences from and inferiority to men – that women are emotional, weak creatures, suited only to a life of domesticity and looking after children. Men and women, so it was said, naturally inhabited 'separate spheres'. The separation of society into two spheres was elaborated upon in the US case of *Bradwell v Illinois* (1873). The case involved a challenge to the refusal to admit a woman to the Illinois bar because she was a woman. In rejecting Bradwell's challenge, Justice Joseph Bradley remarked as follows:

> [t]he civil law, as well as nature herself, has always recognized a wide difference in the respective spheres and destinies of man and woman. Man is, or should be, woman's protector and defender. The natural and proper timidity and delicacy which belongs to the female sex evidently unfits it for many of the occupations of civil life. The constitution of the family organization, which is founded in the divine ordinance, as well as in the nature of things, indicates the domestic sphere as that which properly belongs to the domain and functions of womanhood. The harmony, not to say identity, of interests and views which belong or should belong to the family institution, is repugnant to the idea of a woman adopting a distinct and independent career from that of her husband.
>
> (at 141–2)

Even after the elimination of the most obvious forms of discrimination against women, the law continued to treat women less favourably than men in more subtle ways. Such different treatment – particularly in the public sphere of employment, education and access to goods, services and accommodation – was the focus of so-called 'liberal feminism', which came to prominence during the 1960s and 1970s. Although there are reasons, as we will see, for thinking that the label is inappropriate – for there are many liberals who do not endorse the approach of so-called 'liberal feminism' – the phrase is so entrenched that I will continue to use it to describe a particular approach to sexual equality.

Liberal feminism is premised on the assumption that women are similar to men in their ability to operate in the public world and its primary focus is on the securing of equal opportunity (understood as the absence of legal barriers to advancement) and equal rights for women within the established framework of society. It insists that individuals should be assessed on the basis of their own individual merits, not their membership in a group. Thus whether a particular applicant gets a job should not depend on the irrelevant characteristic of their sex but only on their ability to do the job well. I will call this the 'formal equality' model of sexual equality, meaning by this a model on which sexual equality is guaranteed when the law treats men and women in a formally identical way. On this view, sex-blind or gender-neutral laws are sufficient for sexual equality.

The equal opportunity goals of liberal feminism are encapsulated in anti-discrimination statutes such as the Sex Discrimination Act 1975 (UK). Such acts standardly rule out less favourable treatment on the ground of sex in a limited number of public areas of activity such as employment, education, housing and the provision of goods and services. Less favourable treatment of this kind is often called 'direct discrimination' on the ground of sex.

In fact, anti-discrimination legislation goes further than liberal feminism, in typically also ruling out conduct which, though formally treating men and women in the same way, unreasonably and disproportionately burdens members of one sex more than the other – so-called 'indirect discrimination'. The focus here is on different *impact*, not different *treatment*. If, for instance, an employer made it a condition of employment that an employee not be the primary care-giver of small children, this could amount to indirect discrimination against women, since more women than men are primary care-givers of small children. Though the employer's condition is sex-blind – after all, both men and women need to comply with the condition – the *effect* of such formally equal treatment would be (whether intentionally or not) to discriminate against women. It should be clear that legislation which prohibits indirect discrimination goes beyond 'liberal feminism', with its single-minded focus on eliminating direct sex discrimination or gender-based classifications as the complete solution to sexual inequality. We will return to the concept of indirect discrimination in 8.3.

8.2 The attack on liberal feminism

The formal equality approach to the problem of sexual inequality came under attack relatively quickly. One problem with it, which manifested itself in numerous legal cases brought under anti-discrimination legislation or constitutional guarantees of equality, is the apparent difficulty it has in showing why discrimination on the ground of characteristics that are *unique* to women, such as pregnancy, should be seen as a form of sex-based discrimination. This is because the formal equality approach relies on *comparisons* between the treatment of men and women: it requires the treatment received by members of one sex to be the same as the treatment received by members of the other sex who are in similar circumstances. But men cannot fall pregnant. How, then, can women discriminated against on the ground of pregnancy (by being dismissed from their jobs, for instance) argue that they have been treated less favourably than similarly situated men? Since there appears to be no right extended to a man which they have been denied, it seems that on the formal equality approach they cannot complain of sex-based discrimination.

It should, however, be noted that some feminists argue that the difficulty here is more apparent than real and that the formal equality approach *can* explain why discrimination on the ground of pregnancy amounts to sex-based discrimination. These theorists point out that there are similarities between pregnancy and other physical needs and conditions routinely accommodated by employers in the workplace by the provision of benefits such as sick leave and guarantees of job security. It follows – they say – that there *is* a relevant 'comparator' (a person to whom a pregnant employee can be compared), namely, a temporarily ill employee whom the employer does not dismiss despite his or her temporary inability to work. According to these theorists, pregnant employees who are treated less favourably than other temporarily incapacitated employees *can* therefore complain that they have been discriminated against on the ground of their sex.

A more general problem with the formal equality approach is that most of the inequalities of prestige, wealth and power which characterise the positions of men and women in our society have little to do with sex-based exclusionary treatment in the public world. The ideal of equal access to educational and economic institutions has no doubt been very important in opening up opportunities for women that they were previously denied. Most women continue, nevertheless, to be segregated in the lowest paying, least influential, least valued and least secure occupations, and even those who have high-status and interesting positions generally come up against the 'glass ceiling' and fail to achieve the top positions in their professions, companies or political organisations. Furthermore, many more women suffer from poverty, unemployment and violence than men.

8.3   The male norm

Equal rights to education and employment within the existing system cannot on their own address these sex-based disparities because it is not public discrimination which is the primary cause of sexual inequality, but rather disadvantages suffered by women in areas of life which the formal equality approach tends to ignore – so-called 'private' areas of life. One major source of disadvantage is the fact that women bear the brunt of child-rearing and domestic responsibilities, tasks which our society has historically undervalued and failed to reward. It is much more difficult for women to compete for the positions which society does reward by virtue of the burden of this unpaid form of labour, the inadequacy of child-care facilities, and the expectation of employers that employees should have no family commitments of a kind to interfere with full-time work. The kind of neutrality liberal feminism offers – the right to compete on the same terms as men in a male-dominated world – is therefore of benefit only to a minority of economically and socially privileged women, a group of women whose lives approximate the male norm.

On the liberal feminist view, as Christine Littleton explains:

> the law should require social institutions to treat women as they already treat men – requiring, for example, that the professions admit women to the extent that they are 'qualified', but also insisting that women who enter time-demanding professions such as the practice of law sacrifice relationships (especially with their children) to the same extent that male lawyers have been forced to do.
>
> (Littleton, 1987, p 1292)

But – the critics of liberal feminism ask – why *should* women have to meet workplace standards designed for men in order to claim the protection of the law? Why should sexual equality be a matter of integrating women into a male world? Thus Catharine MacKinnon asks:

> [w]hy should you have to be the same as a man to get what a man gets simply because he is one? Why does maleness provide an original entitlement, not questioned on the basis of *its* gender, so that it is women – women who want to make a case of unequal treatment in a world men have made in their image...– who have to show in effect that they are men in every relevant respect, unfortunately mistaken for women on the basis of an accident of birth?
>
> (MacKinnon, 1987, p 37, MacKinnon's emphasis)

This is an example of what feminists call 'asking the woman question'. As Katherine Bartlett explains, asking the woman question involves looking beneath the surface of the law, so as to expose how the law fails to take into account the perspectives of women or how it disadvantages women (Bartlett, 1990, p 837). Thus feminists ask the woman question when they ask why satisfying, well-paid jobs should be the preserve of workers who are able to work full time by virtue of having minimal domestic responsibilities. In showing how certain apparently neutral rules, which seem to treat men and women equally, are really only of advantage to women who are like men – to whose situation and characteristics the rules are in fact tailored – feminists reveal that men are the assumed subject of the law.

If we now return to the concept of indirect discrimination, it will be clear that its function is precisely to focus attention on practices which are formally neutral but in effect based on a male norm. Laws which prohibit indirect discrimination force employers either to *justify* formally neutral practices the effect of which is to exclude women or to substitute *new* practices which are genuinely fair to women.

But must these new practices be sex-blind or may they treat women and men differently? Some feminists argue that while it is unfair to impose male standards on women, sex-based laws are always illegitimate and we should therefore look for genuinely neutral, sex-blind laws which do not subject women to male standards. They say, in other words, that though sex-blindness is not a *guarantee* of sexual equality, it is nevertheless *necessary* for its achievement. Other feminists disagree. They say that if the law is to be fair to women, there will be occasions on which it should treat men and women differently. We will return to this important issue in 8.6.

8.4   Formal equality and liberalism

Those who criticise the formal equality model hold a conception of equality on which the aim should be redistributive: the aim should be to improve women's social and material circumstances, not merely to ensure that they are afforded the same opportunities as men within the status quo. If men and women are to be truly equal, it is not enough to make place for a handful of 'honorary men' in the boardroom. The deeper social and material disadvantages of women need to be addressed. Laws which are genuinely neutral between men and women will therefore be laws which deliver equality of *results* or *outcomes* – 'substantive' equality, not merely 'formal' equality. They will take account of the 'social fact of gender asymmetry' so as to 'create some symmetry in the lived-out experience of all members of the community' (Littleton, 1987, p 1297).

It is hard to deny that the formal approach to sexual equality is unsatisfactory. The equal rights which it advocates are of the kind famously parodied by Anatole France in 1894, when he wrote of 'the majestic egalitarianism of the law, which forbids rich and poor alike to sleep under bridges, to beg in the streets, and to steal bread'. The formal equality model does not challenge the entrenched injustice and unequal power structures which are built into the status quo. Though it claims to offer neutrality as between men and women, it does not challenge the prevailing male standards and is therefore incapable of delivering on its promises.

But should the formal approach be identified as a *liberal* approach? Though many feminist theorists seem to assume that the limitations of the formal equality model are a function of a liberal outlook, this is because they mistakenly identify liberalism with the view that the state's functions should be kept within the narrowest confines. But, as we now know from Chapter 7, not all liberals take this view. It is, in fact, difficult to define liberalism in a way which does not caricature it or obscure the differences among liberal theorists. While most liberals (though not all) believe in rights as a desirable constraint on government power, they have different views about what rights we have, and this makes for important differences in their views about the legitimate role of the state.

Thus a 'market liberal' like Nozick, who prioritises the importance of individual freedom and has a purely negative conception of rights, which he equates with the absence of state interference, would be likely to identify with the modest goals of 'liberal' feminism. For Nozick, a just society is one in which everyone enjoys the same negative rights to life, liberty and property, regardless of whether everyone is equally able to make use of these rights. Thus Nozick is not worried by the fact that those who are poor may be unable to take advantage of the rights and opportunities which the law formally provides them. It does not, for instance, matter if the poor cannot afford legal representation as long as everyone has the right to a fair trial. Nozick would likewise not be worried by the fact that many women are unable to access the educational and employment opportunities which are in theory open to them.

But other liberals take a different view. Thus Hart says:

> [e]xcept for a few privileged and lucky persons, the ability to shape life for oneself and lead a meaningful life is something to be constructed by positive marshalling of social and economic resources. It is not something automatically guaranteed by a structure of negative rights. Nothing is more likely to bring freedom into contempt and so endanger it than failure to support those who lack, through no fault of their own, the material and social conditions and opportunities which are needed if a man's freedom is to contribute to his welfare.
>
> (Hart, 1982, pp 207–8)

Rawls and Dworkin likewise wish to ensure that equal rights are of equal worth to everyone by improving the condition of those who are worse off in society, thereby providing the material preconditions for the effective exercise of rights. They are sensitive to the unfairness of unequal starting-points in life and believe that it is unjust not to redress the consequent, undeserved inequalities.

This is because, by contrast with Nozick, liberals like Rawls and Dworkin do not believe that we have a right to liberty *as such* – a right which would preclude *any* state interference with people's liberties except to protect rights. Rather, they believe that we have rights to certain *specific* liberties, or, as Rawls calls them, 'basic liberties' (see 7.2). Examples of such rights are the right to freedom of speech, to freedom of religion and to bodily integrity. In Rawls and Dworkin's view, we have rights only to those liberties which are essential to the leading of a meaningful life. Market or economic liberties, such as the liberty to contract and freely to dispose of one's property, are not essential to the leading of a meaningful life, and government may therefore legitimately interfere with them – by passing minimum wage laws, for instance, and other social and economic legislation – in order to achieve desirable social goals (Dworkin, 1977a, p 278). (We took note of a similar point in 7.10.) This view creates the space to take an egalitarian approach to distributive justice – an approach which regards the redressing of undeserved privileges and advantages as a matter of justice, and which therefore agrees that the goals of liberal feminism are too limited.

It is true that in *A Theory of Justice* Rawls does not expressly consider the systemic subordination of women and omits to discuss the issue of injustice within the family. He rectifies this in his later writings, however, in which he makes clear that his principles of justice require the reform of the family, and that he thinks of sex as like social class and natural talent in being a feature which ought not to determine one's life chances (Rawls, 1997, pp 788, 791, 792–3). In testing the justice of legal and social arrangements based on the subordination of women, Rawls would therefore ask whether, if one did not know one's sex, one would choose a society in which sexual differences translate into disparities of power, income, security and status – disparities in 'lived-out experience', to use Littleton's phrase. This question is bound to be answered in the negative, as theorists like Susan Okin observe (Okin, 1989, pp 101–5).

Likewise Mill, whose liberal views on the legitimate role of the law were discussed in 6.2, held views about women's subordination which were radical for his time and there is much in his book *The Subjection of Women* which supports the critique of so-called 'liberal' feminism, as we will see in 8.12. In short, though Rawls, Dworkin and Mill are undoubtedly liberals, they would not identify with the minimalist goals of 'liberal' feminism.

8.5   Individualism and feminism

Martha Nussbaum elaborates on ideas like these, defending a form of liberal feminism which, according to her, provides the foundation for a radical critique of society which is crucial to women's quality of life, not only in Western societies but even more importantly in developing countries, where women's second-class status is even more deeply entrenched (Nussbaum, 1999, p 56). Nussbaum identifies the core of the liberal tradition as consisting in the ideas that everyone – whether rich or poor, female or male, black or white – is of equal worth and equally deserving of respect, and that this requires providing not merely formal equality of opportunity but positive, material support for people to pursue their own lives according to their own views about what matters in life (Nussbaum, 1999, pp 5, 9).

It is often said to be a defect in liberalism that it is 'individualistic' and feminists often argue that individualism is a value associated with men and masculinity. Nussbaum disagrees on both counts. She thinks that individualism is not only a good thing but that its individualism is precisely what makes liberalism good for women. She explains that individualism stresses:

> the basic fact that each person has a course from birth to death that is not precisely the same as any other person; that each person is one and not more than one, that each feels pain in his or her own body, that the food given to A does not arrive in the stomach of B.
>
> (Nussbaum, 1999, p 62)

Another way of putting this is to say that, on an individualistic view, the basic units of moral concern are individual human beings, not larger groups like families, or communities, or states. On such a view, the flourishing of individuals should never be subordinated to the flourishing of groups: the goal of politics should be to improve the lives of individuals, each and every one of them considered as separate individuals. (The connection of this with the discussion of the Kantian basis of human rights in 5.4 will be obvious.) And Nussbaum argues that this is in the interests of women because women's individual well-being has too often been ignored in the service of the goals of others. As she points out:

> [w]omen have very often been treated as parts of a larger unit, especially the family, and valued primarily for their contribution as reproducers and caregivers rather than as sources of agency and worth in their own right. In connection with this nonindividualistic way of valuing women, questions about families have been asked without asking how well each of its individual members are doing.
>
> (Nussbaum, 1999, p 63)

This is even more obvious in poor countries where it is the female members of the family who suffer most from lack of resources. In these countries, statistics show that it is the girls and women who are most often malnourished, whose educational and health needs are most often neglected, and who are most often the victims of violence in the family. Nussbaum concludes that liberalism properly understood is a theory with radical aspirations, focused on fundamental changes to legal and social arrangements, such as workplace norms and the unequal division of labour within the family. Its goal is to remedy the structural and institutional sources of disadvantage which are, as we have seen, the real cause of women's subordinate position in society.

We can sum up the discussion of the last two sections like this: feminists, like the other critical legal theorists discussed in Chapter 4, aim to expose the biases of law, the interests it serves, the way in which it conceals unequal power relationships by presenting itself as in everyone's interests, and the injustices it does. As Gerry Simpson and Hilary Charlesworth say, critical theories of law are distinguished by 'their refusal to accept that law is essentially a benign, neutral and autonomous institution' (Simpson and Charlesworth, 1995, p 86). But critical theorists typically also make another claim, namely, that the critical insights just mentioned undermine liberalism. Thus Simpson and Charlesworth say that critical theories undermine the 'dominant liberal version of law', on which, according to them, law is seen as 'a disinterested reflection of value consensus' within the community (Simpson and Charlesworth, 1995, p 86).

But, as we have seen, liberalism is not committed to the view that the law is rational, disinterested or neutral. Though the law may present itself as securing justice for all, there are many liberals who, recognising its concealed gender-bias, refuse to take its claims at face value. While they believe the state *should* be neutral as between men and women, they do not claim that it actually *is* neutral and they therefore have no difficulty in accepting the views of feminists like MacKinnon that the 'state is male'.

8.6 Difference or cultural feminism

Difference feminism or cultural feminism focuses on women's differences from men, both physical and psychological, which it not only recognises but embraces.

Difference feminism is anti-assimilationist: it is against the idea of assimilating women into a system which it sees as patriarchal. Assimilation, according to difference feminists, forces women to be ersatz men.

The work of the psychologist Carol Gilligan has been influential in the elaboration of difference feminism. She argues that women see themselves as connected with others whereas men see themselves as separate from others, and that this difference leads men and women to reason in a different way or speak in a different voice. When confronted with a moral dilemma, women are more concerned about relationships and needs, the context in which the dilemma arises, and the 'ethics of care'. Men are more concerned about abstract, rigid rules and adversarial and individualistic concepts such as rights and justice.

Gilligan explains how she posed a moral dilemma to a group of children and asked them how they would deal with it. In the scenario, Heinz's wife is dying and needs a drug which he cannot afford. Should Heinz steal the drug from the pharmacy? Jake, an 11-year old boy, sees the problem as a clash of rights. He weighs up life against property, finds life more valuable, and concludes that Heinz should steal the drug. He deals with the situation like a mathematical problem. Amy, an 11-year old girl, wonders why Heinz does not discuss the problem with the pharmacist – for surely he will then give Heinz the drug or at least arrive at a compromise, like a loan? Amy does not see the dilemma in universal terms, as a clash between property and life, but focuses rather on the particular persons, their relationships and needs, and seeks a solution that will satisfy everyone. According to Gilligan, the ethic of justice is commonly thought to represent a 'higher' or more sophisticated stage of moral development, and the female point of view has been correspondingly marginalised and devalued. This neglect of the feminine method of moral reasoning needs, in her opinion, to be reversed (Gilligan, 1982, pp 25–32).

Drawing on these ideas, some feminist legal scholars have argued that the law reflects male values and that it needs to incorporate the ignored values associated with women's voice. Robin West, for instance, argues that law is built on the masculine idea that the individual is physically separate and apart from others – an assumption which is, she says, 'patently untrue of women', who are connected to others through pregnancy, intercourse and breast-feeding. West believes that women differ from men in seeing separation as a threat and intimacy as the most important value. She concludes:

> [w]e need to flood the market with our own stories until we get one simple point across: men's narrative story and phenomenological description of law is not women's story and phenomenology of law. We need to dislodge legal theorists' confidence that they speak for women, and we need to fill the gap that will develop when we succeed in doing so.
>
> (West, 1988, p 65)

Though Gilligan does not explicitly claim that women's heightened concern with relationships and connection to others is natural or rooted in their biology, some cultural feminists do make this claim. West does – she says that the potentiality for motherhood defines women – as does the French feminist and psychoanalyst, Luce Irigaray. Irigaray goes further, making the controversial argument that there should be a separate law for men and women – 'a law of persons appropriate to their natural reality, that is, to their sexed identity' (Irigaray, 1996, p 51). Only if the law recognises special or 'sexuate' rights for women can women enter the public world on equal terms. Among the sexed rights for which Irigaray argues are the right to dignity (which requires an end to the commercial use of women's bodies and the right to valid representations of women in public places); a right to virginity as belonging to the girl and not to her father, brother or future husband; and a right to motherhood (Irigaray, 1991, p 208).

8.7   Criticisms of difference feminism

Difference feminism is controversial because the picture of women's separate identity which it paints is so close to the stereotyped views about women which were used to justify the hierarchical separate spheres ideology. Many feminists worry that women's propensity to care for others and discount their own needs may therefore be an artefact of male domination. Mill had already made this point in 1869. In the *Subjection of Women* he wrote:

> [a]ll women are brought up from the very earliest years in the belief that their ideal of character is … submission and yielding to the control of others. All the moralities tell them that it is the duty of women … to live for others; to make complete abnegation of themselves, and to have no life but in their affections. And by their affections are meant the only ones they are allowed to have – those to the men with whom they are connected, or to the children who constitute an additional and indefeasible tie between them and a man.
>
> (Mill, 1869, p 444)

It is by this means, Mill goes on to say, that men hold women in subjection. MacKinnon provides a contemporary formulation of the same point, when she says: '[w]omen value care because men have valued us according to the care we give them' (MacKinnon, 1987, p 39). If you want to know in what tongue women speak, she adds: '[t]ake your foot off our necks' (MacKinnon, 1987, p 45).

Difference feminism is also controversial in so far as it relies on women's differences from men as the basis for treating them more favourably than men. We have seen that most feminists believe that genuine sexual equality will not be achieved until women's social and economic status is on a par with men's. But how is this to be achieved? Difference feminists commonly argue for 'special' treatment as a means of compensating for the disadvantages from which women suffer and of catering to their special needs. But the opponents of difference feminism fear that giving special benefits to women will reinforce and perpetuate the traditional stereotypes about women's role which have been such an obstacle to their fight for equality.

This debate raises what Martha Minow calls the dilemma of difference or the dilemma that 'we may recreate difference either by noticing it or ignoring it' (Minow, 1987, p 12). Margaret Radin talks in similar terms of the 'double bind' which, she argues, is at the heart of women's issues. The 'double bind' refers to the fact that '[f]or a group subject to structures of domination, all roads thought to be progressive can pack a backlash' (Radin, 1990, p 1701).

Suppose, for instance, that pregnant women are given advantages which other workers are denied. An employer might, for example, guarantee reinstatement in the job after childbirth but not reinstatement for those who have taken time off from work due to illness. On the one hand, this perpetuates the traditional view about women's natural 'destiny' as mothers, a view which contributes to their subordinate position in society. On the other hand, if pregnant women are not given pregnancy-specific benefits, then women are penalised in the workplace because of their biological differences: men can have a family without losing their jobs but women cannot. And this is another kind of obstacle to the goal of sexual equality.

One response to this double bind, made by feminists who are opposed to the use of gender-based classifications in the law, is to say that feminists should concentrate on improving workplace protection for *everyone* – pregnant employees as well as non-pregnant employees, both male and female, who need time off from work on account of physical conditions and needs that affect their workplace participation. Thus Wendy Williams says: '[p]regnancy creates not "special" needs, but rather exemplifies typical basic needs. If these particular typical needs are not met, then pregnant workers simply become part of a larger class of male and female workers, for whom the basic fringe benefit structure is inadequate' (Williams, 1984–1985, p 327).

The controversial nature of the special treatment approach was highlighted in a South African case, *President of the Republic of South Africa v Hugo* (1997). In this case the Constitutional Court of South Africa was faced with a challenge to a Presidential Act, in terms of which President Mandela had exercised his power to pardon convicted prisoners. The Act provided for special remission to be granted to all mothers in prison who had children younger than 12 years old on the day of Mandela's inauguration. The Constitution of South Africa forbids unfair discrimination on the grounds of both sex and gender. Hugo was a male prisoner whose wife had died. He had a child younger than 12 years old at the relevant date. He claimed that the Act unfairly discriminated against him on the ground of his sex and/or gender by treating him less favourably than a similarly situated female prisoner.

The majority rejected his challenge. Goldstone J, who wrote the majority judgment, said that the discrimination was to the advantage of mothers of young children, a group which was vulnerable and had been the victim of discrimination in the past. Furthermore, the point of releasing the female prisoners was to serve the interests of children. Since women are in general responsible for the care of small children in South African society, the release of male prisoners would not have served the purpose as effectively.

Kriegler J, however, dissented, voicing the concerns alluded to above about the dangers in using the law to reinforce the traditional 'separate sphere' stereotypes which paint men as breadwinners and women as mothers and homemakers. Accepting that the less favourable treatment of members of one sex is not necessarily unfair, he nevertheless said that a statute which is likely to promote the continuation of deeply entrenched patterns of inequality is unlikely to be defensible. It might seem that the President had used gender-stereotypes to the advantage of women, but Kriegler J, on looking more deeply, found that the imposition of roles on the basis of 'predetermined...gender scripts' (at para 83) is not in the interests of women and will lead only to more inequality in the long run.

Kriegler J therefore called attention to the complexities involved in deciding whether different treatment for women benefits or harms them. He might have noted, in this connection, that the oppressive labour laws of the past, which, among other restrictions, limited the hours that women could work and prohibited them from working at night, were standardly justified on the basis that they were necessary in order to 'protect' women and were therefore in their interests.

8.8   Radical feminism

The most influential exponent of radical feminism is MacKinnon. She argues that women do not so much speak with a different voice as have no voice at all. The domination of women as a class by men as a class is fundamental to the legal system – indeed, to the whole of society – and the sexual abuse of women is the indispensable mechanism by which women are subjugated. Power and sexuality are therefore central to the radical feminist analysis. MacKinnon rejects both the 'sameness' approach and the 'difference' approach. Whether women are taken to be similar to or different from men, in both cases men provide the standard against which women are judged. MacKinnon, by contrast, takes up the perspective of women: her feminism is therefore 'feminism unmodified', feminism unaffected by anything except the standpoint of subordinated women. She asks not whether women are relevantly like or relevantly unlike men, but whether their treatment perpetuates their inferiority. Sex equality will be achieved only when male dominance over women has been eliminated.

Gender difference is, on MacKinnon's view, just 'the velvet glove on the iron fist of domination' (MacKinnon, 1987, p 8). It is a constructed concept which 'obscures and legitimizes the way gender is imposed by force' (MacKinnon, 1987, p 3). It is the fact of men's power which constructs what we know as feminine – reproducing that power in the process – and gender would consequently have no social meaning in the absence of male domination: 'what a woman "is" is what [men] have *made* women "be" '(MacKinnon, 1987, p 59, MacKinnon's emphasis).

Much of MacKinnon's work focuses on the way in which male sexuality is expressed in ways which objectify and subjugate women, especially through violence, rape, sexual harassment, prostitution and pornography. All are forms of sexual subordination and should therefore, in her opinion, be seen as sex discrimination. MacKinnon's account of pornography is probably best known because it led her to draft legislation allowing anyone who had been harmed by pornography, broadly defined, to sue for damages.

MacKinnon argues that pornography eroticises inequality and the exercise of power:

> pornography is neither harmless fantasy nor a corrupt and confused misrepresentation of an otherwise natural and healthy sexual situation. It institutionalizes the sexuality of male supremacy, fusing the eroticization of dominance and submission with the social construction of male and female...Men treat women as who they see women as being. Pornography constructs who that is.
>
> (MacKinnon, 1992, p 462)

Pornography should be conceptualised, in other words, as an issue of men's power and women's lack of it. Its consumption is thereby seen to be a political issue, rather than a matter of men's personal sexual preferences and choices.

About rape MacKinnon writes:

> [p]erhaps the wrong of rape has proved so difficult to define because the unquestionable starting point has been that rape is defined as distinct from intercourse, while for women it is difficult to distinguish the two under conditions of male dominance.
>
> (MacKinnon, 1989, p 174)

All heterosexual relations, in other words, emerge from MacKinnon's analysis as coercive in a society characterised by male supremacy: there is no clear way of distinguishing between consensual heterosexual sex and rape.

This bleak picture has led some feminists to challenge MacKinnon's picture of women as incapable of anything but helpless, silenced victimhood and as beings whose sexuality is entirely defined in terms of male power – the power, as MacKinnon puts it, 'to make us make the world of their sexual interaction with us the way they want it' (MacKinnon, 1987, p 58). Thus Drucilla Cornell writes:

> women's sexuality is irreducible to the fantasy that we are only 'fuckees'. MacKinnon's reduction of feminine sexuality to being a 'fuckee' endorses this fantasy as 'truth' and thereby promotes the prohibition against the exploration of women's sexuality and 'sex' as we live it and not as men fantasize about it.
>
> (Cornell, 1991, p 2250)

MacKinnon's views about pornography have also proved controversial among feminists, some of whom are opposed to restricting pornography notwithstanding their strong dislike of it on account of the demeaning stereotypes about women that it conveys. This is because they do not accept that pornography is a root cause of women's oppression. Many feminists are also worried that laws restricting pornography would be hijacked by conservative groups wishing to suppress all forms of sexually explicit material, including feminist and lesbian art. Thus Gillian Rodgerson and Elizabeth Wilson point out that:

> [n]o matter how confident feminists may be that they know what they mean, there are those who consider any depiction of women as sexual beings, especially women enjoying being sexual, as degrading; any depiction of homosexuality as degrading; any depiction of women participating in sexual acts as necessarily objectifying them.
>
> (Rodgerson and Wilson, 1991, p 69)

Rodgerson and Wilson also argue that the message of pornography is much more complex and ambiguous than MacKinnon suggests (Rodgerson and Wilson, 1991, p 72).

8.9   Postmodern feminism

The 1990s saw the increasing influence of postmodern feminism. The main ideas of postmodernism will be recalled from 4.9. For our purposes, the most important of these are the following. First, there is postmodernism's distrust of grand, general theories aiming to tell the whole, objective truth, theories for which it wishes to substitute a plurality of small-scale, partial, perspectival accounts. Postmodernists tell us that there are no objective and universal standards of truth and justice discoverable by human reason. There are only different, socially conditioned, subjective interpretations. Second, postmodernism wishes to deconstruct binary oppositions such as male/female, reason/emotion, nature/culture, subverting these traditional distinctions of Western thought. Deconstruction reveals how the one term in the pair has been privileged and the other suppressed, in the process making space for previously excluded and marginalised views.

We see an analogous emphasis on partial perspectives as well as a comparable destabilisation of traditional categories in the case of postmodern feminism. Whereas the feminist views canvassed so far are all, in one way or another, interested in making generalisations about women, and in contrasting the situation of women as such with men as such, postmodern feminism emphasises the differences *among* women and critiques the other theories for what it calls their 'essentialism'. This is the assumption that gender is the fundamental form of oppression in society and that all women, regardless of their other differences, such as race, ethnicity, class, age and sexual orientation, share a common experience of oppression and common interests. MacKinnon, for instance, makes this assumption when she states: '[i]nequality because of sex defines and situates women as women' (MacKinnon, 1989, p 215). And Gilligan likewise makes essentialist assumptions in postulating that there is a distinctively female kind of moral reasoning. For postmodern feminists, by contrast, essential 'woman' does not exist.

Postmodern feminists argue that earlier feminist theories were the theories of privileged, middle-class, white women. Perhaps, for these women, patriarchy is the most fundamental form of oppression, but the experiences of women oppressed by other social forces such as class, race and sexual orientation will necessarily be different. Thus black women are not merely more oppressed than white women, but *differently* oppressed. Theories which stress the uniqueness of the disadvantage suffered by those who are subject to more than one system of subordination are called theories of 'intersectionality' because they hold that different bases of subordination intersect to produce a distinctive kind of disadvantage and a distinctive experience of oppression.

Thus Kimberlé Crenshaw argues that race affects the kinds of gender subordination that black women experience. She gives the example of sexual harassment: black women who complain of sexual harassment come up not only against stereotypes that are faced by white women and black men, but also against the stereotype of black women as sexually promiscuous and unlikely to tell the truth. They also face the commonly held belief that sexually abusive behaviour directed towards black women is less abusive than the same behaviour directed towards white women. They are therefore *uniquely* disadvantaged as black women (Crenshaw, 1992, p 1470).

Larissa Behrendt notes similarly:

> [t]he experiences of minority women have as much to do with racism as sexism. For Aboriginal women, this is illustrated by the experience of rape. When an Aboriginal woman is the victim of a sexual assault, how, as a black woman, does she know whether it is because she is hated as a woman and is perceived as inferior or if she is hated because she is Aboriginal, considered inferior and promiscuous by nature?
>
> (Behrendt, 1993, p 35)

Theorists like Crenshaw and Behrendt argue that the failure to recognise the uniqueness of the experiences of black women silences and excludes them. In this case, however, the silencing and exclusion is not at the hands of men but at the hands of white women: though they claim to speak for all women, they assume an implicit female norm analogous to the male norm they are at such pains to expose. Thus the picture feminists paint of women trapped within the home is, in reality, a picture of the predicament of *white* women: black women have generally worked outside the home. Lesbian theorists make a similar complaint, namely, that feminist theory has spoken only for heterosexual women.

Elizabeth Spelman sums up the difficulties with essentialism as follows:

> [e]ssentialism invites me to take what I understand to be true of me 'as a woman' for some golden nugget of womanness all women have as women;

and it makes the participation of other women inessential to the production of the story. How lovely: the many turn out to be one, and the one that they are is me.

(Spelman, 1988, p 159)

Postmodern feminism therefore wishes to make feminist jurisprudence more inclusive and pluralistic. It renounces the aspiration to general theorising about women, regarding this as impossible, and it pays attention instead to the multiple sources of oppression and the specific forms which oppression takes in different women's lives. Patricia Cain describes its focus like this:

postmodern feminism tells us to beware of searching for a new truth to replace the old... There is no such thing as the woman's point of view. There is no single theory of equality that will work for the benefit of all women. Indeed, there is probably no single change or goal that is in the best interest of all women.

(Cain, 1990, p 838)

8.10   Postmodernism and feminist politics

This, however, raises troubling questions about feminism as a political movement. If theorists cease to use or deconstruct the category 'woman', can they still be said to be offering a form of *feminist* jurisprudence? How will they be able to critique the gender-bias of the law and pursue their political aim of equality with men if the category 'woman' disintegrates into multiple perspectives and points of view, based not only on the gender of those whose perspective it is, but also on their other characteristics, such as race, religion, sexual orientation and class? Must a feminist politics not presuppose that women have common interests?

Furthermore, if we accept the postmodernist view that there is no such thing as objective truth and justice, is it possible to launch a compelling attack on sexual inequality? Which is more likely to advantage the cause of women – the postmodernist belief that there are no universal standards of cognitive and normative legitimacy, or the rationalist premise of 'grand theory' that all social arrangements should be scrutinised and rejected if found to be incapable of rational justification?

Theorists like Sabina Lovibond argue that it is no accident that all the reforming movements of the modern age, Marxism included, have taken their inspiration from rationalist ideas, because these ideas provide a powerful impetus to the liberating demand that traditional and arbitrary hierarchies of power based on criteria such as race, sex and class should be abolished and replaced by social arrangements organised on rational, egalitarian lines (Lovibond, 1989, pp 11–12). Such theories therefore have clear potential to effect social change in the interests of women.

But is the same true of postmodern feminism, which appears to offer no way to distinguish the arbitrary from the non-arbitrary in social arrangements and no way to criticise sexism except from a partisan or self-interested perspective? How, indeed, can one coherently talk of male 'bias' if there is no possibility of challenging the male perspective from an objective point of view? In implying that there is no such thing as an objectively justifiable attack on male domination, might postmodern feminism therefore actually serve the interests of men, by allowing them to claim that their 'truth' is as good as any other? Would it not perhaps be better to impose on men the obligation to explain to women what is *wrong* with the feminist critique, an explanation whose success or lack of it can then be judged in terms of universal criteria of adequate reasoning?

8.11   The public–private distinction

A critique of the public–private distinction is a recurring theme in the works of feminist legal scholars. We have encountered this distinction in Chapter 6, but we need to return to it now and consider it in the context of feminist theory.

We have already taken note of the separate spheres ideology, the distinction which is drawn between the public sphere of male governance and the private sphere of women and children in the home. Feminist legal scholars argue that the relegation of women to the so-called 'private' realm of domestic and family life is one of the most important causes of their subordinate position in society. For one thing, it is the reason why they are expected to bear the brunt of the responsibility for the unpaid work of the home, which, as we have seen, is one of the main causes of women's low employment status, economic dependence on men and inability to participate fully in the public world. Thus women's relegation to the private realm is a primary cause of their second-class public status.

Second, the law has seen fit to regulate the public domain, understood as encompassing state and market institutions, while traditionally regarding it as inappropriate to interfere in the 'loving' or 'intimate' area of family relationships and the home. This has led it to ignore and, in the process, legitimise the way in which women are treated within the home. There are many examples of the law's failures in this area. Probably the best known is the fact that until very recently women were denied a remedy for rape within marriage. At one time husbands also had the right to beat their wives, and even now law enforcement agencies often turn a blind eye in practice to domestic violence – something which would never be tolerated in the context of violence outside the home. The upshot of this hands-off attitude is that male power in the domestic sphere is de facto supported at the same time as its exercise is concealed. As MacKinnon explains:

> [w]hen the law of privacy restricts intrusions into intimacy, it bars change in control over that intimacy . . . It is probably not coincidence that the very things feminism regards as central to the subjection of women – the very place, the body; the very relations, heterosexual; the very activities, intercourse and reproduction; and the very feelings, intimate – form the core of what is covered

by privacy doctrine. From this perspective, the legal concept of privacy can and has shielded the place of battery, marital rape, and women's exploited labor.

(MacKinnon, 1987, p 101)

This kind of analysis underlies the feminist slogan 'the personal is the political'. The slogan calls attention to the fact that private inequality is the source of public disadvantage; that the world of private relationships is not necessarily a world of free choices and maximum autonomy but a world imbued by the politics of power; and that problems faced by women which might seem a matter of their individual, personal circumstances are in fact a function of systemic injustice against women as a group and need to be addressed as matters of public concern. Feminists emphasise 'consciousness-raising' as a method for reaching these insights. This involves the use of shared experience in groups as a way of enabling women to name and understand the forces that oppress them. It is thought that when women share their experiences of subordination, it will become clear that they are not dealing with personal problems but systemic problems, not isolated problems but connected problems. It will become clear that 'the personal is the political'.

There are further aspects to the feminist critique of the private–public distinction. Some feminists point out that it is a *public* decision to treat family life as a private matter. It was, after all, the law which allowed husbands to rape their wives. Others point out that the domestic sphere is, in fact, regulated in many ways which belie the law's official attitude to it. As Nicola Lacey observes:

> in spite of a great deal of rhetoric about privacy in the family sphere, a moment's thought reveals that many aspects of family life are hedged around with legal regulation – marriage, divorce, child custody, social welfare rules, to name but the most obviously relevant areas of law.
>
> (Lacey, 1998, p 74)

Many feminists also make the point that the law's decision not to regulate an area of life has political consequences in just the same way as a decision to regulate. Thus Katherine O'Donovan states: '[n]ot legislating contains a value-judgement just as legislating does. Law cannot be neutral; non-intervention is as potent an ideology as regulation' (O'Donovan, 1985, p 184). Thus when the law refuses to intervene in the domestic sphere the effect is to entrench and give legitimacy to the status quo. A connected claim is that the state should be held responsible for its hands-off approach to the domestic sphere and the inequalities and violence which flow from this indifference.

8.12   Liberalism and the public–private distinction

The feminist critique of the private–public distinction as spelt out in 8.11 is powerful. But feminist theorists typically also go further, saying that because liberals defend a private sphere of freedom of action, the feminist critique of the private–public distinction amounts to a critique of liberalism. Hilaire Barnett puts the point like this:

> liberalism...contributes to the problem which women face. By distinguishing between the public sphere of life which is legally regulated, and the private sphere of life, which is largely legally unregulated, liberalism carves out a haven for domestic violence.
>
> (Barnett, 1998, p 258)

Margaret Davies writes to similar effect:

> [l]iberal thought has been blind to harms perpetrated in private (the 'private' having been constructed as precisely that place where harm does not happen), and the victims of these harms are typically women and children. Feminist critiques of liberal thought have pointed out that the family is one of the central spheres of women's oppression.
>
> (Davies, 2002, p 218)

But are liberal views about the importance of a private realm really at odds with the feminist critique of the public–private distinction? As we know, Mill was a strenuous defender of the private realm, meaning by this a realm in which the law should not interfere and in which we should enjoy perfect freedom of action (see 6.2). At the same time, in the *Subjection of Women*, Mill vigorously objected to the way in which the law sanctions inequality and violence in the family. He observed that 'the wife's position under the common law of England is worse than that of slaves in the laws of many countries' (Mill, 1869, p 462), listing all the ways in which the life of a married woman amounts to servitude under the law, and especially stressing the law's acceptance of marital rape. In this connection he wrote:

> no slave is a slave to the same lengths, and in so full a sense of the word, as a wife is. Hardly any slave...is a slave at all hours and all minutes...Above all, a female slave has (in Christian countries) an admitted right...to refuse to her master the last familiarity. Not so the wife: however brutal a tyrant she may unfortunately be chained to...he can claim from her and enforce the lowest degradation of a human being, that of being made the instrument of an animal function contrary to her inclinations.
>
> (Mill, 1869, p 463)

How could Mill defend the private–public distinction while also seeming to accept the feminist critique of the family as a site of women's oppression? The answer to this is that the private realm that Mill and other liberals defend is not the same private realm that feminists attack.

Liberals do not, contrary to the claims of many feminists, identify the private realm with a *place* – the home. Nor do they identify it with the realm of conduct to which the law turns a blind eye. Theirs is not a *descriptive* claim about the areas of life which the law does not, in fact, regulate but a *normative* claim about the areas of life which the law *should* not regulate. For liberals, the private realm is the realm in which the law ought not to interfere. For Mill, if we are not violating anyone's rights or failing to perform our positive obligations the law should leave us alone.

'Private' is therefore just a label liberals apply to conduct which they believe we are morally entitled to engage in without interference. By no means does this coincide with the realm of family or domestic relationships which are often, as we have seen, characterised by harmful conduct, especially to women and children. Liberals therefore do not say that the realm of the family *is* a realm of freedom, nor that it *should* be. On the contrary, they say that the state is obliged to protect us from harmful conduct regardless of where it occurs. Liberals will therefore agree with feminists that when the state refuses to intervene in the domestic realm this is a political choice and an abdication of responsibility. They will also agree with feminists that when the domestic sphere is wrongly described as 'private' the label serves to mask the oppression and exploitation of women and children.

Liberals may also go on to argue that their defence of a private realm, understood as a defence of the right to make self-regarding decisions without interference from the state, serves the interests of women in granting them the right to make decisions about their own bodies, something frequently denied them by the law. One example is provided by statutory rape laws which punish under-age sex with girls but not boys. As Frances Olsen notes about such laws:

> [b]y refusing to grant women autonomy and by protecting them in ways that men are not protected, the State treats women's bodies – and therefore women themselves – as objects. Men are treated differently. Their bodies are regarded as part of them, subject to their free control.
>
> (Olsen, 1984, p 406)

Another example is laws which restrict access to abortion in the early stages of pregnancy. As we saw in 6.7, the liberal notion of privacy provides a way to attack such laws. Indeed, it was precisely on this basis that the Supreme Court of the United States struck down anti-abortion laws in the well-known case of *Roe v Wade* (1973).

It should be noted, though, that the use of the liberal notion of privacy to support the right to abortion is controversial. MacKinnon, for instance, argues that it is a mistake to defend the right to abortion by appealing to privacy. She claims that the conceptualisation of abortion as a private choice in the case of *Roe v Wade* led the Supreme Court in the later case of *Harris v McRae* (1980) to uphold the validity of a law which prohibited the use of government funds to finance abortions for poor women. She writes: '[f]reedom from public intervention coexists uneasily with any right that requires social preconditions to be meaningfully delivered' (MacKinnon, 1987, p 100). She suggests, in other words, that if we understand the right to abortion in negative terms, as a right to choose abortion free of state interference, then we will be less inclined to believe there is a positive obligation on the state to fund abortions for those who cannot afford them.

Is this correct? Some theorists argue that it is not. Dworkin, for instance, agrees with MacKinnon that if we are to achieve genuine sexual equality, it is not enough that abortion should be legal. Women must also be able effectively to exercise their right to abortion and the state should therefore finance abortions for poor women. But Dworkin argues that this is not incompatible with seeing abortion as a matter of 'sovereignty over personal decisions'. On the contrary: 'recognizing that women have a . . . right to determine how their own bodies are to be used is a prerequisite, not a barrier, to the further claim that the government must ensure that the right is not illusory' (Dworkin, 1993, p 54).

8.13   Rights

Feminist scholarship is characterised by an ambivalence about the value of rights and about the notion of justice, which is said by some feminists to be a gendered concept. Feminists influenced by the CLS view that rights are too individualistic (see 4.12), as well as by the claims of writers like Gilligan (see 8.6), argue that the notions of rights and justice reflect a competitive, male perspective on the world. They say that we should care about other people more, and press our own individual claims less. As Deborah Rhode explains, these feminists believe that:

> [a] preoccupation with personal entitlements can divert concern from collective responsibilities. Rights rhetoric too often channels individuals' aspirations into demands for their own share of protected opportunities and fails to address more fundamental issues about what ought to be protected. Such an individualistic framework ill serves the values of cooperation and empathy that feminists find lacking in our current legal culture.
>
> (Rhode, 1990, p 633)

On the other hand, as Rhode also points out, other feminists agree with the critical race theorists (see 4.13) that rights have an empowering aspect, especially for members of disadvantaged groups. These feminists are likely to be sceptical about notions like 'co-operation' and 'empathy' which, as we have seen, have been used to subject women to the exercise of male power. They are also likely to point out that the law's failure to protect women in the domestic sphere suggests that what women need is not less rights-protection – not fewer 'personal entitlements' – but more. Consider, for instance, the importance to women of the recent recognition that married women have the right to refuse to have sex with their husbands. And consider the way in which the ability of women to control their own fertility depends on the right to abortion. On the basis of these and similar examples, many feminists are loath to give up on the language of rights, which they see as a necessary protection in circumstances in which love and affection have run out.

Defenders of rights furthermore argue that rights do not serve only to protect us against interference from other people, as writers like Gilligan suggest. As we saw in 5.2, most contemporary rights-theorists believe that rights have just as important a role to play in protecting material well-being as in protecting freedom. It is only libertarians like Nozick who argue that we do not have a right to positive assistance from other people. Most rights-theorists therefore agree with those feminist writers who stress the importance of care and empathy in adequate human relationships.

8.14   Adjudication

So far we have focused on feminist views about the way in which the content of the law is skewed towards male interests. But feminists have also launched a powerful attack on the stereotyped sexist assumptions and gender-bias manifested by judges in the course of applying the law. Regina Graycar gives a number of examples in an article entitled 'The Gender of Judgments: An Introduction' (Graycar, 1995, pp 269–71). Three of these will serve to make the point. In them we see one judge commenting on a woman's appearance and its supposed connection with the instincts he judges to be 'properly maternal'; another assuming that women who pursue careers make poor custodial parents; and a third expressing the view that it is legitimate for men to use some degree of force in persuading their wives to consent to sexual intercourse. In this way legal discourse not only reflects but contributes to the construction of gender differences. The three examples are as follows.

First, Graycar refers to the case of *Udale v Bloomsbury Area Health Authority* (1983), in which the court had to decide whether a woman who had four children and did not want any more, and who became pregnant after a negligently performed sterilisation, was entitled to damages for the cost and upkeep of the child. The judge described her as 'a motherly sort of woman, nice looking but rather overweight... She is not only an experienced mother but, so far as I am able to judge, a good mother, who has all the proper maternal instincts' (at 526).

Second, Graycar discusses a custody dispute between two parents, both doctors, in which the judge said: 'the major question mark hanging over the wife... is whether she would be prepared to sacrifice her career for the sake of the children... My own assessment of her is that she wants her cake and eat it too.' In her decision, the judge awarded the wife custody on a conditional basis: if she resigned her job and came back to court pregnant two months later, she would be awarded custody; otherwise custody would be given to the father who was working full time (quoted in *Swaney v Ward* (1988) at 712).

And in a third case, which involved a prosecution of a husband for five counts of rape of his wife, the judge directed the jury as follows: '[t]here is, of course, nothing wrong with a husband, faced with his wife's initial refusal to engage in intercourse, in attempting, in an acceptable way, to persuade her to change her mind, and that may involve a measure of rougher than usual handling. It may be, in the end, that handling and persuasion will persuade the wife to agree' (quoted in *Case Stated By DPP (No 1 of 1993)* (1993) at 264).

In addition to revealing the gender-bias of many judges, feminist theorists have also contributed to the theory of judging. In particular, many feminists argue that good judging involves flexibility and sensitivity to details and to context rather than rigid reliance on very generally framed, bright-line rules which are more attuned to the abstract similarities in successive situations than the concrete differences. This approach goes back to Aristotle, though it also has obvious affinities with Gilligan's notion of the ethics of care. Aristotle thought that the exercise of practical wisdom cannot be identified with the following of abstract rules applicable without further reflection to subsequent cases. Though abstract rules may be useful as rules of thumb, or provisional guides to decision-making, we must be prepared to jettison them when they are not appropriate to the particular situation now before us. Nussbaum describes Aristotle's view like this:

> [t]he subtleties of a complex ethical situation must be seized in a confrontation with the situation itself, by a faculty that is suited to address it as a complex whole. Prior general formulations lack both the concreteness and the flexibility that is required. They do not contain the particularizing details of the matter at hand, with which decision must grapple; and they are not responsive to what is there, as good decision must be.
>
> (Nussbaum, 1990, p 69)

Minow and Spelman have recently defended a contextual approach to judging. In their article, 'Passion for Justice', they attack the idea of 'justice by computer'. They use the analogy of computer programmes that do not allow bank customers to withdraw more money on a given day than the programme allows. The machine does not and cannot care whether the customer has a need or justification unanticipated by the programme's writer. A system of justice by computer would be similarly unyielding, in being unable to consider how its decisions will affect particular people or to reconsider its initial judgment in light of unanticipated effects (Minow and Spelman, 1988, p 42). Good judging would, by contrast, according to them, be responsive to individual human beings and open to changing and unique circumstances which may require conceiving a case in new terms.

In their subsequent article, 'In Context', Minow and Spelman spell out the feminist potential of sensitivity to context. It is, they say, 'the particular particularities associated with legacies of power and oppression that we mean to highlight by the interest in context' (Minow and Spelman, 1990, p 1601). So, in instructing judges to look at context, Minow and Spelman are calling attention to the experiences and needs of groups which have been subject to domination, enjoining judges to consider features like race, gender and class which more abstractly framed rules ignore.

This point brings us full circle, returning us to the formal equality approach with which this chapter began. As we saw, the formal equality approach regards gender-neutral rules as a guarantee of sexual equality. It thereby ignores the differences between men and women and their different situations and characteristics. A more contextual approach would investigate the impact of the rule on the particular parties to the dispute, which would include attention to the question of whether their gender makes them disproportionately susceptible to the rule's impact.

Bibliography

Alexy, R, 'A Defence of Radbruch's Formula', in Dyzenhaus, D (ed), *Recrafting the Rule of Law: The Limits of Legal Order*, 1999, Oxford and Portland Oregon: Hart Publishing, pp 15–39.

Aquinas, *Summa Theologica*, 1947, New York: Benziger Brothers, Inc.

Atiyah, P, 'Justice and Predictability in the Common Law' (1992) 15 *University of New South Wales Law Journal* 448.

Austin, J (1832), *The Province of Jurisprudence Determined*, Rumble, WE (ed), 1995, Cambridge: Cambridge University Press.

Austin, J (1863), *Lectures on Jurisprudence*, Campbell, R (ed), 5th edn, 1885, London: John Murray.

Barnett, H, *Introduction to Feminist Jurisprudence*, 1998, London and Sydney: Cavendish Publishing Limited.

Bartlett, K, 'Feminist Legal Methods' (1990) 103 *Harvard Law Review* 829.

Behrendt, L, 'Aboriginal Women and the White Lies of the Feminist Movement: Implications for Aboriginal Women in Rights Discourse' (1993) 1 *Australian Feminist Law Journal* 27.

Bell, J, *Policy Arguments in Judicial Decisions*, 1983, Oxford: Clarendon Press.

Bell, J, 'Legal Education', in Cane, P and Tushnet, M (eds), *The Oxford Handbook of Legal Studies*, 2003, Oxford: Oxford University Press, pp 901–19.

Bentham, J (1789), 'An Introduction to the Principles of Morals and Legislation', in Harrison W (ed), *A Fragment of Government and An Introduction to the Principles of Morals and Legislation*, 1960, Oxford: Basil Blackwell, pp 113–435.

Bentham, J (1795), 'Nonsense Upon Stilts', in Schofield, P, Pease-Watkin, C and Blamires, C (eds), *Rights, Representation, and Reform: Nonsense Upon Stilts and Other Writings on the French Revolution*, 2002, Oxford: Clarendon Press, pp 317–401.

Beyleveld, D and Brownsword, R, 'The Practical Difference between Natural-Law Theory and Legal Positivism' (1985) 5 *Oxford Journal of Legal Studies* 1.

Beyleveld, D and Brownsword, R, 'Normative Positivism: The Mirage of the Middle-Way' (1989) 9 *Oxford Journal of Legal Studies* 463.

Bix, B, *Law, Language, and Legal Determinacy*, 1993, Oxford: Clarendon Press.

Bix, B, *Jurisprudence: Theory and Context*, 3rd edn, 2003, London: Sweet and Maxwell.

Bottomley, S and Parker, S, *Law in Context*, 2nd edn, 1997, Sydney: Federation Press.

Buchanan, AE, *Marx and Justice: The Radical Critique of Liberalism*, 1982, London: Methuen.

Cain, P, 'Feminism and the Limits of Equality' (1990) 24 *Georgia Law Review* 803.

Campbell, TD, 'Democracy, Human Rights and Positive Law' (1994) 16 *Sydney Law Review* 195.

Campbell, TD, *The Legal Theory of Ethical Positivism*, 1996, Aldershot: Dartmouth.

Cicero, *De Republica De Legibus*, Keyes, CW (trans), 1928, London: William Heinemann Ltd; Cambridge, Mass.: Harvard University Press.

Coase, R, 'The Problem of Social Cost' (1960) 3 *Journal of Law and Economics* 1.

Cohen, GA, *Karl Marx's Theory of History: A Defence*, 1978, Oxford: Clarendon Press.

Coleman, J, 'Negative and Positive Positivism', in Cohen, M (ed), *Ronald Dworkin and Contemporary Jurisprudence*, 1984, Totowa, N. J.: Rowman and Allanheld, pp 28–48.

Coleman, J, 'Incorporationism, Conventionality, and the Practical Difference Thesis', in Coleman, J (ed), *Hart's Postscript: Essays on the Postscript to* The Concept of Law, 2001a, Oxford: Oxford University Press, pp 99–147.

Coleman, J, *The Practice of Principle: In Defence of a Pragmatist Approach to Legal Theory*, 2001b, Oxford: Oxford University Press.

Cooke, R, 'The Road Ahead for the Common Law' (2004) 53 *International and Comparative Law Quarterly* 273.

Cornell, D, 'Sexual Difference, the Feminine, and Equivalency: A Critique of MacKinnon's *Toward a Feminist Theory of the State*' (1991) 100 *Yale Law Journal* 2247.

Cotterrell, R, *The Politics of Jurisprudence: A Critical Introduction to Legal Philosophy*, 1989, Philadelphia: University of Pennsylvania Press.

Crenshaw, K, 'Race, Gender and Sexual Harassment' (1992) 65 *Southern California Law Review* 1467.

Davies, M, *Asking the Law Question: The Dissolution of Legal Theory*, 2nd edn, 2002, Sydney: Lawbook Co.

Delgado, R, 'The Ethereal Scholar: Does Critical Legal Studies Have What Minorities Want?' (1987) 22 *Harvard Civil Rights – Civil Liberties Law Review* 301.

Denning, AT, *The Discipline of Law*, 1979, London: Butterworths.

Derrida, J, *Positions*, Bass, A (trans), 1981, Chicago: University of Chicago Press.

Devlin, P, *The Enforcement of Morals*, 1965, London, Oxford, New York: Oxford University Press.

Dworkin, R, *Taking Rights Seriously*, 1977a, London: Duckworth.

Dworkin, R, 'No Right Answer', in Hacker, PMS and Raz, J (eds), *Law, Morality and Society: Essays in Honour of HLA Hart*, 1977b, Oxford: Clarendon Press, pp 58–84.

Dworkin, R, 'What is Equality? Part II: Equality of Resources' (1981) 10 *Philosophy and Public Affairs* 283.

Dworkin, R, 'Law as Interpretation' (1982) 9 *Critical Inquiry* 179.

Dworkin, R, 'A Reply by Ronald Dworkin', in Cohen, M (ed), *Ronald Dworkin and Contemporary Jurisprudence*, 1984, Totowa, N. J.: Rowman and Allanheld, pp 247–300.

Dworkin, R, *A Matter of Principle*, 1985, Cambridge, Mass.: Harvard University Press.

Dworkin, R, *Law's Empire*, 1986, Cambridge, Mass.: Belknap Press.

Dworkin, R, *Life's Dominion: An Argument about Abortion and Euthanasia*, 1993, London: HarperCollins Publishers.

Dworkin, R, *Freedom's Law: The Moral Reading of the American Constitution*, 1996, Cambridge, Mass.: Harvard University Press.

Dworkin, R, 'Thirty Years On' (2002) 115 *Harvard Law Review* 1655.

Dworkin, R, 'Hart's Postscript and the Character of Political Philosophy' (2004) 24 *Oxford Journal of Legal Studies* 1.

Feinberg, J, *Harmless Wrongdoing*, 1990, New York, Oxford: Oxford University Press.

Finnis, J, *Natural Law and Natural Rights*, 1980, Oxford: Clarendon Press.

Finnis, J, *Fundamentals of Ethics*, 1983, Oxford: Clarendon Press.

Finnis, J, 'On Reason and Authority in *Law's Empire*' (1987) 6 *Law and Philosophy* 357.

Fish, S, 'Working on the Chain Gang: Interpretation in Law and Literature' (1982) 60 *Texas Law Review* 551.

Fitzpatrick, P and Hunt, A, 'Introduction', in Fitzpatrick, P and Hunt, A (eds), *Critical Legal Studies*, 1987, Oxford: Basil Blackwell, pp 1–3.

Frank, J, *Law and the Modern Mind*, 1930, New York: Brentano's Publishers.

Fuller, LL, *The Law in Quest of Itself*, 1940, Chicago: The Foundation Press, Inc.

Fuller, LL, 'The Case of the Speluncean Explorers' (1949) 62 *Harvard Law Review* 616.

Fuller, LL, 'Positivism and Fidelity to Law – A Reply to Professor Hart' (1958) 71 *Harvard Law Review* 630.

Fuller, LL, *The Morality of Law*, revised edn, 1969, New Haven and London: Yale University Press.

Gabel, P and Kennedy, D, 'Roll Over Beethoven' (1984) 36 *Stanford Law Review* 1.

George, RP, *Making Men Moral: Civil Liberties and Public Morality*, 1993, Oxford: Clarendon Press.

Gilligan, C, *In a Different Voice: Psychological Theory and Women's Development*, 1982, Cambridge, Mass. and London, England: Harvard University Press.

Gray, JC, *The Nature and Sources of the Law*, 2nd edn, 1972, Gloucester, Mass.: Peter Smith.

Graycar, R, 'The Gender of Judgments: An Introduction', in Thornton, M (ed), *Public and Private: Feminist Legal Debates*, 1995, Melbourne: Oxford University Press, pp 262–82.

Greenawalt, K, 'Discretion and the Judicial Decision' (1975) 65 *Columbia Law Review* 359.

Grotius, H (1625), *De Jure Belli ac Pacis*, Kelsey, FW (trans), 1925, Indianopolis, New York: Bobbs-Merrill.

Hare, RM, 'Rawls' Theory of Justice', in Daniels, N (ed), *Reading Rawls: Critical Studies of* A Theory of Justice, 1975, Oxford: Basil Blackwell, pp 81–107.

Harris, JW, *Legal Philosophies*, 2nd edn, 1997, London, Edinburgh, Dublin: Butterworths.

Hart, HLA, 'Positivism and the Separation of Law and Morals' (1958) 71 *Harvard Law Review* 593.

Hart, HLA, 'Immorality and Treason', in Dworkin, R (ed), *The Philosophy of Law*, 1977, Oxford: Oxford University Press, pp 83–8.

Hart, HLA, *Essays on Bentham*, 1982, Oxford: Clarendon Press.

Hart, HLA, *Essays in Jurisprudence and Philosophy*, 1983, Oxford: Clarendon Press.

Hart, HLA, *The Concept of Law*, 2nd edn, 1994, Oxford: Clarendon Press.

Holmes, OW, 'The Path of the Law' (1897) 10 *Harvard Law Review* 457.

Holmes, OW, *The Common Law*, 1923, Boston: Little, Brown and Company.

Horwitz, M, 'The Rule of Law: An Unqualified Human Good?' (1977) 86 *Yale Law Journal* 561.

Howarth, D, 'Making Sense out of Nonsense', in Gross, H and Harrison, R (eds), *Jurisprudence: Cambridge Essays*, 1992, Oxford: Clarendon Press, pp 29–53.

Hutchinson, AC, 'Introduction', in Hutchinson, AC (ed), *Critical Legal Studies*, 1989, New Jersey: Rowman and Littlefield Publishers, Inc., pp 1–11.

Irigaray, L, 'How To Define Sexuate Rights?', in Whitford, M (ed), *The Irigaray Reader*, 1991, Oxford: Basil Blackwell, pp 204–12.

Irigaray, L, *I Love To You: Sketch for a Felicity Within History*, Martin, A (trans), 1996, New York and London: Routledge.

Kant, I (1785), *The Moral Law – Kant's Groundwork of the Metaphysic of Morals*, Paton, HJ (trans), 1948, London: Hutchinson University Library.

Kelly, JM, *A Short History of Western Legal Theory*, 1992, Oxford: Clarendon Press.

Kelman, M, *A Guide to Critical Legal Studies*, 1987, Cambridge, Mass. and London, England: Harvard University Press.

Kelsen, H, 'The Pure Theory of Law and Analytical Jurisprudence' (1941) 55 *Harvard Law Review* 44.

Kelsen, H, *General Theory of Law and State*, Wedberg, A (trans), 1945, New York: Russell and Russell.

Kelsen, H, 'What is the Pure Theory of Law?' (1959–1960) 34 *Tulane Law Review* 269.

Kelsen, H, *Pure Theory of Law*, Knight, M (trans), 1967, Berkeley, Los Angeles, London: University of California Press.

Kennedy, D, 'Form and Substance in Private Law Adjudication' (1976) 89 *Harvard Law Review* 1685.

Kramer, MH, *In Defense of Legal Positivism: Law without Trimmings*, 1999, Oxford: Oxford University Press.

Kymlicka, W, *Contemporary Political Philosophy: An Introduction*, 1990, Oxford: Clarendon Press.

Lacey, N, *Unspeakable Subjects: Feminist Essays in Legal and Social Theory*, 1998, Oxford: Hart Publishing.

Littleton, C, 'Reconstructing Sexual Equality' (1987) 75 *California Law Review* 1279.

Llewellyn, KN, 'A Realistic Jurisprudence – The Next Step' (1930) 30 *Columbia Law Review* 431.

Llewellyn, KN, *The Bramble Bush*, 1930a, New York: Oceana Publications, Inc.

Llewellyn, KN, *The Common Law Tradition*, 1960, Boston and Toronto: Little, Brown and Company.

Locke, J (1690), 'An Essay Concerning the True Original, Extent, and End of Civil Government', in Laslett, P (ed), *Two Treatises of Government*, 1970, Cambridge: Cambridge University Press.

Lovibond, S, 'Feminism and Postmodernism' (1989) 178 *New Left Review* 5.

Lukes, S, *Marxism and Morality*, 1985, Oxford: Clarendon Press.

Lyons, D, *Ethics and the Rule of Law*, 1984, Cambridge: Cambridge University Press.

Lyons, D, 'Original Intent and Legal Interpretation' (1999) 24 *Australian Journal of Legal Philosophy* 1.

Lyotard, J-F, *The Post-Modern Condition: A Report on Knowledge*, Bennington, G and Massumi, B (trans), 1984, Manchester: Manchester University Press.

MacCormick, N, *H L A Hart*, 1981, London: Edward Arnold.

McCoubrey, H and White, ND, *Textbook on Jurisprudence*, 2nd edn, 1996, London: Blackstone Press Limited.

MacKinnon, CA, *Feminism Unmodified: Discourses on Life and Law*, 1987, Cambridge, Mass. and London, England: Harvard University Press.

MacKinnon, CA, *Toward a Feminist Theory of the State*, 1989, Cambridge, Mass. and London, England: Harvard University Press.

MacKinnon, CA, 'Pornography, Civil Rights and Speech', in Itzin, C (ed), *Pornography: Women, Violence and Civil Liberties*, 1992, Oxford: Oxford University Press, pp 456–511.

Marx, K (1843), 'On the Jewish Question', in Karl Marx and Friedrich Engels, *Collected Works*, vol 3, 1975, London: Lawrence and Wishart, pp 146–174.

Marx, K (1846), *The German Ideology*, in Karl Marx and Friedrich Engels, *Collected Works*, vol 5, 1976, London: Lawrence and Wishart, pp 19–93.

Marx, K (1847), *The Poverty of Philosophy*, in Karl Marx and Friedrich Engels, *Collected Works*, vol 6, 1976, London: Lawrence and Wishart, pp 105–212.

Marx, K (1859), 'Preface to *A Contribution to the Critique of Political Economy*', in Karl Marx and Friedrich Engels, *Selected Works*, vol 1, 1958, Moscow: Foreign Languages Publishing House, pp 361–5.

Marx, K (1867), *Capital*, vol 1, 1974, London: Lawrence and Wishart.

Marx, K (1875), *Critique of the Gotha Programme*, in Karl Marx and Friedrich Engels, *Selected Works*, vol 2, 1958, Moscow: Foreign Languages Publishing House, pp 13–48.

Meyerson, D, 'Contradictions in Critical Legal Studies' (1991) 11 *Oxford Journal of Legal Studies* 439.

Meyerson, D, *False Consciousness*, 1991a, Oxford: Clarendon Press.

Meyerson, D, 'Does the Constitutional Court of South Africa Take Rights Seriously? The Case of *S v Jordan*' (2004) *Acta Juridica* 138.

Mill, JS (1859), *On Liberty*, in Fawcett, MG (ed), *Three Essays: On Liberty, Representative Government, The Subjection of Women*, 1912, London, New York, Toronto: Oxford University Press.

Mill, JS (1869), *The Subjection of Women*, in Fawcett, MG (ed), *Three Essays: On Liberty, Representative Government, The Subjection of Women*, 1912, London, New York, Toronto: Oxford University Press.

Minow, ML, 'Justice Engendered' (1987) 101 *Harvard Law Review* 10.

Minow, ML and Spelman, EV, 'Passion for Justice' (1988) 10 *Cardozo Law Review* 37.

Minow, ML and Spelman, EV, 'In Context' (1990) 63 *Southern California Law Review* 1597.

Moore, M, 'The Interpretive Turn in Modern Theory: A Turn for the Worse?' (1989) 41 *Stanford Law Review* 871.

Murphy, L and Nagel, T, *The Myth of Ownership: Taxes and Justice*, 2002, New York: Oxford University Press.

Nagel, T, 'Libertarianism without Foundations', in Paul, J (ed), *Reading Nozick: Essays on Anarchy, State and Utopia*, 1981, Oxford: Basil Blackwell, pp 191–205.

Nozick, R, *Anarchy, State and Utopia*, 1974, Oxford: Basil Blackwell.

Nussbaum, MC, *Love's Knowledge: Essays on Philosophy and Literature*, 1990, New York and Oxford: Oxford University Press.

Nussbaum, MC, *Sex and Social Justice*, 1999, New York and Oxford: Oxford University Press.

O'Donovan, K, *Sexual Divisions in Law*, 1985, London: Weidenfeld and Nicolson.

Okin, S, *Justice, Gender and The Family*, 1989, New York: Basic Books.

Olsen, F, 'Statutory Rape: A Feminist Critique of Rights Analysis' (1984) 63 *Texas Law Review* 387.

Perry, SR, 'Hart's Methodological Positivism', in Coleman, J (ed), *Hart's Postscript: Essays on the Postscript to* The Concept of Law, 2001, Oxford: Oxford University Press, pp 311–54.

Posner, R, 'The Economic Approach to Law' (1975) 53 *Texas Law Review* 757.

Posner, R, 'Utilitarianism, Economics, and Legal Theory' (1979) 8 *Journal of Legal Studies* 103.

Posner, R, *The Economics of Justice*, 1981, Cambridge, Mass. and London, England: Harvard University Press.

Posner, R, *The Economic Analysis of Law*, 6th edn, 2003, New York: Aspen Publishers.

Postema, GJ, *Bentham and the Common Law Tradition*, 1986, Oxford: Clarendon Press.

Radin, M, 'The Pragmatist and the Feminist' (1990) 63 *Southern California Law Review* 1669.

Rawls, J, *A Theory of Justice*, 1971, London, Oxford, New York: Oxford University Press.

Rawls, J, *Political Liberalism*, 1993, New York: Columbia University Press.

Rawls, J, 'The Idea of Public Reason Revisited' (1997) 64 *University of Chicago Law Review* 765.

Raz, J, *The Authority of Law: Essays on Law and Morality*, 1979, Oxford: Clarendon Press.

Raz, J, *Ethics in the Public Domain: Essays in the Morality of Law and Politics*, 1994, Oxford: Clarendon Press.

Rhode, D, 'Feminist Critical Theories' (1990) 42 *Stanford Law Review* 617.

Rodgerson, G and Wilson, E, *Pornography and Feminism: The Case against Censorship*, 1991, London: Lawrence and Wishart.

Rumble, WE, *American Legal Realism: Skepticism, Reform and the Judicial Process*, 1968, Ithaca, N.Y.: Cornell University Press.

Sandel, MJ, 'Book Review of *Political Liberalism*' (1994) 107 *Harvard Law Review* 1765.

Schauer, F, 'Easy Cases' (1985) 58 *Southern California Law Review* 399.

Schauer, F, 'Causation Theory and the Causes of Sexual Violence' (1987) 4 *American Bar Foundation Research Journal* 737.

Schauer, F, 'Formalism' (1988) 97 *Yale Law Journal* 509.

Schauer, F, *Playing by the Rules: A Philosophical Examination of Rule-Based Decision-Making in Law and in Life*, 1991, Oxford: Clarendon Press.

Schauer, F, 'Positivism Through Thick and Thin', in Bix, B (ed), *Analyzing Law: New Essays in Legal Theory*, 1998, Oxford: Clarendon Press, pp 65–78.

Scheffler, S, 'Conceptions of Cosmopolitanism' (1999) 11 *Utilitas* 256.

Schubert, G, *The Judicial Mind: The Attitudes and Ideologies of Supreme Court Justices 1946–1963*, 1965, Evanston: Northwestern University Press.

Simmonds, NE, *Central Issues in Jurisprudence: Justice, Law and Rights*, 1986, London: Sweet and Maxwell.

Simmonds, NE, 'Law as a Moral Idea' (2005) 55 *University of Toronto Law Journal* 61.

Simpson, G and Charlesworth, H, 'Objecting to Objectivity: The Radical Challenge to Legal Liberalism', in Hunter, R, Ingleby, R and Johnstone, J (eds), *Thinking About Law: Perspectives on the History, Philosophy and Sociology of Law*, 1995, Sydney: Allen and Unwin, pp 86–132.

Singer, JW, 'The Player and the Cards: Nihilism and Legal Theory' (1984) 94 *Yale Law Journal* 1.

Smart, JJC, *An Outline of a System of Utilitarian Ethics*, 1961, Melbourne: Melbourne University Press.

Smart, JJC, 'Distributive Justice and Utilitarianism', in Arthur, J and Shaw, WH (eds), *Justice and Economic Distribution*, 1978, New Jersey: Prentice-Hall, pp 103–15.

Smart, JJC and Williams, B, *Utilitarianism For and Against*, 1973, Cambridge: Cambridge University Press.

Spelman, EV, *Inessential Woman: Problems of Exclusion in Feminist Thought*, 1988, Boston: Beacon Press.

Sunstein, CR, 'Justice Scalia's Democratic Formalism' (1997) 107 *Yale Law Journal* 529.

Taylor, C, 'Alternative Futures: Legitimacy, Identity and Alienation in Late Twentieth Century Canada', in Cairns, A and Williams, C (eds), *Constitutionalism, Citizenship and Society in Canada*, 1985, Toronto: University of Toronto Press, pp 183–229.

Taylor, C, 'The Politics of Recognition', in Gutmann, A (ed) *Multiculturalism*, 1994, Princeton, N.J.: Princeton University Press, pp 25–73.

Thompson, EP, *Whigs and Hunters: The Origin of the Black Act*, 1975, London: Allen Lane.

Twining, W, 'General and Particular Jurisprudence – Three Chapters in a Story', in Guest, S (ed), *Positivism Today*, 1996, Aldershot: Dartmouth, pp 119–46.

Unger, R, 'Legal Analysis as Institutional Imagination' (1996) 59 *Modern Law Review* 1.

Veljanovski, CG, *The New Law-and-Economics: A Research Review*, 1982, Oxford: Centre for Socio-Legal Studies.

Waldron, J, *'Nonsense upon Stilts': Bentham, Burke and Marx on the Rights of Man*, 1987, London, New York: Methuen.

Waldron, J, *The Law*, 1992, London and New York: Routledge.

Waldron, J, 'All We Like Sheep' (1999) 12 *Canadian Journal of Law and Jurisprudence* 169.

Waldron, J, *Law and Disagreement*, 1999a, Oxford: Clarendon Press.

Waldron, J, 'Normative (or Ethical) Positivism', in Coleman, J (ed), *Hart's Postscript: Essays on the Postscript to* The Concept of Law, 2001, Oxford: Oxford University Press, pp 411–33.

Walker, G de Q, *The Rule of Law: Foundation of Constitutional Democracy*, 1988, Carlton, Victoria: Melbourne University Press.

Waluchow, WJ, *Inclusive Legal Positivism*, 1994, Oxford: Clarendon Press.

Walzer, M, *Spheres of Justice: A Defense of Pluralism and Equality*, 1983, New York: Basic Books.

Ward, I, *Introduction to Critical Legal Theory*, 2nd edn, 2004, London, Sydney, Portland: Cavendish Publishing Limited.

Weinreb, LL, *Natural Law and Justice*, 1987, Cambridge, Mass.: Harvard University Press.

West, R, 'Jurisprudence and Gender' (1988) 55 *Chicago University Law Review* 1.

Williams, G, 'The Case That Stopped a Coup? The Rule of Law and Constitutionalism in Fiji' (2001) 1 *Oxford University Commonwealth Law Journal* 73.

Williams, P, 'Alchemical Notes: Reconstructing Ideals from Deconstructed Rights' (1987) 22 *Harvard Civil Rights – Civil Liberties Law Review* 401.

Williams, W, 'Equality's Riddle: Pregnancy and the Equal Treatment/Special Treatment Debate' (1984–1985) 13 *New York University Review of Law and Social Change* 325.

Wolfenden Report, 1957, Cmd 247.

Wolff, J, *An Introduction to Political Philosophy*, 1996, Oxford, New York: Oxford University Press.

Index

communitarianism 113–14; critique of
liberal conception of self 127, 164;
critique of rights 127, 128–9
consequentialist reasoning 40, 120;
see also utilitarianism
constitution: Australia 14; South Africa
74, 184; United Kingdom 14, 29, 38;
United States 14, 51, 52, 68, 130
contractarianism 158–60
contract law 99, 104, 112; contradictions
in 112
convention, consensus of 17–18
conventional rules 4, 20, 51–2, 53
conviction, consensus of 17–18
Cooke, Lord 38
Cornell, Drucilla 186
cosmopolitanism 164
Cotterrell, Roger 13, 15
coup d'etat *see* political revolutions
Crenshaw, Kimberlé 188
criminal law: Devlin's view on use of
137–9; Mill's view 134–7; perfectionist
view 140
Critical Legal Studies (CLS) movement 5,
104; criticisms of 115–16; influence of
Marxism on 89, 113; influence of
postmodernism on 105; intellectual
roots 104–5; rejection of liberal values
113–14; views on legal doctrine
111–13
critical race theory 5, 89, 104, 114–15,
173, 194

Davies, Margaret 192
deconstruction 105, 108–9, 187
Delgado, Richard 114–15
democratic formalism *see* formalism
democratic positivism *see* ethical
positivism
Denning, Lord 72
Derrida, Jacques 106, 108–9
Descartes, René 106
Devlin, Lord 6, 137, 142; criticism of
140–1; critique of Mill 137–9
difference principle *see* Rawls
discrimination 8, 107, 114, 125, 142, 174,
176, 184; direct 175; indirect 175, 177;
legislation against 175; racial 117;
sex-based 175–6, 186
Dworkin, Ronald 3, 4, 17–18, 49–54,
57–9, 62, 63, 66, 75–88, 91, 97–8, 99,
100, 102–3, 112, 115, 121–4, 136–7,
144–50, 163, 179, 194;

and controversial nature of law 4, 18,
53, 77, 78, 80, 84, 85–6; criticism of
Critical Legal Studies 115; criticism of
judicial discretion 75–6; criticism of
Posner 102–3; criticism of Raz 57–8;
criticism of realism 91, 97–8; distinction
between convention and conviction
17–18; distinction between judging and
legislating 84–5; distinction between
policies and principles 85; distinction
between rules and principles 76–8;
influence of Kant on 124; interpretive
approach to law 78–81; law as integrity
81–4, 97–8; objections to inclusive
positivism 53–4; objection to difference
principle 162–3; on positivism and
plain facts 49–50; rights 85, 97, 121–2,
123, 136; sense in which natural lawyer
53, 87; views on abortion 144–8, 193;
views on euthanasia 148–51

economic analysis of law 5, 89, 98–9, 104;
Coase's view 99–100; criticisms of
102, 103, 104; Kaldor-Hicks efficiency
101; transaction costs 99–100, 103;
wealth maximisation 99, 101–3;
see also Posner
essentialism 187,188
ethical positivism 59–60, 82
ethnocentrism 129
European Convention on Human
Rights 132
euthanasia 6, 23, 133, 148–50; active
148, 150; liberal approach 149–50;
non-voluntary 148; passive 148–9;
voluntary 148–50; *see also* suicide,
assisted
exclusive positivism *see* positivism

Feinberg, Joel 129, 139, 140
feminism 173; and adjudication 195–7;
Case Stated by DPP (No 1 of 1993)
(1993) 196; difference feminism
181–5; and individualism 180–1;
intersectionality 188; liberal
feminism 174–5; liberal feminism,
criticism of 175–6; postmodern
feminism 187–90; pregnancy
discrimination 175–6; *President of the
Republic of South Africa v Hugo* (1997)
8, 184; radical feminism 185–6;
special treatment approach 107, 183–4;
Swaney v Ward (1988) 195;